THE CRUCIBLE OF A JAILER

THE CRUCIBLE

OF A

JAILER

HOW TO SERVE AND SURVIVE SUCCESSFULLY

ZACHARY GRAHAM

Copyright © 2019

Published by Prairie Eagle Publishing

All rights reserved. In accordance with the U.S. Copyright Act of 1976, the scanning, uploading, and electronic sharing of any part of this book without permission of the publisher constitute unlawful piracy and theft of the author's intellectual property. If you would like to use material from the book (other than for review purposes), prior written permission must be obtained by contacting the author. Thank you for your support of the author's rights.

Disclaimer: The thoughts and opinions expressed within are solely those of the author and are not meant to be legal advice. Consult legal counsel before using any techniques, tactics, or expressed suggestions. In no way should these be interpreted as views held by anyone else or as representative of any legal entity mentioned. All anecdotes and stories are factual, but names or any identifying information of people have been removed in order to protect their privacy. In addition to this, the author learns something new every day and reserves the right to modify views and conclusions at any time.

First Edition
978-1-7331167-0-1 (E Book)
978-1-7331167-1-8 (Paperback)
978-1-7331167-2-5 (Hardback)

Library of Congress Control Number: 2019908408

Acknowledgments

THEY TOOK TIME OUT OF their busy lives to look at my chapters, make suggestions, and improve this work. I'm extremely grateful for the time they have given me! To protect their identities, I would like to thank, through their officer numbers, these wonderful people:

07007, 07057, 05004, 17023, 17003, 13009, 13010, 04043, 02007, 01005, 17020, 15072, and 83025

I would like to thank R. Crawford for looking at specific chapters and giving his thoughts.

I would like to thank my rough-draft copyeditor, A. Wright. Your eye for detail and your non–law enforcement view were invaluable to advancing my work to a peer-review stage.

I would also like to thank Molly from Inkbot Editing for helping make polish this work and for the many great suggestions.

Dedication

To those that helped me grow, and to those that held me back.

To those that gave me guidance, and to those that gave only admonishments.

To those that believed in me and in my future, and to those who discounted me.

To those that gave and give me kind words, and to those who've yelled at me in anger.

To my parents who were perfectly human in their imperfections but still dared to be parents.

To my grandparents who guided me with the patience they couldn't give their children.

To my wife who has endured with me, for me, and because of me.

To my children who must endure fractured time with me and endure my imperfection.

This is dedicated to all who have shaped me, and therefore, this book.

JUSTICE IS AS FRAGILE AS any child. And, because Justice is a child containing our dreams for a more equitable future, it must be nurtured and protected. In order to be blind to personal circumstances, give weight to the facts and testimony, and then effect consequence with the precision of a blade; it must be given our utmost attention and assistance. All who assist must walk a very narrow path all the while trembling with the great responsibility entrusted to them.

CONTENTS

Chapter 1:
FROM SUSPECT TO DEPUTY — 1

    A Born Suspect — 2
    From Suspect to Soldier and College Graduate — 5
    From Former Suspect, Soldier, and College Graduate to Jail Deputy — 7
    The First Year of Work — 10
    The Second and Third Years — 12
    The Fourth and Fifth Years — 14
    Years Six through Nine — 15
    What You Should Get from This Book — 16
    Chapter 2 Prep — 17

Chapter 2:
A GLANCE OVER THE LEGAL SYSTEM — 18

    The Legal System — 18
    Basic Enforcement of the Law — 22
    How Criminal Courts Work — 27
    Justice, Freedom, Jail, or Prison (Corrections) — 30
    Chapter 3 Prep — 34

Chapter 3:
The Social Contract and the Monopoly of Force — 35

    What Exactly Is the Monopoly of Force? — 35
    Violence Influences Effectively — 36
    Why It's Important That Governments Maintain the Monopoly of Force — 36
    Monopoly of Force and Law Enforcement — 37
    Monopoly of Force in a Jail — 38
    Use of Force in State Statutes — 39
    The Social Contract — 40
    Chapter 4 Prep — 40

Chapter 4:
Being Arrested—A New Identity   42

    A New Identity   42
    Am I a "Criminal" Now?   43
    Breaking the Facade   44
    The "One and Done"   45
    The "Career Criminal"   45
    Public Perceptions   46
    Legislator Perceptions   47
    Citizen to Inmate   47
    Chapter 5 Prep   47

Chapter 5:
Jail Security Operations   49

    From Booking to Administrative Segregation   50
    Chapter 6 Prep   56

Chapter 6:
The City within a City   57

    Jail Management   57
    A Multidisciplinary Approach   61
    Jail Programs   65
    Chapter 7 Prep   68

Chapter 7:
Being a Jailer—A New Identity   69

    What Is a Jail Deputy?   69
    Will You Become a Different Person?   70
    Wearing, Then Not Wearing, a Badge   71
    Public Perception   72
    Public Expectations   72
    Legislative Perception   74
    Inmate Perceptions   75
    Breaking the Facade   75
    The Jailer Identity   76
    Jailer Archetypes   78

Chapter 8 Prep 85

Chapter 8:
Learning to Be a Jailer 86

Learning to Be a Jailer 86
Anecdotes from the Jail 91
Chapter 9 Prep 95

Chapter 9:
Inmate Management 96

The Short-Term Inmate 96
The Pre-Trial Inmate 97
Direct-Supervision Philosophy 98
Influencing Incarcerated Citizens (Inmates) 99
How This Applies to Jails 105
Chapter 10 Prep 106

Chapter 10:
Problem Solving and Decision Making 107

Paid to Observe and Listen 107
Paid to Think 108
Paid to Decide 108
Paid to Respond 109
Responding Well 109
Action Phase 113
Prioritizing Tasks 116
Anecdotes from the Jail 117
Chapter 11 Prep 121

Chapter 11:
Conflict 122

Verbal Conflicts 123
Psychological Conflicts 124
Physical Conflicts 126
Staff Conflicts 127
Conflicts with Yourself 128
Anecdotes from the Jail 130

Chapter 12 Prep	*133*

Chapter 12:
Communication   *134*

A Challenge of Meaning	*134*
Saying No by Saying Yes	*135*
Word Choice, Vocabulary, and State of Mind	*136*
Context Is a Must	*137*
Nonverbals Are King	*139*
Communicating State of Mind	*139*
Communicating Intended Action	*140*
Communicating Possible Action	*140*
Being on Stage	*141*
Anecdotes from the Jail	*142*
Chapter 13 Prep	*144*

Chapter 13:
Inmate Ethics   *145*

The Career Criminals	*145*
One-and-Done Citizens	*146*
Repeat Offenders	*146*
Effects of Career Criminals on the Housing Areas	*147*
Inmate Ethics	*148*
Anecdotes from the Jail	*154*
Inmate Archetypes	*155*
Chapter 14 Prep	*164*

Chapter 14:
Lies and Excuses   *165*

Lies, Human Nature, and Law Enforcement	*165*
How Inmates Use Lies	*168*
Anecdotes from the Jail	*174*
Chapter 15 Prep	*176*

Chapter 15:
Discipline   *177*

Structure and Order	*178*

    Predictable Consequences   *178*
    Humility   *178*
    Responsibility   *179*
    Self-Control and a Cost-Benefit Analysis   *179*
    The Start of a Conversation   *180*
    Establishing a Reputation   *181*
    Failing to Establish a Strong Disciplinary Reputation   *182*
    Being Badge-Heavy   *183*
    Alternative Disciplinary Actions   *184*
    Writing Disciplinary Forms or Reports   *184*
    Progressive Disciplinary Process   *185*
    Discipline for Minor Rule Violations   *187*
    Discipline for Major Rule Violations   *188*
    Appeals and Hearings   *188*
    Anecdotes from the Jail   *189*
    Chapter 16 Prep   *191*

Chapter 16:
Use of Force and Physical Assaults   *192*

    Responsibilities with the Monopoly of Force   *193*
    Use of Force in State Statutes   *193*
    Types of Force and Definitions   *195*
    What Is Reasonable?   *195*
    Use of Force in Jail   *199*
    Liability with Use of Force   *200*
    Training in Use of Force   *200*
    Physical Assaults and Officer Safety   *201*
    Use of Force: An Incident Breakdown   *205*
    Chapter 17 Prep   *211*

Chapter 17:
The Special Emergency Response Team (SERT)   *212*

    The Corrections Special Operations Group (CSOG)   *213*
    Pre-Deployment of SERT   *213*
    Deployment of Team: The Cell Door Opens   *214*
    Anecdotes from the Jail   *215*
    Chapter 18 Prep   *220*

Chapter 18:
Jail Investigations — 222

    A Learning Curve — 223
    Agency and County Support — 224
    Basic Jail Investigations — 224
    Court Proceedings — 226
    An High Volume System — 226
    Challenges to Investigations in a Jail — 227
    Learn to Think Like a Defense Attorney — 227
    Learn to Argue Your Conclusions and Expectations — 229
    Learn to "Fire and Forget" — 229
    Chapter 19 Prep — 230

Chapter 19:
Mental Health and Jail — 231

    Idle Hands and Minds — 232
    Mental Health Care in Jails: A Community Issue — 233
    Mental Health Training — 234
    Anecdotes from the Jail — 236
    Chapter 20 Prep — 237

Chapter 20:
Psychological Stress and Assaults — 239

    "You Chose to Work There!" — 239
    Violence Is Influential — 240
    Psychological Stress — 242
    Psychological Assaults — 242
    Stockholm Syndrome — 243
    Traumatic Transference — 244
    Anecdotes from the Jail — 245
    Chapter 21 Prep — 247

Chapter 21:
Challenges and Preparation — 248

    Competency Challenge — 248
    Identity Challenge — 249

Worldview Challenge	*249*
Stress Management Challenge	*250*
Preparing for the Challenge	*261*
Conclusion: The Crucible of Service	*267*
Additional Resources	*269*
Online Resources	*269*
Books	*269*
Bibliography	*273*

Chapter 1:
FROM SUSPECT TO DEPUTY

As I began writing this book, one question kept running through my mind: "Why should anyone who reads this believe what I'm telling them?"

I started thinking about the countless conversations I've had with those outside of law enforcement, remembering their dismissive skepticism once they learned that I was a deputy[1]. So, I decided to reveal more of the person behind the title.

Some people take on their law enforcement identities to such a degree that they no longer see themselves as separate from their jobs. I've found that I have taken on some of the characteristics of a person in law enforcement, but not overly so. I've come to strongly support some ideas in law enforcement, but I still oppose others.

I am not my job or my job title. I'm not my former jobs, either—as much as I've been influenced by my past jobs and my career, I'm not sure how much those experiences define me as a person. (I will, however,

---

1   In my agency, all the jailers are called deputies because they're sworn in by the sheriff. However, in other agencies they could be called corrections officers, corrections deputies, jail deputies, or jailers. All of these titles refer to those whose mission is essentially the same, and I use the terms "jail deputy," "deputy," and "jailer" interchangeably in this book.

gladly take the title of father, as nothing else in this world could have changed me so much for the better.)

A BORN SUSPECT

I'm from the wrong side of the tracks, so to speak. Being born to a mother of mixed European and Native American ethnicity and a father of Scottish ancestry (whose family were racists) in the 1970s meant that I was subject to societal disapproval from an early age in rural Colorado. However, that wasn't the only scarlet letter I had—I also carried the P for poverty.

Government cheese, food handouts from other family members, long bouts of eating only Cream of Wheat, hole-filled clothing and shoes, and the societally induced shame of food stamps didn't seem so bad until I reached school age. That was when I discovered I was poor—other kids were eager to let me know. I was also soon informed that people had low expectations for my behavior and life path.

I learned early on that money meant a person had opportunities and the lack of money had the opposite effect. Having to miss out on summer sports and school outings made this clear to me and reinforced my "otherness." It also pointed out how seemingly little influence my parents or I had on my destiny. Some of my teachers, beginning in junior high, asked me which prison I thought I would go to when I was eighteen. Other teachers supported me and told me I could do something with my life.

My "otherness" was further reinforced by cousins from my father's side who would sometimes utter racial slurs toward us as a sign of their "superiority." My father would also urge me (through chiding and lectures) not to adopt any language or customs from my mother's side of the family. After all, I was "lucky" to have white skin, and therefore (even though he never said it directly), I needed to hide and deny the "non-whiteness" of myself and my heritage. I was "lucky" to be able to blend in.

I didn't belong to one group because I was *not* "white." I didn't belong to another group because I *was* "white." I didn't belong because I was poor. I didn't belong because my father was not a "good man," but a person with a prescription-drug addiction and criminal tendencies (even though he seemed to avoid getting caught). My mother married him only to later find out that she would suffer emotional, mental, and sometimes physical abuse at his hand. As a child I observed what happened to her and was subjected to similar treatment. Since these things happened in a rural community, they didn't escape notice of the locals, who, in turn, made judgments about my future.

While at elementary and junior high (middle school now), I got into my share of fights. I never started them, but I sought to end them. Using violence to end violence was normal for me, even though I despised it. I never liked the feeling of being angry, or the anxiousness that preceded a fight. However, I eventually discovered that "crazy" tends to trump "violent," and I used "crazy" to avoid fights and still win. By win I mean that I parlayed being "crazy mean" into helping those most under threat of bullying and violence band together for safety. I would then only need to intervene on rare occasions to stop bullies.

In addition to the food insecurity I lived with, housing insecurity would also sometimes raise its head. Frequent moves and temporary homelessness (camping "for real") would happen. High school came, and some key people encouraged me to make the most of my life. When I was old enough to get a job, I purchased my own car and worked full-time while going to school. I worked hard because I wanted to get somewhere with my life. Still, societal expectations remained, and some people looked to prove themselves "right" about me. The town police and state patrol saw me as a suspect—after all, the apple doesn't fall far from the tree, does it? I would often get pulled over (three to four times on a bad day), and each time they would search my car for the drugs they were sure I was selling. It wasn't uncommon for the state patrol to drive next to me for several miles, looking my car up and down for the next technical violation to pull me over for.

Not only did I have to try to make many repairs, on no budget, to my beat-up car in order to avoid further citations, I still had to pay for insurance, fuel, school costs, and the like. The mere sight of a police car would (and occasionally still does) send an electric shock through my body. The local police at the time seemed to view me with suspicion and skepticism. They appeared to be looking for any wrongdoing on my part, like hunters looking for prey. Because of this, I didn't get the feeling that they were protecting me so much as hunting me and waiting for me to make the slightest wrong move. I wasn't a "bad guy"; I was a good kid at a less-than-ideal starting point, looking to improve my life.

Unlike the city police and state patrol, the sheriff's deputies pretty much ignored me. I was never hassled by them. When I was fourteen and did break the law, it was the sheriff's deputies who came to get my statement and process me. I never felt like they were after me. Instead, they conducted an investigation and tried to find out the truth. At the time, I didn't understand why I was in trouble. I learned that even though I was defending myself, I'd solved my "problem" using illegal means. I was processed through the system and was lucky enough to get off with a couple of years' probation and several weeks of community service. To this day, that decision affects me—I've had to explain it to nearly every employer. I guess you could say it was another scarlet letter, but I learned that I didn't want to go through that process ever again.

Despite the challenges I faced during high school, some people encouraged me, and through their support and that of two Rotary Clubs I was given the opportunity of a lifetime: I was able to get my graduating credits completed early and spend a year abroad as a foreign exchange student to Australia. This wouldn't have been possible, regardless of all the extra work I was doing at the time, without the sponsorship of those in Rotary. I'll never forget, and forever honor those special people who helped and mentored me throughout that time in my life.

While I was an exchange student, I expanded my family and learned through observation and personal experience that those who work hard can achieve a lot in life. Even though I was still faced with the same challenges, biases, and marginalization that came with my status and identity, I felt freer to challenge the perceptions of those around me, as well as the perceptions that had been keeping me bound to self-limiting thoughts and negative thinking.

FROM SUSPECT TO SOLDIER AND COLLEGE GRADUATE

After high school, in the mid 1990s, I went into the military. My parents had been in the army, my father during the Vietnam era and my mother during the Gulf War. My grandfathers on both sides were in World War II—the military was called "the service" then, as you were expected to give to your country. I hoped that I could heed that call to service and, should I survive, have a chance at college and a career. At the time, there weren't many avenues for funding an education. Shortly after this, under President Clinton, it seemed like everyone was getting grants and money for school.

I went into service, and after training I was assigned to a station in Germany. We were activated as part of the NATO intervention to help stop the killing in Bosnia. While there, I learned a little about the history of the conflict and saw a great deal of suffering. I saw some of our soldiers making miracles happen while others perpetrated evil deeds. There was exploitation of women and children as well as other questionable conduct. Of course, it was a small minority of soldiers, but it happened enough to have a lasting impact on me. I'd always thought of us (U.S. soldiers) as "the good guys," so it was difficult for me to see these things. I wanted to protect people, yet I felt powerless because I was the youngest and most junior of our unit. As a result, I exited my service alive but not unscathed, and I'll always carry those memories with me.

When I left the service, I went to a community college to begin my education and then attended a state university. I wanted to be a pilot, but the GI bill wouldn't allow students to use it to get a private pilot's license at the time. So, I pursued a degree in anthropology with an emphasis in forensic archaeology (applying the archaeological method to modern crime scenes) because archaeology was always a passion of mine. It was also during this time that I married a wonderful woman who stood by me through one of the roughest times in my life.

Having seen the brutality of war, I decided that I wanted to reconstruct crimes, recover the human remains, and bring them as evidence for prosecution. I soon discovered that I would have to get an advanced degree to be considered for work in this field. Furthermore, I was unsure that I wanted to work almost exclusively with the dead. I interned with a sheriff's office (focusing on investigations) and enjoyed it so much that it changed my direction. At that point, I wanted to go into police investigations right after I graduated, but I discovered that one must first go through patrol and then move gradually up the ranks to become a detective.

I eventually completed a master's degree focusing on anti-human trafficking. I thought I might be able to use my mind to develop methods and practices to deal with this violent issue, but I was passed up by several federal agencies for a variety of reasons. Sometimes I was beat fair and square by more qualified candidates. Sometimes I was given no response at all. Sometimes the rejections felt prejudicial—one agency's contact told me that since I was a "white" male with a master of arts, I shouldn't expect a call back, but if I got a master of science degree I should reapply.

I needed a break from school, so I decided to apply to the same sheriff's department I'd previously interned with. My plan was to start in the jail, work my way to patrol, and then go into investigations where I could use my degree and skills to help people.

FROM FORMER SUSPECT, SOLDIER, AND COLLEGE GRADUATE TO JAIL DEPUTY

When I first became a jail deputy, I was around thirty-two years old. It seemed like a step back at first, but I was willing to work hard to reach my goals. Learning to work inside a jail was different than any other job I'd had, yet the people inside were very familiar to me. In some ways it was like returning to visit the violent personalities I'd run into in my youth. In other ways I found it a true test of character. The challenge has been to not let it become a negative experience, but instead one that reminds me of what I'm thankful for.

Testing, Interview, Selection, Integrity Interview, Polygraph, and Second Interview

When I went through the hiring process, applicants had to take a written test just to get a chance at an interview. The test was about memory, judgment, and English composition—I had to brush up on my English grammar in order to do well. Afterward, I was given an interview to determine if I was to go further in the process. In the interview, an investigator spoke with me about my goals and my application. After the interview I was given a provisional job offer and a background packet to fill out, and an investigator with the sheriff's office visited my family and friends to ask them about me.

I then had another interview where they asked me if the information I'd provided was correct and complete (this is known as an integrity interview). Following this, I had to take a polygraph test. The polygraph was the most nerve-racking experience of the whole process. Having never taken the test before, I was unsure of its usability or accuracy. After going through the baseline checks, I began to believe it could pick up on my subconscious thoughts, making me doubt my own memory! After the polygraph I had a final interview with a board made up of jail staff before being given a full offer of employment and a seat in the field training program.

Many people don't make it past the background and integrity interviews—for whatever reason, they omit things they shouldn't, and in some cases, they even admit to criminal activities. However, having passed all previous requirements, I was accepted into the agency and scheduled to attend the jail's mini-academy.

Mini-Academy

A mini-academy is just what it sounds like: a condensed version of several fields of education. Its job is to provide a basic level of information to the new employee, as well as advise them about actions that are outside the scope of their training and not under the legal protections of the agency.

For example, if you're trained to respond to a resistant inmate using a control hold, but instead you use a favorite move you saw on the World Wrestling Entertainment network, you will have stepped outside the scope of your training. As a result, your actions aren't protected, as they aren't what the agency taught you. Furthermore, it's likely that the agency will prosecute for official misconduct and assault.

The interdisciplinary nature of the work requires many classes, and it takes significant effort to weave them together toward the goal of the agency. To me, the most difficult parts of the mini-academy were the number of PowerPoint presentations and the information overload. Once the mini-academy was completed, I began my field training program.

Field Training Program

The first step in learning any new job is training, followed by more training. Surprisingly, in the jail's field training program, there didn't seem to be much emphasis on learning the laws that apply to criminal charges—instead, it focused on safety and the basics of being in law enforcement. There was great emphasis on communication, management of difficult people, and some constitutional law regarding inmate rights and liability. As I found out later, the real law training happens after both the field training program and the peace officer standards and training (POST) academy are completed.

When I went through the field training program, it was designed to ready a new jail deputy to work in different types of housing areas. The downside to this was that after being "checked off," or cleared to work, in one housing area, you could find yourself working that area until a field training officer (FTO) was available to continue your training. The jail later moved to a skill-based program that focused on building a stronger foundation in the specific skills needed for certain areas, while also providing coaching and guidance.

New Stressors

In the field training program I went through, there were several different types of stressors radiating at the same time. There was a "safety" stressor as I tried to figure out how to be as safe as possible in an environment where I could be injured or have to fight for my life. There was a "proficiency" stressor that attacked my mind as I constantly tried to get my accuracy and speed up regarding documentation and general operations. There was a "judgment" stressor that came with repeatedly having someone over my shoulder critiquing my every word, action, inaction, and decision. There was a "liability" stressor that became more and more potent as I began to realize just how much I really didn't know. (Furthermore, I realized how being ignorant of the law could result in both personal financial loss and federal prison time.)

There was a "skills" stressor that raised its head when I wanted to do my best in arrest control, tactics, firearms, active listening, interviewing, and discipline so others could rely on me. Believe it or not, there was also a stressor for trying to figure out how not to be fooled or manipulated by inmates on a constant basis. I'll discuss this in a later chapter.

Then there were the biological hazards, verbal abuse, emotional abuse, and physical and psychological assaults by inmates. There was also the occasional verbal abuse or disapproval from some citizens who didn't like law enforcement or were against me because their loved one was incarcerated. There was the stress of adapting to the authority entrusted to me and a stressor for physically adapting to different shifts. Jails operate twenty-four hours a day, seven days a week. It isn't uncommon to work multiple twelve-hour shifts a week and change from day to night shifts every couple of months. In my jail, we worked at least a twelve-hour shift, and my internal clock was set to check on people every fifteen minutes. It was often difficult to sleep between shifts as my body adapted to this clock of enhanced awareness. I also had to adapt to the longer-than-average recovery time after work due to the mental stressors. I noticed that my muscles were often tight and my mood sometimes changed when it was my last day off and I had to go to work the next day.

Nearly everyone new to working in a jail begins to gain weight despite active lifestyles, and a few people have early increases in blood pressure. Personal-life stressors go on top of all of the work stress, including family issues, history or "baggage," housing, moving, relationships, and any other thing that could possibly cause stress.

THE FIRST YEAR OF WORK

After training under an FTO for a few months, I was cleared to work on my own. It was great to not have anyone looking over my shoulder, yet I felt that I had to be even more on my game once I was alone. Training was over, yet my education had just begun. It took the better part of the first year to feel like I finally understood the requirements of my job and was able to meet them.

Being former military, it was difficult to work with people who were used to ignoring rules and even their own common sense. Much like herding cats, there's an art to influencing them to do what they should be doing. For the first year, this type of behavior contributed greatly to my daily stress because in the military, a leader or manager would be held accountable for the actions of those they look after. In a jail, many inmates find it sporting to do anything that resists authority. This can make running a housing area difficult. My military mind was constantly worrying that I would be judged by how the inmates were acting, and I was stressed by those thoughts.

Learning Discipline

Because military-style corrective disciplinary techniques aren't allowed or particularly effective in jail, I worked hard on using the progressive disciplinary model taught to me in the field training program in order to attempt to alter the behavior of inmates. While trying to learn to communicate effectively with inmates, avoid manipulation, enforce discipline, and influence their behavior, it was not uncommon for me to write ten or more infractions during my shift.

I still had a military mindset, and I wanted to make sure my supervisors didn't think I wasn't enforcing discipline. I also wanted inmates to know that I would follow through with discipline and not ignore their behavior. Because of this, I established a reputation for being strict. Despite being trained to enforce disciplinary actions every time I found infractions, I soon found that I was also expected to use discretion and "pick my battles."

Instead of relaxing and picking my battles when sent out on my own, however, I pushed myself even harder to discover infractions and avoid manipulation. Since everyone seemed to have an excuse for their behavior, I felt that they were trying to trick me into not enforcing discipline. As a result, I rarely allowed these excuses or reasons to interfere with the issuing of discipline. Since I was new to the field and still learning how to influence career criminals and repeat offenders, I was more likely to use discipline in order to attempt to gain compliance.

After my first year, I slowly developed a sense of making light of minor rule violations and allowing the person to comply in their own time when possible. This allowed them to be "publicly" defiant, yet come into compliance in order to avoid disciplinary action. It seemed that most inmates would do what I asked as soon as they thought the "public" spotlight was off of them. I also found that my reputation for being strict was of benefit at that point, because it would seem like I was being cool or generous for allowing them a little more time to comply rather than issuing discipline immediately.

Dealing with Authority

Even as I issued discipline, I didn't want to do so in an unjust way. As a new jailer, I was worried about how I would respond to the authority given to me. My fear was that "power tends to corrupt, and absolute power corrupts absolutely." However, jailers aren't given as much authority as one might think. Since I wasn't POST-certified yet, my authority was largely limited to the safe and secure operation of the facility. This meant that my actions had to be constitutional, in line with agency policy, and deemed reasonable to those who worked in the field with similar training. I didn't want to let the little bit of authority entrusted to me change me and then negatively impact my life or relationships.

Since I was conscientious of this, I would repeat quotes to myself in order to check myself. One of my favorite quotes, attributed to Abraham Lincoln, seems to fit law enforcement perfectly: "Nearly all men can stand adversity, but if you want to test a man's character, give him power." It reminded me that just because I had the authority to do something didn't mean I should do it.

THE SECOND AND THIRD YEARS

After about a year, I felt that I'd learned the basics of my job and I wanted to become more proficient so I could handle more situations on my own. My second year was all about improving the quality of my work and expanding my knowledge. I wanted to make myself more of an asset to the agency, so I pushed myself to learn—I began studying as many policies and procedures as I could. I attempted to gain extra duties, but I hadn't established myself enough to be allowed to do those duties yet.

I was holding my own, working the housing areas like the others, and feeling good about my abilities. However, I began to notice that I was using the methods given to me by my FTOs as a crutch. I then started to branch out and try different techniques and tactics in order to find my own style. Of course, this was a process that would take several years.

At this point, I still planned to become peace officer standards and training (POST)–certified as soon as possible, since this certification was required to move into patrol and then into investigations. The challenge was that there was no longer an in-house POST program, and my work schedule didn't allow the time I needed to complete the certification.

A Career Instead of a Stepping Stone

Throughout years two and three, I was still wrestling with the idea that I could be working at the jail for a very long time. If I wanted to continue on my original path, I would have to find some alternative means to achieve POST certification, since I couldn't go on leave without pay. My wife and I were expecting a child and we had bought a house. I felt my priorities shift from a career push to preparing to be a father.

Between the second and third year, I was still focused on learning policies and procedures and being there for my family. By the third year, I was given the opportunity to begin training people in cultural diversity as part of the mini-academy. My degree in anthropology lent to this, as well as my life experience. My goal was to teach a brief history of bias and demonstrate how to be more open in moments of misunderstanding or distrust in order to help inmates comply voluntarily.

Family continued to be a top priority during this time, and any new parent knows the perpetual lack of sleep that comes with the first year of a child's life. Balancing my work and home life was challenging during this time, but rewarding.

Inside the housing areas I began to notice that a direct approach with some very difficult inmates often had a negative effect. However, I didn't favor using indirect approaches because I was still being very firm, and I thought indirectness might confuse people. Developing these skills, for me, took time.

General Trends I Noticed

Some of my colleagues had consistently expressed the fact that they found this work very difficult, and that maybe it wasn't for them. During the second and third years, many of these colleagues began to leave. Stress, job dissatisfaction, life events, or the agency's culture pushed some people to reevaluate their career choice and move on to another employer. In some ways, these individuals were very wise—they knew themselves and what they wanted in their lives, and they saw that it was time to move on. Others needed more time to make this decision.

THE FOURTH AND FIFTH YEARS

During my fourth year, I began teaching another class for mini-academy and became an FTO. I had decided to stay in the jail, and I was enjoying the challenges and new responsibilities. I decided to put in for a promotion around this time, as I wanted to put my education to good use. It wasn't that I didn't have enough challenges in the housing areas; I just wanted the additional challenge of turning policy ideas into real-world processes.

In my fifth year, I finally had the opportunity to attend the reserve POST academy because I had enough seniority to be able to pick a compatible schedule. Reserve POST isn't a full certification (it's more of an introduction to policing), but I was happy for any opportunity to learn.

Also in my fifth year, I began working on modifying our field training program to become more skills-based (as opposed to area-based), as I mentioned earlier. This journey required more than a year's worth of work outside of the job and resulted in significant changes to the program. I fully committed to the career around this time, but I tried to keep my work identity at work and my home identity at home.

When I first started working this job, I thought I was going to be the same person I always was. This was, of course, not totally true—I'd already changed in many ways by this point. I was less trusting of people and more concerned than ever for the safety of my family and myself. Family and friends noted the changes in me and I could tell they were saddened by it. I was no longer extremely trusting and jovial; I was now skeptical of many people and always tired.

YEARS SIX THROUGH NINE

By the time I hit my sixth year, time began to accelerate. I suspect that some of this acceleration had to do with aging, but some of it also had to do with my increasing workload. I took on many duties that benefited the agency but were not absolutely necessary. I completed the POST academy and dove into investigations within the jail.

My first case was a felony involving witness tampering, and I saw it all the way through trial and conviction. Because it was my first case, I had a lot of competing thoughts and emotions regarding the process. I was very conscientious that my investigation and actions would impact another human being negatively. Even though he was clearly in the wrong by threatening and coercing the witness to not show up to trial, I could still feel the weight of the consequences to this person. I then had to put my training and critical thinking skills to work in order to collect evidence and present the case to the district attorney (DA) in a complete and professional manner. The justice system doesn't function if every witness can be intimidated without consequences, and this man was convicted by a jury. He did threaten to harm me for holding him accountable for his own actions.

During years seven and eight, I knuckled down and really concentrated on my job, training others, investigations, evidence collection, interview and interrogation courses, and continuing to try and climb the ranks within the agency. During my seventh year my last grandfather passed away, and halfway through my eighth year my grandmother passed as well. My grandmother's death was particularly hard-hitting for me, but it also made me look to make changes in my life for the better.

I had thought on and off again about writing this book since my fifth year in service. When my grandmother passed, I had to stop what I was doing for a couple of weeks, take stock of my life, and remind myself what really mattered. I'd gotten so busy that I'd slowly and steadily begun to push aside what was important to me. I had put some of the things that should've been first in my life off to the side. My grandmother's death reminded that I needed to keep those things in the proper place. As a result, I began writing this book shortly before the beginning of my ninth year. It started with me just writing my thoughts as they would occur to me. Those thoughts expanded into several paragraphs, and then chapters. Before I knew it, I had a book full of thoughts and experiences.

During my ninth year, I spent a great deal of time just getting what had been stored up inside me out onto paper. Of course, I also continued to train people, conduct criminal investigations, and run housing areas, but I focused on trying to give back by sharing my experience with those who are also following this path.

WHAT YOU SHOULD GET FROM THIS BOOK

If you're becoming (or thinking about becoming) a jailer, this book will give you more to think about, as well as some additional tools and resources to help you adapt to your new career and explain your job to others.

The first six chapters of this book outline the societal framework in which the work of being a jailer takes place. Chapter 2 outlines the criminal process, while chapter 3 shows why the monopoly of force is necessary in order to keep citizens safe. Chapter 4 outlines how an average person will enter, and then be challenged by, the current legal system and the jail. Chapter 5 speaks to jail operations specifically, while chapter 6 outlines why it takes many hands to operate a jail appropriately.

Chapters 7 to 21 are dedicated to topics a new jailer needs to know: chapter 7 begins with what it's like to become a jailer, while chapters 8 to 20 build upon this and provide more insight. Chapter 21 then brings these challenges into a more condensed form and provides some guidance on how to prepare for them.

CHAPTER 2 PREP

The next chapter provides a very brief outline of the legal system. Each state and county have their own way of conducting legal processes, but in a general sense, some of these are consistent. I'm not a specialist in law or legal procedure, but I've made some interesting observations that may be of use to a person with little to no familiarity with any legal system.

Chapter 2:
A GLANCE OVER THE LEGAL SYSTEM

WHEN I FIRST BECAME A jailer, the only things I knew about the legal system came from the experiences I'd had growing up and, of course, what I'd seen on TV. I felt that the enforcement of law tended to be by the letter and not the intent. Furthermore, it seemed like the simple act of being charged with a crime changed one's status in their own eyes and those of their family, friends, and the public at large. The legal system appeared to be a large, unknowable juggernaut that could alter a person's life path permanently with little to no warning.

After working in the field for a time, I began to see that the legal system operates on some basic constitutional rules, and that the consequences can be staggering if a person is unfamiliar with the basics of criminal law. I also saw how breaking the law does change your status, but it isn't the end of the road; instead, it's a chance to change and grow in the process. I've also come to realize that the more I work in this field, the more questions I have than answers, especially concerning legislative solutions to behavioral problems.

THE LEGAL SYSTEM

This chapter is an extremely abbreviated version of the criminal legal system, and is not designed to do anything other than give you an idea of how things work in general. My goal for this chapter is to make the criminal legal process a little more understandable to the average person who has little to no experience with it.

Over the last two hundred years, there have been some expansions and changes in the American criminal legal system that have resulted in additional protections for the rule of law and due process. This has created additional challenges by solving a bureaucratic mess with additional bureaucratic processes that mire the system with further steps and requirements—basically patching up an existing process rather than building a new one from scratch.

Due Process

One goal of the American legal system is to give everyone the same "due process." This process has to be equal for all people, so individual circumstances are largely irrelevant. (And if individual circumstances are highlighted, it can be seen as giving someone preferential treatment.) Because of this, the "individual" can be lost in the process—he or she is instead seen by the system as a widget to be moved along in the process from point A to Z.

The due process we have today has evolved with the investigation of new types of crimes and challenges to certain processes, such as evidence collection. The goal of due process is to reduce bias in the investigation, prosecution, and adjudication of crimes in a way that ensures that a person's constitutionally guaranteed rights aren't infringed upon by the enforcement arm of a governing body. However, the meaning of due process changes with the latest interpretations of the law by district courts and the U.S. Supreme Court.

The U.S. uses the Constitutional due process largely because the more individualized the system, the more costly and unwieldy it is, since it has to accommodate each person rather than the masses it's designed for. As a result, due process removes individual choices and severely restricts freedom, making those who go through it unsure of what, if anything, they have control or influence over. This can be very disconcerting and frustrating to a person used to having their independence.

Why Do We Have a System?

Why do we have a system in the first place? Well, if there aren't any processes for the redressing of wrongs or perceived wrongs, then the strongest, most violent, and most influential people will determine what happens when there's an issue.

Due process is an attempt to preserve liberty, reduce vigilantism, avoid kangaroo courts, and level the playing field for all citizens. This approach to law isn't without its flaws, but it's a worthy ideal to work toward. Despite the challenges, our system is one of the better systems out there, and it's still evolving.

Where Does the Law Come From?

At any point in time, someone might see something that seems like it should be illegal but isn't. As a result, there begins to be public pressure toward elected officials to make changes. These officials get together, discuss the issue, and a judgment is made on whether that behavior or action should or shouldn't be outlawed.

For example, after several hundred innocent people were killed by drunk drivers, citizens got together to decide how best to dissuade others from drinking and driving. Those citizens decided they wanted the drunk drivers to be held accountable. As a result, they pressured their local officials, elected or otherwise, to solve the problem. But what was the true cause of the problem, and how could it be solved?

For example, were bars and breweries to blame? Was it alcohol consumption? Was it alcoholism? Was it the poor decision making of those impaired by alcohol? Was it education in that people, once they knew the consequences to others, would no longer choose to drive drunk? Was it the automotive manufacturers' fault for not installing additional safeties? Was it a lack of public transport available? Was it the other drivers on the road who should just get out of the way of the drunk people? Was it how the roads were made, or the current traffic code?

Furthermore, how would legislation help once the problem was identified? A government can't truly legislate behavior in a free society, but it can create consequences for when a person decides to disregard a law. But how effective is legislation as a preventative measure when you can only provide an "on paper" consequence? Furthermore, once a citizen has made the poor decision, been caught, and the case has been taken to court for adjudication, how will the new law actually change their behavior and the behavior of others?

Additionally, what is the appropriate consequence for a citizen who violates the new law? How many times is the citizen allowed to violate the law before the consequences compound? Or should we wait for a drunk driver to kill someone first in order to hold them more accountable? How can we balance individual rights and still try to prevent the potential deaths of innocent victims?

These are just some examples of the types of questions that legislators have to answer. The formation of law is a messy process with many views and opinions involved, and in addition to this, election politics, information found and presented, business lost, business pending, and many other outside influences make the lawmaking process that much more contentious.

Who Makes the Law Work?

The citizens in the community elect officials who make law. These elected officials then decide what they think the problems are, what's going to be legal, what's going to be illegal, and the consequences for noncompliance. However, no matter how many laws or rules the lawmakers make, simply putting it on paper won't convince all of the people to follow those laws. Furthermore, your average person isn't going to turn themselves in when they break a law. As a result, the government requires an enforcement arm. The word enforcement implies that the use of force can be used, if necessary, to bring someone into compliance with the law.

Law enforcement officers have some authority to make limited decisions about the enforcement of law, but they mostly investigate violations to present to the district attorney, or DA. The DA is an elected official who is largely responsible for the enforcement of law at the judicial level, as he or she has the power to investigate and bring cases to prosecution. Because the DA and his or her assistants may not have enough time or resources to keep up with the number of violations, the local sheriff's office and other municipal policing agencies help with observation, evidence collection and submission, and the apprehension of offenders.

BASIC ENFORCEMENT OF THE LAW

So what happens when a person breaks the law and is investigated? Here's an example of the basic process:

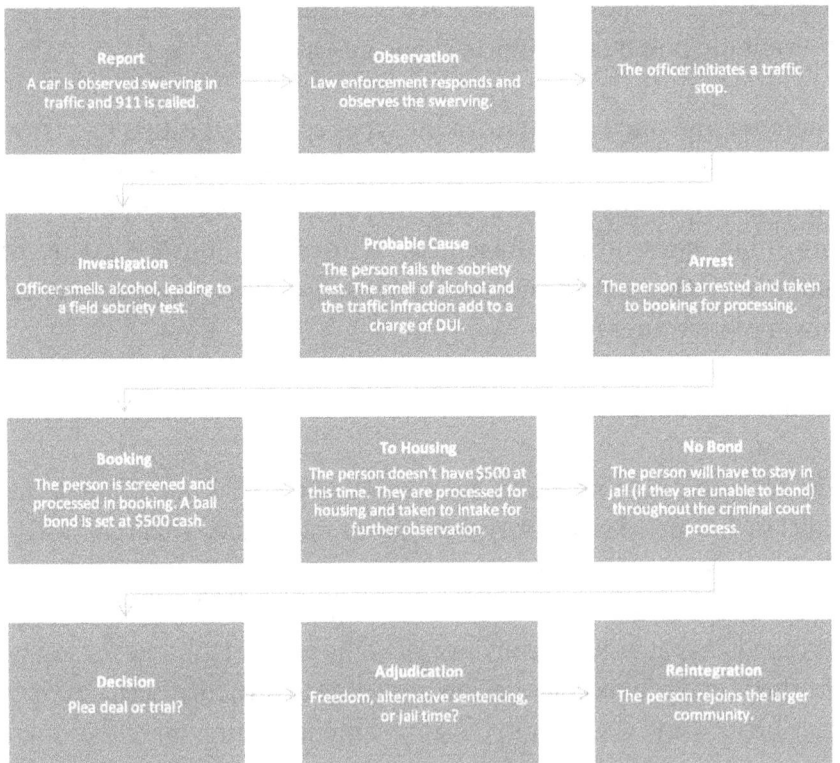

This process may seem simple, but the officer must collect information and evidence in a way that maintains due process, chain of custody, and other protections outlined in the U.S. Constitution.

Decisions and Actions That May Be Illegal

At some point in time, every one of us will have a momentary lapse of reason. That is to say, we'll ask a question we already know the answer to, or turn right when we know to turn left. In some cases, a person throws caution to the wind and leaps before looking. Sometimes, leaping before looking can be sheer fun—other times, the consequences can be lifelong.

Looking at cause and effect seems simple, but some actions have delayed consequences. In an aviation accident where pilot error is suspected, for example, it isn't usually the immediate action surrounding the accident that's the problem. Often, it's a series of poor decisions that severely limit the options available to the pilot at a critical moment. In the majority of cases, it's simply too late to "turn the ship," so to speak.

Many of our decisions will affect us later. There are people who are unable to see, or who choose not to address, the potential consequences of their actions. As a result, they tend to think that life just happens to them and that they're "victims" of the system.

Some of the events in our lives can't be controlled, but our reactions to those events can be. A person generally has no influence over when someone they love dies, for instance. But they do have influence over their relationships and job performance. A healthier approach to these two things can sometimes help reduce the stress of the uncontrollable event (the death of a loved one).

In times of stress, however, some people elect to forget things for a minute or take a break from "adulting." This reaction to stress is fine if it's addressed in a healthy way, such as taking a break to exercise or meditate. However, many choose alcohol.

Let's look at a person who's had the hardest week of their life. A close family member has died, a relationship is breaking down, and their job isn't going as well as they would like. As a result, they decide to have a few more drinks than normal and go for a hike to clear their head. The future is put into motion as they jump into their car and head to the nearest trail.

In this case, the origin of the decision to drink and drive came from avoiding or not properly addressing life events. This then led to a heightened amount of stress after the death of a family member. The person's previously established pattern of avoidance then led to a decision to drink. The alcohol, paired with the avoidance, then led to a decision to drive drunk, which then locked the person into a path likely to produce a very negative consequence.

Law Enforcement Investigates Actions for Legality

A law enforcement officer observes a vehicle swerving from side to side and going over the road lines. The officer sees this swerving as a violation of the traffic code but reasonably suspects that the person is distracted, careless, impaired, or having a medical issue. As a result, the officer will pull the person over for the traffic violation and use that time to investigate the other possibilities. The investigation contains voluntary and involuntary steps depending on state law and the evidence observed.

The Action Is Determined Unlawful

As the investigation begins, the officer determines that alcohol is probably the cause of the traffic violation after looking into the driver's eyes and smelling alcohol in the car. To test this theory, the officer conducts a field sobriety test, which indicates that the person is impaired. The officer arrests the driver and takes him to jail or the station for a more precise test called an Intoxilyzer. This test confirms that the person is intoxicated.

The officer then completes paperwork showing the evidence for the violation of law, preserves the evidence, and issues formal charges. The person is then processed into jail at a booking window.

Individual Is Arrested and Presumed Innocent

U.S. law states that an individual is presumed innocent until proven guilty. This doesn't mean that the person is free to go—presumed innocence doesn't excuse a person from the legal processes of the criminal justice system when they're accused of a crime. After an investigation, the law violation is documented, charges are filed, and the person is booked into the jail.

The booking process requires that the person be fingerprinted and photographed, and their personal information is placed into a database. They're given a jail number as well as a few other numbers as required by local, state, and national criminal databases. Their clothes are taken away and they're issued jail clothes.

Although there are occasions where a jail deputy or contracted medical or counseling staff member will step in and see to a person's comfort, the new inmate's personal needs are secondary to the jail's processes.

Those who have been in a jail know what this means. It means you won't have your soft bed and pillow. You won't be able to shower whenever you please. You won't have access to the products you're used to. Your medications might not be honored if they aren't acceptable to the contracted company that oversees medical services, and brand names will likely be replaced by generics. Mental health counselors will be there to make sure you don't harm yourself and to point you to outside resources or begin paths to assistance and medication, but they're not there to solve your problems for you while you're inside.

Despite all of this, you are still presumed innocent until proven guilty. Again, this doesn't mean that you aren't subject to the processes involved in the investigation and prosecution of a criminal case. Innocent until proven guilty is, like many other legal processes, a legal status rather than a state of being. The status of being innocent until proven guilty simply means that you won't be subject to the processes limited to those who have been convicted of a crime, such as those within the department of corrections.

Being innocent until proven guilty means you'll be considered a pre-trial detainee and will remain in a jail (if you don't bond or bail out) rather than going to a prison throughout your trial. While you're in a jail or detention facility, the staff there are charged with making sure you survive to have your day in court. They aren't there to cater to you, assist in your legal defense, make you comfortable, or investigate your case further in order to exonerate you. However, they're also not there to judge, punish, or cause additional harm if it's avoidable.

Individual Is Given a Bond or Bail as a Promise to Go to Court

Sometimes a person may not have to be taken farther inside the jail after booking—the person may be eligible to get a bond and get out. A bond (also known as bail) is a promise to show up to court under some sort of penalty or exchange of property. Sometimes, should the arrest occur on a Friday, Saturday, or Sunday, the person may have to spend the weekend in jail and then see a judge to have a bond set. These bonds vary in monetary amounts and have several classifications, a few of which are listed below:

Personal Recognizance (PR) Bond
- Sign yourself out with a promise to pay the court money if you don't appear in court

Personal Recognizance/Cosigner (PR/CO) Bond
- You need another person to sign you out, and both parties are on the hook for the money if you don't appear in court

Cash Only (CA) Bond
- You need the stated cash amount to leave the jail, and you'll lose it if you don't appear in court

Cash, Property, or Surety (CPS) Bond
- You need cash, property, or a bail bond agent to sign out, and you'll lose the money or property if you don't show up in court

Continuing with our DUI example, let's say that the person was given a personal recognizance bond and released with a future court date. Now that the process has been put into motion, the courts will begin reviewing evidence, interviewing witnesses, collecting victim statements, and preparing for trial.

This is the beginning of a long legal process—a speedy trial is defined as being completed within one hundred eighty days from the entering of a plea. Attorneys on either side will also usually ask for more time to get their cases ready, which pushes the decision back even further.

HOW CRIMINAL COURTS WORK

It's difficult to generalize about this subject because so much depends on a state's procedures. However, there are some very general processes for prosecuting misdemeanors and felonies. Criminal cases are different than civil cases, as the burden of proof for a civil (non-criminal) case is the "preponderance of the evidence," while for criminal cases it's "beyond a reasonable doubt."

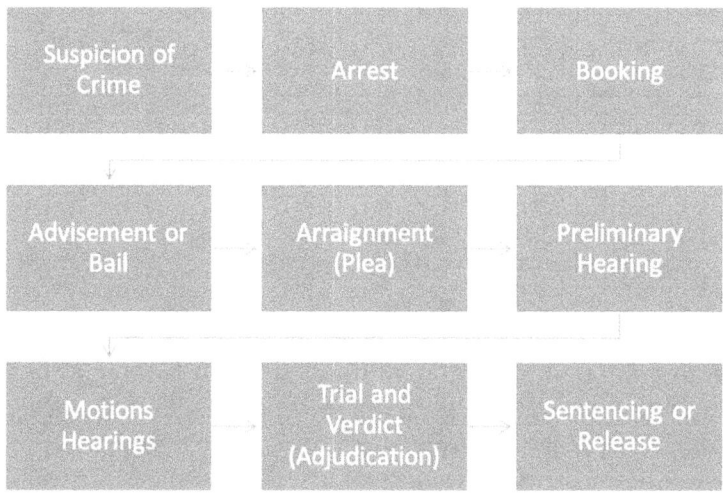

Misdemeanors

If a person has been charged with a misdemeanor, the first step is an initial appearance and arraignment before a magistrate or a judge of a lower court. Many limited-jurisdiction courts combine the initial appearance and the arraignment.

Initial Appearance

- The charges are read to the defendant and the penalties are explained
- The defendant is advised of their right to a trial by jury
- The defendant's right to legal representation is explained, and the judge or magistrate assigns a court-appointed attorney if the defendant can't afford to hire one
- If the basic elements for the charges have been met, the judge or magistrate sets bail conditions

Arraignment

- The defendant enters a plea
  - If the defendant enters a not-guilty plea, a trial date will be set
  - If the defendant pleads guilty or no contest (nolo contendere[2]), a date will be set to sentence the defendant for the crime

Felonies

The process for felonies is very similar to the one above except there's the additional step of a preliminary hearing to review evidence, due to the more serious nature of the charges. Because of this, the arraignment

---

2   A plea of no contest, or nolo contendere, means that the defendant neither disputes nor admits guilt. This is treated like a guilty plea, and the defendant agrees to accept punishment for the crime. Many U.S. states have restrictions on its use.

occurs after the preliminary hearing and can't be combined with the initial appearance.

Initial Appearance

- The charges are read to the defendant and the penalties are explained
- The defendant is advised of their right to a preliminary hearing and a trial by jury
- The purpose of the preliminary hearing is explained
- The defendant's right to legal representation is explained, and the judge or magistrate assigns a court-appointed attorney if the defendant can't afford to hire one
- A plea is not entered at this time; the judge or magistrate sets the amount of bail

Preliminary Hearing

- The prosecution must demonstrate that there's sufficient evidence, or probable cause, to prove that the person committed the crime they're charged with (defendants usually must be present for this, but they don't generally give evidence in their defense)
- If the court finds no probable cause, the charges are dismissed
- If the court finds probable cause, a date for the arraignment is set

Arraignment

- The defendant enters a plea
    - If the defendant enters a not-guilty plea, a trial date will be set
    - If the defendant pleads guilty or no contest (nolo contendere), a date will be set to sentence the defendant for the crime

Trial and Verdict (Adjudication)

If the case goes to trial, the person who has gone through the system now faces one of these results:

Case Dismissed

- This is due to lack of evidence, exculpatory evidence (evidence that shows innocence or brings doubt of guilt) that's brought to light, or other legal technicalities

Not Guilty

- Found not guilty

Guilty

- Found guilty

Plea Bargain

- Admission of guilt in exchange for a mitigated sentence

JUSTICE, FREEDOM, JAIL, OR PRISON (CORRECTIONS)

What Is Justice?

Imagine for a moment that a person steals your car. What is "justice" in this situation? First, you probably want your car back. If it's damaged, you would like it fixed or replaced. And you'd likely want the person to be punished somehow for the crime.

When it comes to property, justice is often seen as the replacement of that property (or a monetary equivalent) along with some sort of time consequence for the person responsible. Justice for property crimes seems easy compared to those classified as "crimes against the person."

What is justice when it comes to crimes against people? How can the system ever make things right for the victims of assault or murder? Is "justice" simple retribution in these cases? Is it an eye for an eye? I don't have the answers to these tough questions, but I do think it's important to find ways to help the victims and their families in addition to ensuring due process for the accused.

This leads us to other important questions, such as:

- Should justice be punitive or corrective? Is it possible for justice to be punitive for some crimes and corrective in others?
- What rights do victims really have? The state ensures the rights of the accused, but what about the rights of the citizens who were victimized?
- When it comes to repeat offenders, is there a point when that person signals their inability to be anything other than a predator who generates victims? How can sentencing deal with that?

These are hard questions with elusive answers, and they represent just a small fraction of the moral and ethical dilemmas facing those who work in the justice system.

Justice: Freedom

A not-guilty verdict or a dismissed case means that the individual doesn't have to go to jail or prison, serve probation, or be given alternative sentencing. Although a relief, the process has likely taken a financial, physical, emotional, and mental toll on the person and their family. A not-guilty verdict seldom results in "the people" (the state or federal government) making everything right with the accused—by that I mean restoring losses in time and resources. Instead, the victory and the maintenance of one's freedom is the reward.

A not-guilty verdict also doesn't mean that the prosecutor or the police believe in the innocence of the accused; it just means they couldn't prove their case "beyond a reasonable doubt" to that particular jury.

Justice: Prison or Jail

When a person is found guilty, the preparation for the sentencing phase begins. There's usually an evaluative process for determining sentence length that includes factors such as the impact of the sentence on the defendant, victim impact statements, and opinions from both the prosecution and defense. Generally, misdemeanors and petty crimes will see a small amount of jail time and alternative sentencing programs. Felony convictions usually result in prison time.

Are Prisons Actually "Corrective"?

Prisons now often fall under the umbrella of "corrections." The word implies that prison somehow corrects the behavior of individuals. It also implies that there is some level of rehabilitation going on inside the walls. I can't speak to this as I've never worked in a prison, but with so many repeat offenders and career criminals coming through the jail, there's room for skepticism.

Given the sheer numbers of incarcerated persons and the costs that go into their housing, feeding, medical care, mental health care, and monitoring, the funding for more advanced rehabilitation and reeducation programs is unlikely to exist in most prisons.

The truth is often messier than the vision: it would be nice to incarcerate offenders and be able to change their worldview, give them a truly fresh start upon their release, and have them suddenly become productive, non-offending citizens. However, repeat offenders' characters were years in the making, with educations in violence and predation that allowed for these tactics to become legitimate survival strategies in their minds.

Many people want there to be a way to give offenders more opportunities and outlets for change. How that can be achieved—and who gets those limited resources—is constantly debated in the world of law enforcement and corrections. Still, even if there were great programs for change while in prison, reintegration strategies would have to follow suit or the efforts made would be much less effective.

Justice: Reintegration with the Community

Reintegration into the community is a challenge that both jails and prisons face. There is a simple mechanism for people to enter the system, a complex, due process–driven legal process to decide guilt or innocence, and a corrections portion that allows for the holding of people from the beginning of the process until the sentence is served. Then, after all is completed and the sentence is served, many people are simply released back to where they came from. Often, this release comes with probation, parole, court-mandated classes, and fines still to be paid. However, these aren't all that a person takes with them: they now have a public conviction that employers will ask about.

There are some programs that address reintegration from prisons to halfway houses, which prepare individuals for release into the community. When people are removed from their social structures and placed into the corrections community, there are expectations for those people to change. Despite losing their jobs and possibly some friends or family members, becoming financially dependent, being given a new inmate identity and education, living with societal restrictions, having to disclose their criminal records when applying for employment, paying additional fines, fees, or restitution, and reporting to parole or probation officers, we expect them to return to normal life without complaint and to show newfound appreciation for their freedom, as well as continued responsibility.

This isn't to say that I think such individuals are being treated poorly or asked to do an excessive amount of work, necessarily—after all, they've breached a public trust and should earn their way back into society. I'm just not sure how effective the current process is in being a path to regaining freedom, status, and a fresh start.

CHAPTER 3 PREP

The will of the people, as carried out through elected officials and the lawmaking process, needs an enforcement arm. However, these enforcement arms—including the DA's office, the criminal court system, and corrections—only work when people recognize the legitimacy of the monopoly of force granted to them. If everyone has the same level of authority for the use of force, who will keep the peace? The next chapter will look at the monopoly of force and why it's necessary.

Chapter 3: The Social Contract and the Monopoly of Force

COMMUNITY MEMBERS VOTE FOR THEIR representatives who, in turn, make laws that require enforcement. Because the elected government is expressing the will of the people, there's an implied social contract between the community, their legislators, and law enforcement officials in regard to the requests for, drafting of, passing of, and enforcing of laws and codes.

Citizens entrust their elected representatives to work with the law, but the lawmakers do not, after making a law, roam the streets to enforce it. Instead, they pass this duty to DAs and law enforcement officers. An unenforced law may be seen as an admission that the law shouldn't exist in the first place. Therefore, elected representatives need to have the ability to enforce the laws they have collectively decided on. Giving lawmakers physical power through law enforcement officials gives them the means to attain a monopoly of force.

WHAT EXACTLY IS THE MONOPOLY OF FORCE?

A monopoly of force, in this case, means the exclusive control and use of violence or force by the state or government through its agents.

Old Westerns seem to capture this relationship more clearly: both the bad guy and the sheriff tend to be "tough" men who will use violence to achieve a result. The difference between these two characters, however, is that the sheriff was elected by the people to use violence or force in order to keep the "bad guys" accountable to the laws of the people.

In today's society, some people think that using violence to stop violence is a backward way to deal with crime. However, it's the monopoly of force that gives law enforcement the power to deal with violent predators when words or counseling fail or are ineffective.

VIOLENCE INFLUENCES EFFECTIVELY

When I was a child, I saw violence. Some children see much more violence than I did, yet many people can't imagine what it's like to grow up in a place where violence is the norm. My point is that even if you dislike violence or have never seen or experienced it in real life, a person learns quickly that violence *is* an effective means of coercive influence. Those who are willing to utilize physical and psychological violence effectively often have much greater influence than those who try to get along with others and "follow the rules."

Violent criminals see the use of force as their primary means of communication, an expedient way to influence those who follow the rules. They also tend to see rule-followers as easier to prey on or influence. Predators use violent words and actions to pick out victims who are seen as weak, unable, or unwilling to defend themselves.

WHY IT'S IMPORTANT THAT GOVERNMENTS MAINTAIN THE MONOPOLY OF FORCE

Between the government and a local crime lord, who would you want to have the power over—and responsibility of—ensuring public health and safety and enforcing due process? I don't know about you, but I'd rather have the government, law enforcement, and the court system providing those services than random people carrying out their own versions of justice.

Governments use the monopolization of force to maintain order for the sake of public safety. If the government didn't have the monopoly of force, anyone with enough violent power could challenge the government for control, causing a breakdown of law and order. As a result, violent criminal leaders could control portions of a city or area.

However, the monopoly of force only works when it's given to governments and their agents by the people. In general, if the government, through a law enforcement agency, has the monopoly of force, then security reaches more people. If you haven't heard Gary Haugen speak on security and poverty, it's worth looking him up—I've included a link to his TED talk in the resources listed at the end of this book.

MONOPOLY OF FORCE AND LAW ENFORCEMENT

It's easy to think that law enforcement is only about catching "bad guys" and then keeping them in jail. However, it goes far beyond that. The societal impacts of law enforcement may be better understood when they're observed in the context of dealing with civil unrest, or when there's a high-profile murder in your area.

If or when the community becomes dissatisfied with some process or event, protests tend to begin. Law enforcement soon arrives to both protect the right to peaceably assemble as well as the rights of those who aren't protesting. For example, a business owner may find a protest going on in their private parking lot, in which case they can call on law enforcement to encourage the protesters to relocate to the public sidewalk.

Civil processes for the redressing of wrongs is vital to the rule of law because a violent response will almost always work against the interests of those protesting. The public tends to identify with protesters who assemble peaceably in order to be heard. The same public become much less empathetic to those who riot and set private property on fire. During criminal processes such as a high-profile murder, the accused has to be protected until their guilt is determined through the judicial process. As a result, those who are innocent don't have to worry as much about being harmed before all of the evidence is brought forward at trial. The importance of law enforcement goes well beyond collecting evidence and catching offenders.

Violence, as used in a protest, is a direct challenge to the local government's monopoly of force. As a result, it's expected that law enforcement officers respond to restore this monopoly. If the local or state governments lose control, the federal government might institute martial law and sanction the use of extreme military force to maintain order. If you're the type of person who prefers local government control rather than martial law, you can appreciate why the civil arm of the government's monopoly of force—law enforcement—exists.

MONOPOLY OF FORCE IN A JAIL

A jail is a city within a city. Jailers use the monopoly of force to provide a safe place to hold people who are moving through a system designed to have similar processes to address their violations of law. Jailers must keep people in a locked facility so they can't continue to offend, and also to maintain order and safety and assist in the provision of food, medical care, and the like. As a result, jailers play a significant part in governmental monopoly of force. Without jails holding violent offenders for the legal process, it seems likely that street justice would be used to resolve issues better left to the courts.

When working in a jail, there's no question that jailers should have the monopoly of force because it allows them to do their jobs. Without it, they couldn't ensure the basic safety of citizens both inside the jail and out.

The people kept inside a jail are someone's father, mother, brother, sister, uncle, aunt, son, or daughter, and it's the jailer's job to ensure they get to trial, make things right, and get back to their lives. If the jailers didn't have the monopoly of force inside the facility, then the strongest or most influential inmates would determine what would happen to them instead of the courts.

USE OF FORCE IN STATE STATUTES

Law enforcement is created and governed by statutes. Even the use of force is contained in state statutes that outline how force can be used and for what purpose. In Colorado, there are several statutes regarding the use of force. These include everything from the parental use of force, defense of property, and the use of deadly force. Some sections, or specific statutes, address the use of force for law enforcement, jails, and corrections. Some specific statutes for Colorado jails and corrections are outlined below:

Jails

- C.R.S. 18.1.703 B

  - "A superintendent or other authorized official of a jail, prison, or correctional institution may, in order to maintain order and discipline, use reasonable and appropriate physical force when and to the extent that he reasonably believes it necessary to maintain order and discipline, but he may use deadly physical force only when he reasonably believes it necessary to prevent death or serious bodily injury."

Corrections

- C.R.S. 17-20-122

  - "Justification of officer. If an inmate sentenced to any state correctional facility resists the authority of any officer or refuses to obey any officer's lawful commands, it is the duty of such officer immediately to enforce obedience by the use of such weapons or other aid as may be effectual. If in so doing any inmate thus resisting is wounded or killed by such officer or such officer's assistants, such use of force is justified and any officer using such force shall be held guiltless; but such officer shall not be excused for using greater force than the emergency of the case demands."

- C.R.S. 17-20-123.

  - "Insurrection—duty of citizens. It is the duty of all the officers and other citizens of the state, by every means in their power, to suppress any insurrection among the inmates sentenced to any correctional facilities under the supervision of the executive director and to prevent the escape or rescue of any such inmate there from, or from any other legal confinement, or from any person in whose legal custody such inmate may be. If, in so doing or in arresting any inmate who may have escaped, such officer or other person wounds or kills such inmate or other person aiding or assisting such inmate, such officer or other person shall be justified and held guiltless; but such officer or other person shall not be excused for using greater force than the emergency of the case demands."

THE SOCIAL CONTRACT

Since at least the time of Socrates there have been arguments surrounding the moral and political obligations a person has to society. Philosophers like Hobbes, Locke, Rousseau, Rawls, and Gauthier all wrote about this "social contract" if you feel compelled to learn more about it.

It does seem that, with our representative republic through the Constitution, the people can expect some services in exchange for peaceful political processes. I must note, however, that for many career criminals and predators, there is no contract that they recognize, except that witnesses shouldn't talk to law enforcement. This type of division between law enforcement and the people increases the length of the shadows criminals operate in, making everyone less safe.

Governments need the monopoly of force to maintain order and services, enforce the law, and to provide a secure environment for daily life, commerce, and change. Since we're in a representative republic, this is done through the consent of the people through elections and ballot voting. The people expect that this force will be used reasonably and without bias. They also expect that those enforcing the law will be reasonable about law enforcement, use of force, providing security, and offering protected spaces where peaceable assemblies can hold their elected officials accountable.

I do think that everyone should learn about these processes so they can understand the very difficult position law enforcement officers are in and appropriately use their rights to vote and peaceably assemble when their representatives need more guidance or accountability.

CHAPTER 4 PREP

The monopoly of force is maintained by the government in order to ensure that everyone is given the opportunity for due process rather than resorting to street or vigilante justice. Still, the person who made a mistake, poor decision, or intentionally victimized another now has to deal with a new identity as they're thrust into the legal system to determine guilt or innocence and bear the consequences of that determination. In chapter 5, we will look at this new identity and the challenges it brings.

Chapter 4: Being Arrested—A New Identity

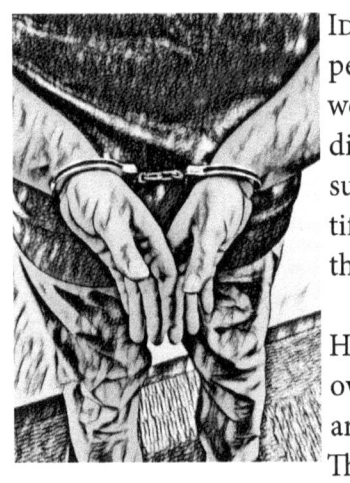

IDENTITY IS A COMPLEX THING. No one appears to be all one thing or another; instead, we seem to identify ourselves through many different, changing lenses and by taking on sub-identities. Sometimes I feel that we identify ourselves more by what we aren't rather than what we are.

However, with a major event, our view of our own identity as well as those of the people around us can change suddenly or drastically. This sudden change of identity can make for unique challenges that are difficult to deal with and process. Suddenly going from Tom "the life of the party" to Tom "the criminal" is difficult, as people have expectations of who you are. More importantly, when a person's view of their own identity rapidly changes, it can be challenging for them to process it emotionally. Very few people, as children, aspire to be incarcerated or to work in an environment that sustains those incarcerated.

A NEW IDENTITY

Some people go through their whole lives never knowing who they really are. Some seem to know who they are from a young age and act accordingly. Some people change who they are to fit each situation. Others become someone else due to an accident or a poor decision.

And then there are those who are given a new classification by professionals or the state.

State labels are nothing new. At birth we're assigned the gender and ethnicity that other people, agencies, and social networks tie us to. Each identity has an expectation of certain behaviors, thought processes, or codes of conduct attached to them. Sometimes we're given or reap a new identity that follows us for the rest of our lives—these identities often come as a result of a poor decision. I'm an example, as I mentioned in the first chapter of this book, of how a mistake can result in lasting consequences.

I was only fourteen when I was investigated and charged with a crime, but the consequences have stayed with me for life. I had to deal with those emotions and my confusion the best I could and keep believing I was a good person—I could have easily found a path to prison if I'd believed my mistake meant there was no other path. Instead, I had the will to make other choices and the luck not to do overly stupid things as I got older.

When I was first hired on as jailer, I would have the occasional nightmare that I was being put into a housing area as an inmate but had no idea what I was charged with. It was my mind's way of dealing with stress and encouraging me to make good decisions, but it was also a way for me to empathize with the incarcerated citizens I saw every day at work. Few people truly know what it's like to question who you are and whether or not you can accept who you've become.

AM I A "CRIMINAL" NOW?

A single poor decision can have lifelong consequences. I've seen many recently jailed people wrestle with what the experience means about them and the system. They tend to wonder if they're bad people, if they're criminals now, if their whole lives have gone down the tubes, and if their lives are still worth living. Some also become angry at the arresting officers for not taking their particular cases into account.

This shift in their view of themselves can be earth-shattering. The change in how they view the system and how it functions can have an equally life-altering effect. This experience often results in the breaking of the facade of who they are, what the system is, and how it functions, which can be very alarming. Having been a soldier, and deployed, I can identify with such life-altering experiences that change a person's worldview and their perception of self.

BREAKING THE FACADE

It's hard for some people to see themselves having a lapse of reason that could result in poor choices—maybe this is because some want to believe they're smarter or better than those who end up in jail. However, let's imagine a person who's made a series of poor decisions that has led to their arrest. They're likely to be on an emotional roller coaster as they replay the events in their mind and are processed into a system that is foreign to them.

This person may demand to know why they're being arrested, as the mere act of handcuffing someone can be seen as implying guilt. Then, after the handcuffs go on, the person begins to reevaluate everything. The world they've been living in, once as fast-paced as a shooting star, suddenly slows to a crawl. Simple movement between spaces, or access to those they trust for advice or encouragement, is restricted as any phones or communication items are likely to have been taken from them. They're then driven through their community in the back of a police car. This car arrives to a large garage door and drives into a large enclosure. The door closes behind the car and the person is escorted into the jail or police station where they begin answering questions.

Their information is then added to governmental databases throughout the country and the accusation of their law violation is recorded for the courts and public records. If the person is lucky, they leave quickly after being given a bond and a phone call. If they're unlucky, they remain in jail until they get bonded out or have their day in court.

In any case, the person now has the new identity of "inmate." While in booking they're given booking numbers, a state ID number, a "master name index" number, and likely an FBI or even a DOC (department of corrections) number if they're convicted and sent to prison. Their name and number are now used to identify them as they're shuffled through the legal process as required by law. They may also be dealing with a shattered facade of who they thought they were. They probably desperately want to be understood in the context of the events leading up to their decision, not just the fact that they broke the law in the process. In essence, they want to be seen as having acted reasonably for the situation and mitigate societal judgments for their choices.

THE "ONE AND DONE"

For the majority of people, the breaking of this facade is enough to get them to change their behavior so they never go to jail again. Depending on the charges, the "one-and-done" citizen may be able to return to their work and family with little more than a story and community service. Sometimes, however, they must climb the social mountain with the scarlet letter "F" for felon, making for a far greater degree of difficulty throughout the remainder of their lives.

THE "CAREER CRIMINAL"

For the minority, jail temporarily saves their lives (from homelessness or addiction, for example) and is like a second home. For others, jail is a path to criminal credentials, a place to meet up with friends, or a brief stop before prison. The "career criminal" tends to embrace the criminal identity, whatever that entails.

The point of this identity is to gain status and influence. Career criminals tend to view the world around them as being made up of predators and prey. Therefore, those who have more status and influence inside that world have less chance of becoming prey and a stronger demand for respect.

Many of these "high-status" career criminals generally expect two things when they go to jail or prison:

1. Officers should treat them as if they're a respected CEO of a company
2. All others should fear and obey them

Respect for your "average" career criminal is much the same, except they expect less grandiose treatment by law enforcement and more of a "mutually assured destruction" mentality toward other inmates in order to avoid becoming prey. Mutually assured destruction simply means that both will most likely suffer significant injuries or losses as a result of a conflict. Many do this by making it known that they will fight to the bitter end, regardless of the outcome.

PUBLIC PERCEPTIONS

Generally, people expect those accused of crimes to be removed from sight, kept in good health, given access to legal counsel, and prevented from committing more crimes. However, there's sometimes an expectation that the person should pay for their crime in a way that's more akin to revenge rather than making things right.

As soon as someone is arrested, the public seems to think they disappear into jail and are then subjected to other criminal acts by "worse" criminals, resulting in everlasting shame. Frankly, I just don't see that happening. Sure, there can be further predation inside the jail, but I haven't seen evidence that this is a frequent occurrence.

Being convicted of a crime does have repercussions beyond the jail walls, since many convicts have to list their accusations or convictions on job applications. In my experience, for the public, it's largely "out of sight, out of mind" until someone they know is accused of a crime or victimized by a criminal. Upon the citizen's release from jail, there's also a "not in my backyard" mentality on reintegration.

LEGISLATOR PERCEPTIONS

Legislators are politicians who write the law, set guidelines for its enforcement, and then allocate funds for this process. Those accused then become involved in a legal process where everyone is intended to be equal (due process) and allowed the same access to legal defense. Legislators may initially write a law based on a moral judgment or public pressure, but that usually gives way to pressures to ensure that such laws don't violate civil rights.

After this, there are further changes in policy or law that attempt to lessen the cost of enforcement if possible. Legislators can then show that they're "tough on crime" yet "fiscally responsible." The long-term effects that this approach has on the lives of those in the community (victims, perpetrators, and witnesses) are part of the equation but somehow seem secondary. It's little wonder to me why there's an erosion of public trust toward the government and its enforcement arm.

CITIZEN TO INMATE

As the average citizen is being booked into a jail, I'm sure they have moments of disbelief about what's happening. In addition to this, the average person has no idea about the legal process and if what they're experiencing is normal.

Having had a really bad day and in need of emotional support, these citizens are highly motivated to try and get themselves out on bond. However, they must wait for the many gears within the system to turn in order to allow any movement. If they can't bond out, they go into some sort of intake area in the jail and then there's little doubt that they have become an "inmate."

CHAPTER 5 PREP

The whole process of being arrested and investigated for a crime is challenging for anyone to deal with. It also brings with it a level of stress that few people are used to. The new identity felt after having gone to jail, and the future consequences for their decisions, are often overwhelming for people.

For jailers, it becomes normal to see people on their worst days yet still hold them accountable for their behavior while they're going through a challenging process. In the next chapter, we'll explore the basic operations of a jail, starting with the booking process.

Chapter 5: Jail Security Operations

I'll admit, I knew very little about how jails operated when I first started. I have no doubts that if I'd never worked in one and was arrested, I would be somewhat confused by the process. My previous military experience would've made this less of an issue, but your average person doesn't have a similar frame of reference to draw upon.

Jails have a general process for how the accused enter the facility. In most cases, they're booked in, interviewed for additional risk factors, moved to intake for observation, cleared for movement to general population or another appropriate housing area, and then relocated to segregation should their behavior or severity of charges call for it.

When I was a new jailer, it took time for me to see how this process worked and, more importantly, why it was in place. This chapter is on how and why a person can be moved from one type of housing area to the next. This process is likely to vary between jails based on size, resources, and agency philosophy. Some of these steps may apply to your local jail and others may not.

FROM BOOKING TO ADMINISTRATIVE SEGREGATION

Being arrested is usually seen as one of the more negative experiences the average person can have. In the United States, it's likely that a less-than-stellar decision is what leads to law enforcement becoming involved in a particular event. An officer will arrive at the location of the event, stop or detain those involved, conduct an investigation, and then determine if there is sufficient evidence to sustain "probable cause" that a crime was committed. The officer then writes a document stating how the accused's actions meet the elements of the crime, according to the criminal statutes of the state. It takes time to sort out the details, preserve evidence, collect witness statements, and document the investigatory process. When enough evidence has been collected to make it more than likely that the crime was committed by a specific person, the officer can make an arrest.

The person is then transported to the jail (in some sort of restraint for officer safety) to ensure that their information is processed and their access to their victim or future victims is restricted. This happens regardless of whether the accused believes they have done anything wrong. I've seen, many times, those accused failing to see the trail of victims created by their decisions—they often shout that they're the true victim. Sometimes, the accused can be both victim and perpetrator.

Next, the process of determining whether the evidence collected is enough to secure a conviction "beyond a reasonable doubt" begins.

JAIL SECURITY OPERATIONS | 51

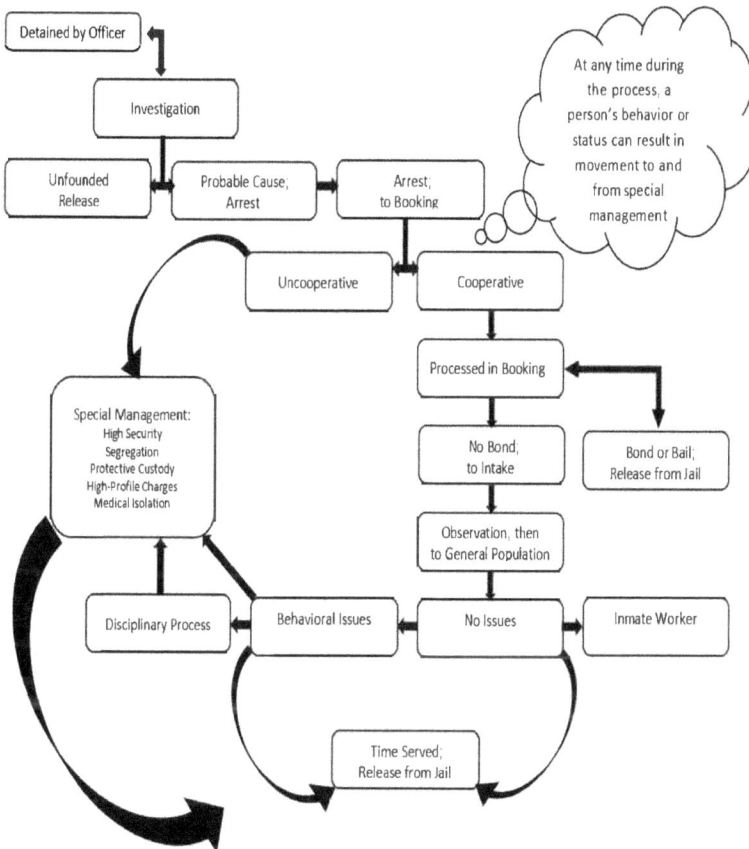

Booking

There are two types of arrivals in booking: uncooperative people and cooperative people. Uncooperative people are generally doing one of the following:

- Being physically assaultive
- Being verbally assaultive (making threats)
- Refusing to cooperate with the booking process

If a person is uncooperative, a team of deputies is assembled, a plan of action is made, and the process of moving the person from the vehicle into the facility begins. The transport will often be recorded on video, and a thorough search for weapons or contraband will be completed.

Often, clothing layers are removed for safety, as people can become quite emotional and seek to harm themselves with an article of their own clothing. After this, the person is placed in a cell and checked on frequently. When the person has demonstrated that they're stable enough and ready to cooperate, the booking process is completed and the inmate is generally taken to an intake area for further evaluation.

Cooperative people are either brought in by the arresting officer, transported from another agency, or have turned themselves in. They generally have handcuffs on, but they can also have other types of restraints until they've completed the first part of the booking process. They're searched by the arresting officer and they turn in any extra clothing, valuables, and their shoes. Some jails have the arresting officer complete an inventory of items, while others may have a specialist do that. A jail deputy will then conduct another search upon entry. The person will then complete the second part of the booking process, which often includes fingerprinting, an iris scan, a photograph, and, if required by statute, a DNA swab. If they have a bond and can get it posted, they will leave the jail. If not, they will likely be strip-searched or body-scanned (similar to an airport scanner), showered, given jail clothes, and taken into an intake area.

Intake

Upon arrival in intake, the inmate is given items necessary for their stay. Sometimes this includes blankets, basic hygiene products, and items with which to eat. They remain in intake until they're cleared for general population by both the medical and counseling teams. This is where things are more complicated than it would first appear. Inmates are classified according to medical, psychological, and physical needs, and some will spend more time being assessed before being cleared for general population.

For example, people coming off of drugs, alcohol, tobacco, and other substances may need additional medical monitoring before being allowed to leave the intake area. Other people are in an emotional crisis, have recently attempted to self-harm, or, as outlined in the previous chapter, think they've lost everything because of their arrest and believe they should end their lives. This results in an "emotional instability watch," meaning that the person will be closely monitored by deputies and counseling staff before being cleared for general population.

Some inmates are already dealing with serious health issues when they arrive in jail. As a result, care must be given as to where they'd best be housed, without giving them preferential treatment (which would go against due process).

After an individual is cleared for general population, they're moved from the intake area.

General Population

Jails have limited space and resources regarding how they manage the general population. As a result, they sometimes have to get creative when it comes to housing assignments. Some are divided according to a criminal classification system, others by charges, and others (if they're blessed with abundant resources) by pre-trial and convicted areas. In my jail, general population is a mixture of classifications because our philosophy focuses mainly on the behavior of the inmate rather than the charges. This isn't true in every case, however—murderers or suspects in high-profile cases may start out in our segregation area for safety.

Our general population areas consist of two types of operations: regular and privileged. In our regular general population housing area, we have rotational lockdown. This is where only a certain portion of the housing area is allowed out of their cells at any given time. This type of rotation is largely for the safety and security of the inmates as well as the staff. We switched to rotational lockdown because of the ever-growing ratio of inmates to staff and an increase in negative inmate behaviors. It was safer is reduce the number of inmates out at any given time than attempt to maintain control with ratios that can be as high as ninety inmates to one staff member. (As a side note, there are jails where this ratio is much higher.)

In our privileged general population area, inmates who behave well are allowed to be out all day (even at a ratio of eighty inmates to one staff member), and the housing areas are larger with an open layout. Inmates are expected to be better behaved or be moved back to the rotational lockdown areas for safety. We also have an area specifically for inmate workers. In that housing area, the inmates have cell door control because they have communal restrooms rather than cell restrooms. They're given alarm clocks to assist them in waking up and getting to work on time inside the jail.

In our jail, convicted inmates are mixed with those who are pre-trial because of the jail's size and resources. In the intake area, any special needs or accommodations are usually discovered and planned for before the inmates are moved to general population. Because of limited resources and our behavior-based housing philosophy, we can have a citizen accused of murder housed in the same area as a person who failed to pay their "dog at large" ticket.

Admittedly, moving an alleged murderer to general population doesn't happen immediately—when they're first brought into custody, they're likely to be housed in the high-security or segregation area for an extended evaluation of their behavior. This is done because it's safer for both them and the staff. As time progresses, it's possible for this person to be moved to general population if their behavior is consistently appropriate.

Inmate Workers

Many jails have some form of classification system for inmate workers. In our jail, we give these inmates more responsibilities and an opportunity to demonstrate self-discipline. These inmates work in the kitchen, do laundry and maintenance work, and assist with various programs and other needs. In exchange for this work, they're given extra time off their sentence and more housing area privileges. There are enough perks to being an inmate worker that these people tend to follow the guidelines required of them.

Special Management and Protective Custody

Anyone who needs some type of special consideration may require a special management plan. We've already discussed those with emotional instability, but we also see individuals who have altered mental states, suffer physical or mental disabilities, or require special management due to gender dysphoria. Some of them will end up in special cells or areas, while others will be placed in protective custody to keep them and others safe. We have a number of devices, medical and otherwise, that can be issued to or used by those who require additional support. Some medical devices brought in by the arrestee or their family members will be approved to enter the facility if a legitimate medical need is determined.

We have a housing area largely dedicated to those who have mental health needs or who are found to be less able to tend to their own safety in general population. Even this area doesn't have enough beds to house as many of these inmates as we have, however, resulting in spillover into other areas. For those who require mental health treatment and are extremely violent, segregation is the only place we can safely house them. Throughout the facility we have a limited number of cells for those with disabilities. For others who require medical isolation or need additional safety because of gender dysphoria, we must be creative in our use of cells within a housing area or we must move whole sections of the jail to accommodate these few inmates.

In the time I've worked in the jail, I've noticed an increase in the number of individuals with disabilities being incarcerated. Some people may have an increased medical need for items such as continuous positive airway pressure (CPAP) machines, oxygen tanks, wheelchairs, walkers, braces, and a host of other devices that are quite challenging to have in a secured place like a jail. This is especially true for smaller jails like ours that don't have the resources for a dedicated infirmary. Crutches and canes have a way of becoming weapons, and metal and electronic pieces often disappear from wheelchairs and medical devices. Jailers don't like these additional medical devices in their areas because of the increased safety risks they pose. However, because many inmates really do need this equipment and bed space is always at a premium, we must deal with it the best we can.

Administrative Segregation and High Security

Administrative segregation (ad seg) is a status that removes a person from general population. People moved to ad seg status upon arrival tend to have violent charges and have often violently resisted arrest, causing injuries to officers. However, an inmate can also earn a spot in ad seg for repeatedly disregarding facility rules or causing area disturbances. If the inmate is sufficiently violent and willing to physically assault a deputy, they will likely find themselves on ad seg status and tagged as "high security."

In our jail, an inmate dressed in red is a visual indicator that they're on high security status. It's a reminder that the inmate has made credible threats toward or injured staff. They may have also fashioned a weapon while being housed in the facility or have a violent criminal history.

Your average person likes to confuse ad seg with solitary confinement. These aren't the same thing. Ad seg inmates in our jail can talk with other inmates, and when they're behaved enough to not assault others, they can reduce their classification level until they're allowed to be out with other inmates again.

CHAPTER 6 PREP

Jail operations go beyond the basic processing and moving of incarcerated citizens, and it requires cooperation between many people, businesses, contractors, and agencies. This type of cooperation results in an enclosed society that operates like its own city. The next chapter will outline the many other sections, or units, within the jail that are required to ensure the safety and security of inmates and staff.

Chapter 6: The City within a City

When I first started my career, I concentrated on safety and working my housing area. In the first year, I sometimes felt that volunteer services, programs, and counseling were somewhat of a hindrance. After I learned the basics of my job, however, I changed my point of view rather quickly. I now see that all sections of the jail form a team that essentially manages a small city, and that this large and diverse team works together to ensure both the safety and security of everyone. I also feel that this team effort is vital to managing the stress of all those inside the facility.

JAIL MANAGEMENT

Jails can be small enough to only house a few cells—they can even be small enough that a deputy might be making all of the inmate meals. Jails can also be so large that they compare with prisons in their scale of operation. In the jail where I work, we're large enough to have contracted services but small enough that we have very few specialty housing areas. Each jail will have a unique style of operation even though they fall under the same constitutional guidelines.

A large jail is a city unto itself. Deputies are on the front line of the operation, but the job would be much harder, if not impossible, without all of the planning, resource allocation, training, and support provided. At the top of jail operations is the sheriff, but she or he is likely too busy to be directing the jail personally, so this task may fall to a facility administrator.

Facility Administrator

These administrators or designees tend to be deputies of higher rank, such as a captain or lieutenant. They are responsible for making sure the jail is run as well as possible, as safely as possible, and as securely as possible, given the resources devoted to it.

Facility administrators oversee the sworn staff, civilian staff, and any contracting entities. They build the case to request additional resources, which the sheriff then presents to the county commissioners and voters. Administrators also make the case for policy changes that could help to more effectively manage inmate populations. Such a task can seem monumental and never-ending. It requires a large commitment, lots of energy, and good organization skills. As a result, administrators are reliant upon others to expertly manage their respective areas of responsibility.

Because of the demanding nature of their work, administrators are unlikely to maintain a detailed knowledge of the challenges faced by the deputies and other front-line staff members. As a result, they're less likely to identify with what the average deputy is going through or how policy changes affect them. This can foster a belief by the front-line staff that those promoted eventually become too detached. After all, these administrators were likely to be, at one time, front-line staff themselves. The truth is that administrators must focus on other challenges that require complex solutions.

While administrators have the same basic skill sets that every supervisor must have (such as strong management, communication, and leadership abilities), their area of influence is greater, bringing increased liability. Policy decisions made by administrators will influence the front-line staff, who, in turn, will influence the hundreds of people under their care. A misstep or ambiguous change in policy can have serious consequences if a less-than-fully-trained staff member attempts to implement it or a veteran isn't properly informed of the change. This requires additional skills in resource procurement and allocation, logistics, risk management, and litigation. They focus in this way so they can provide the training and resources necessary for the front-line staff members to continue their good work.

Jail Deputies

Jail deputies ensure that inmates get access to food, medicine, emergency care, counseling, protection, and programs, and that their cells and areas are repaired as needed. In addition to this, deputies attempt to watch out for the safety of those who are having difficulty managing themselves or are being victimized by others. If the agency employs deputies who have low personal and professional standards, there will likely be an increased risk of tragedy and litigation.

Being on the front line means consistently dealing with a vast array of negative behaviors, attitudes, and aggression that the rest of the staff may only face on an occasional basis. The deputy must be able to step in and be a counselor, bodyguard, investigator, and program facilitator, and they may even need to give CPR in an emergency. The jailer is often one of the first people that newly booked citizens in the jail come in contact with, and they're often the last person they see when they leave. Deputies often wish them luck when they leave, and (not to sound inhospitable) hope they don't come back.

First-Line Supervisors

First-line supervisors, usually corporals or sergeants, are responsible for ensuring that the front-line deputies get the day-to-day guidance, training, supplies, and support they need to do their work. The tradeoff for this support is an expectation that the deputies remain professional and in compliance with agency expectations. First-line supervisors are also the first line in ensuring that the administrator's vision is being worked toward.

Most events, complaints, and quality-control issues are handled by the first-line supervisors. For reviews of the use of force and complaints against staff by citizens and other employees, we have a professional standards unit.

Professional Standards Unit

A professional standards (or internal affairs) unit is vital in the effort to ensure that both jailers and citizens have a way to reveal less-than-professional conduct and fix it. There are times when a jailer's conduct is questionable or their actions violate policy to such a degree as to constitute a breach of the public trust in the authority given. A professional standards unit will investigate the actions of staff in relation to policies and the law. The investigation will determine if that staff member will remain an employee of the sheriff's office and if criminal charges will be brought.

In my jail, inmates can file grievances as the first step in a process designed to solve problems at the lowest level possible. However, these are also screened by the professional standards unit, and should a trend reveal itself or require more investigation, an inquiry begins. I find this part of the agency to be more of a support system than a concern—we all need help keeping standards high.

Master Control

Inside the jail there is often a group of individuals who monitor radio traffic and operate doors. Sometimes this is done within the housing area at a separate control point, and sometimes there's a central area in the building dedicated to this. Some jails combine the housing area controls and the general master controls.

Often, these individuals are watching cameras, controlling important access points, and assisting greatly in the facility's emergency operations. Where I work, the master control team operate as gatekeepers, additional eyes during emergency situations, and dispatch for the jail.

Support Personnel

It takes many people working together to ensure that inmates receive the proper treatment while in jail. Providing for their basic needs also greatly reduces tension.

Just as in any community, jail is a collection of people housed in close proximity to each other and operating with varying levels of stress and coping skills. A jail, however, has a higher level of tension when compared to the community at large. Being a community, it requires some support in providing for orderly operation.

Where I work, we have various supply companies, contracted kitchen, medical, and counseling staff, and companies that provide money and telephone management. In addition to these contracted companies, we have inmate programs staff, booking specialists, pre-trial staff, maintenance staff, veterans affairs and Medicaid representatives, and various volunteers. We have sections that run payroll, records, transportation, and notary services to inmates. On top of this is all of the court staff, such as clerks, investigators, public defenders, DAs, and judges. All of these sections support the criminal justice system and the mission of the jail.

A MULTIDISCIPLINARY APPROACH

Sometimes it seems like the public expects law enforcement to toss citizens into a jail cell and "throw away the key." However, the era where this was acceptable treatment is long over. Today, citizens expect jails to meet inmates' physical, mental, and emotional needs to a reasonable standard during their time in jail. At the same time, there's also some expectation that inmates are supposed to be "uncomfortable" as a deterrent against future incarcerations.

Still, you'd be surprised at the amenities that inmates expect to have access to when they're in jail. Some people literally expect Starbucks and McDonald's, along with continued access to their phones and Facebook, unlimited phone calls, and instantaneous service for their demands. Sometimes these inmates complain to their families, saying that they aren't being fed or given access to medical care even though they are. As a result, the families of these inmates are, rightly, very concerned when they call into the jail to yell about how the treatment their loved one is receiving will result in litigation. At times it can seem that society "sort of" wants the inmates to be held accountable for their actions, but in a way that doesn't inconvenience them.

Inmates have the right to reasonable access to medical services, food, light, hygiene, and safety. My jail works hard at providing access to as many services as safely as possible. Separating programs, resources, and responsibilities among sections within the jail reduces stress for everyone, and allows the inmates to have more access to those resources than they would if only the deputies were responsible for them. (However, during an emergency or unusual event, deputies must to be able to fill in for any of the other sections, often at a moment's notice.)

The jail where I work is constantly looking toward the future. Our administrators see the strong need for community involvement that supports inmates and hopefully reduces recidivism. There are ongoing efforts to provide space at or near the jail for other governmental and non-governmental organizations that provide services or at least a gateway to those community resources. Our jail eventually wants to have a release process that helps citizens reintegrate back in the community and avoid future jail stays.

Food Services

It's easy to take food choice for granted. But when a person is arrested and taken to jail, this choice is often limited to the items on an issued tray. Nearly everyone who comes into jail will say that the food isn't good. Many are so used to processed and fast food that kitchen-made items just don't seem to compare. Some think that not having the foods they like means they're being starved, or that they're entitled to the food they had outside.

When inmates do complain about the food, I sometimes cringe and think of how, for supposedly tough people, entitled and petty they sound. One day, when my "word filter" failed me, I replied to an inmate that I would rather the money be spent on school meals for kids instead of adults who should know better. I urged him to appreciate what he was given, as life is full of things to appreciate if you look for them.

Also, I had to eat those free school meals as a kid, and I find the food provided by the jail to be quite reasonable. Just like in school, there are days where it isn't to everyone's liking, but it's their choice to eat or not. In the military, sometimes green eggs and spam was considered a fantastic meal. I guess it's all about perspective. Still, if the meals are truly and consistently bad, this can lead to unrest, so it's important to have a reasonable standard for meal service.

Medical Services

When I was in the military, there was a social expectation that one avoids going to see the medical team. In fact, you could have a fractured bone and 90 percent of the time you were just prescribed Motrin and told to drink a lot of water.

The jail normally takes a similar approach, in that the inmates are given ibuprofen and water as a treatment for most ailments. At first this approach may not seem right, until you see the sheer amount of med-seeking and drug abuse that takes place. The medical team needs to get their patients to a baseline so they can evaluate them for further and appropriate treatments.

Inmates suffering drug or alcohol withdrawal tend to be given some medication to prevent damaging seizures and other events. The medical team works to get inmates off of whatever illegal or non-prescribed medications they were on in order to stabilize their condition and evaluate for further treatment.

The medical professional's license is on the line, so they will conduct their own evaluations and, given the evidence, use their company guidelines for providing medical care. Although medical staff do seek additional information from the inmates and even call their primary-care physicians or pharmacies, further care is at their discretion. Once inmates are stabilized, medical staff members begin looking at access to other treatments, but it may be a much slower process than treatment on the outside.

Emergent medical needs are taken care of quickly, but the trick is determining whether or not the "emergency" is designed to lure staff into a cell or send the inmate to the hospital for an escape attempt. Sometimes inmates also have an expectation that all their medical needs will be taken care of without cost to them.

Despite months or years of self-neglect, inmates believe their issues can be magically fixed by jail nurses and doctors. They then get very angry when they find that a jail medical section doesn't do elective treatment or surgeries. More often than not, there's only one nurse to every one hundred fifty to three hundred inmates. Yet those inmates expect the nurses to remember their personal circumstances, maintain their basic health care, and accept crude remarks or creepy statements as compliments.

As jailers, we report our observations of medical issues to nursing staff and document interactions of medical note. Because we aren't trained medical professionals, we can't assume that inmate complaints are fictional. Instead, we pass along the inmate's concerns and let medical staff make treatment decisions. Practicing medicine in a jail isn't easy, and the staff don't have the resources that private practices have. That being said, the nurses I've met in the jail tend to be of high quality and they do make the right decisions when emergent or critical situations require additional resources.

Counseling and Mental Health Services

Jails are, more and more, being filled with those who have difficulty coping in the community due to mental health issues. It's important for jails to work toward some sort of continuity of care for these citizens, as it's part of public safety. This approach also helps to stabilize, then increase, the functionality and safety of those with disabilities.

Our counseling staff must be flexible when it comes to treating people in order to get them started on the care they need. Jail counselors triage, stabilize, and then try and get people on the right track. As you can imagine, this isn't easy, as there aren't many funded mental health resources.

When I first started working inside the jail, there was a common view that the counselors were too quick to believe inmate stories and "over-empathize" with them. Some also thought that counselors were looking for ways to absolve inmates of their culpability. It didn't take long to realize that this was not the reality.

In truth, mental health professionals bring specialized knowledge regarding behavior and thought processes into a field that traditionally views all citizens as being responsible for their decisions in every respect, regardless of circumstance. Since jailers are greatly interested in generating voluntary compliance, the techniques used by those in the counseling field are highly valued. Furthermore, their view on behaviors can assist in formulating special management plans for difficult or especially challenged individuals.

JAIL PROGRAMS

There are some jailers (and some people in general) who think inmates should be locked in cells all day. However, even in ancient times, authorities understood that idle hands and minds are cause for concern and often trouble. Roman armies did more than just fight, they were also "engineer" armies. When they weren't preparing for or engaging in the bloody business of war, they were kept occupied by building roads, aqueducts, government buildings, and other projects. By putting the focus and energies of the troops into engineering pursuits, the leaders mitigated the risk of them causing trouble.

Program staff inside jails provide a similar function. They can, at the very least, provide a distraction, but their goal is to give inmates new life skills or a change in worldview in order to help them change their path. Inmates are often worried about their families, their future, the legal process, and whether or not their lawyer is truly working for them. They also worry about threats from or problems with other inmates—they might be bunked above or below someone they absolutely detest, yet they're expected to not buckle from the stress. Leaving their pod and cell for an hour here or there can be a welcome distraction, and, if the program is right, an outlet for negative thoughts or energy.

Depending on the program, inmates can come away with new tools to mitigate destructive behaviors. It isn't that these programs will supplant years of bad decision making, but sometimes a person is ready to change, and they just need information on how to turn their lives around. As a jailer, I greatly appreciate the programs because they keep inmates busy, reduce the number of inmates in the housing area for that time, and reduce tension. I also like how some programs challenge world views, prompting some inmates to change their path. I can't imagine the jail without such programs, and when I do, I imagine higher tension and increased stress and violence.

Jail Commissary

Many jails have items that inmates can purchase in order to make their incarceration a little easier. These commissary programs are either run by an internal unit or a third-party vendor, and they provide another level of services and options to inmates and their families who wish to support them while they're in jail. Food items sold in the commissary can be used on days when the provided meal isn't to the inmate's liking.

Commissary items do introduce a challenge to security as these items are often gambled away or coerced from those who receive them. Some items should also never be allowed in a jail—anything that can be used as a weapon will, eventually, be turned into one by an inmate. However, despite the difficulties, jails still try to ensure the safety and security of inmates while providing some additional levels of service.

Jail Maintenance

Jails need to maintain a number of critical systems twenty-four hours a day, seven days a week. The general use and abuse of equipment results in a near constant need for repairs. Equipment designed by those with little front-line experience often leads to design flaws, which result in costly modifications in order to maintain safety and security. Infrastructure built by the lowest bidder may last a few years, but as time passes, it can become more and more difficult to get parts.

The women and men who work in maintenance are absolutely critical to the safe and secure function of a jail. Their jobs never end, and there are always issues with balancing the demands of the facility versus the availability of money, parts, and time.

The citizen who finds him or herself in jail has to deal with the end result of these challenges—I've heard many inmates complain about the heating and shower systems, beds, and other maintenance-related aspects of the jail. Since jailers are the most visible representatives, inmates complain to us as if we're responsible and have the ability to fix it. The truth is, the citizens of the county are responsible for the jail's funding, and this has a direct impact on what the jail can and can't do. It's far easier for citizens to approve funding for the improvement of the facility than for a sheriff to scrounge up cash internally to make improvements or change a bad jail design.

CHAPTER 7 PREP

As with many process-based governmental interactions, the system and its processes are a source of friction to the accused, the victims, and those inside the system. Those who work inside the system are the "grease" that allows the wheels to keep turning despite this friction. However, just like the system creates a new identity for the accused, the jailer is also given a new identity that they too have to work through.

Chapter 7: Being a Jailer—A New Identity

As I talked about in chapter 4, identity is complicated—we're more than our sex and skin color, or any other physical attributes. We're spiritual, emotional, and intellectual. We're so many things that it seems like many people try to simplify it for themselves and others.

However, even with all its complexities, a sudden change in how we or others see ourselves is difficult to process. Making the transition from "Joe the mechanic" to "Joe the cop" isn't easy for Joe or those who know him best.

A person joining law enforcement will have their own expectations of how they're supposed to be and act now. Their friends and family members will also have expectations of how they're going to be, and will perhaps even fear who they might become. Strangers might only see their badge, and their identity may then be limited to that person's experience with law enforcement officers or what they've seen on television.

WHAT IS A JAIL DEPUTY?

One time I was attempting to de-escalate a situation with an inmate who'd been brought to booking from our segregation area. He had broken the cell lights and light covers repeatedly, and sharp pieces of plastic and glass were all over the floor. He didn't want to talk to anyone and would repeatedly spit on the window when someone tried to speak with him. I went up to the cell window and he spit on the glass where my face was. Instead of leaving, I told him that we had something in common. He stopped for a moment, his face and eyes filled with rage, yet I sensed I had a chance to talk with him.

I told him that neither he nor I had ever expected to be in a jail when we were children. I didn't expect to be working in one, and he didn't expect to be on the other side of that door. After I said this, his facial expression changed, his body became more relaxed, and we got into a long conversation about life.

Although I'm sure there are a few people out there who always wanted to be a jailer, the vast majority in the field didn't imagine themselves ever having this job. People who enter law enforcement, in general, want to make a difference, and they imagine themselves running into the line of fire to save a family or stop a murderer. Jailers are similar to police officers in that they run to troubled areas, try to stop people from hurting themselves or others, and investigate criminal activity.

Jailers must also slip into many roles, including counselor, case manager, disciplinarian, mental health worker, educator, and investigator, and then they must file charges like a patrol officer. Being a jailer is different than being a patrol officer in that the "beat" a jailer walks is much smaller than in a real city, but there are higher concentrations of citizens who make poor decisions or are quick to deliver violence.

WILL YOU BECOME A DIFFERENT PERSON?

After several years of being a jailer, I could safely say that I'd been influenced by my job. I found that I had slowly begun isolating myself in an attempt to cope with the higher stress levels that came with feeling at risk. One example of this was that after being threatened multiple times in my work week, I developed a reluctance for going out in my community because I was sure to see a handful of people I'd recognize or that I could tell recognized me, and I couldn't be sure if one of them would try and make good on a threat.

The reality is that I meet hundreds of people in a year and remember very few of them. I feel that I've placed my family at risk because some inmates have threatened to harm them just because I'm doing my job. As a result, I've changed how I view and respond to the world around me and those most important in my life. Those who have known me the longest have told me that I've changed.

WEARING, THEN NOT WEARING, A BADGE

There's something about a uniform and a badge that makes people feel more important and professional. The badge and uniform symbolize the authority given to you on behalf of the sheriff and the government—that authority will be maintained provided that your decisions and orders fall within the framework laid out in the statutes. I feel a stronger sense of duty and legitimacy when I put on my uniform and go to work.

I've observed an interesting phenomenon between those currently wearing the badge and those who've retired or accepted a civilian position (support positions like those in records or master control). Often, those who've come off the line tell me that they no longer receive the same level of respect from their colleagues as those who continue to wear a badge.

Some of the civilian staff in the jail have had far more experience as uniformed jail deputies than those in the early part of their careers. Yet their experience may be overlooked because they no longer have a bright, shiny star on their chest.

I'm not sure why this happens, but there may be an assumption by some officers that those without badges have nothing valuable to contribute. My guess is that, without a badge, these civilians are assumed to be as undereducated in the policing field as the general public. Furthermore, a general separation between civilians and law enforcement may be at work here. The remedy is simple, however: try not to marginalize anyone. You haven't walked a mile in their moccasins.

PUBLIC PERCEPTION

Each agency or jail has its own unique operations, ethos, culture, and personalities driving it. There's no perfect way to do things, and many agencies have differing philosophies. As a result, jails will vary significantly in reputation and retention. Some members of the general public have an anecdotal and imaginative view of what it's like in jail, or what it's like to work in a jail. Many think that all law enforcement agencies are the same despite the obvious evidence to the contrary.

Some people want to believe that all jailers or those with badges are power-hungry, sleep with their badges on, and get sadistic enjoyment from watching the emotional pain of others. It's easy to let our imaginations run wild and think about all the ways that a person with power and protection from the law could cause harm. This fear is valid given the general non-education regarding how jails operate. The reality is, in my agency at least, that jailers are just as restricted—sometimes more so—than those they watch over. Jailers are also given a great deal of responsibility, for which they can be held accountable at any time.

Other people understand that working in a jail is a difficult job and will give jailers praise when they encounter one. Since jailers tend to work inside a locked facility, however, these encounters are very rare, contributing to a sense of social isolation and a perception that there's a lack of social appreciation for their work.

PUBLIC EXPECTATIONS

The problem with public expectations of law enforcement is that the law and real life are rarely so orderly. I've heard members of the public criticize the actions of law enforcement officers as if they were some high-speed, highly trained, Delta-Force operators with years of experience. The citizenry seems to forget that officers aren't trained for ten years in every skill before being added to a patrol or jail roster.

Most officers are from the community they serve and aren't highly trained ninja warriors with special-forces shooting skills, Jedi reflexes, and psychic abilities that allow them to know who intends to do what and when. These are your average neighbors, sons, daughters, and spouses who have signed up to do a very difficult job with some additional training and education. They learn that a person with violent intentions will have the advantage of action versus reaction, and that they may not see it coming.

In movies, jailers are often given the identity of the "badge-heavy asshole" who couldn't make it as a street officer or was picked on as a kid. When other media sources (or the agencies themselves) don't contradict this, or the media selectively shows stories supporting this view, this identity is given weight in the general public.

As a result, those who work in a jail may be branded with that identity by the public whether or not it has any basis in reality. If the average citizen doesn't know or understand what it takes to be a jailer, or anything about the lives of jailers, then how do we expect them to get an accurate picture when fiction rules the airwaves?

The work inside a jail is much harder than most people imagine. Jailers have more interactions with difficult people for longer intervals of time during their shift than your typical patrol officer. Jailers will, at some point, have a serious crime committed in their housing area. They then have to investigate, collect evidence, write the report, write disciplinary actions for all involved, file charges, and then receive further guidance or criticism from those expecting polished, detective-level work.

Jailers have to do these investigations while continuing to run their housing areas—they don't get a break or downtime. They rarely get time to de-stress or debrief. Despite the crime that was just committed, jailers must make sure that inmates have as much access out of their cells as possible while ensuring their safety and security.

A patrol officer will spend a few minutes to a few hours with a citizen, victim, or suspect. A jail deputy will get to know an accused citizen over a few days to a few years. As a result, many more jail deputies are recognized in public by former inmates, despite being out of uniform, than the standard patrol deputy. The result is a reduced sense of anonymity while being out in public, and therefore, a reduced sense of safety. In essence, a jailer sacrifices the safety and freedom that comes with anonymity as a result of their public service. Furthermore, there's little to no consistent public recognition for their efforts, adding to their sacrifice.

LEGISLATIVE PERCEPTION

Jailers must, for all individuals under their care, make the laws and policies work in order to ensure due process. As you can imagine, citizens in general aren't happy with the circumstances around their arrests, nor the processes they must go through thereafter.

Those who legislate these processes have difficulty tailoring the law for the masses, let alone each individual, and have difficulty accepting criticism from enforcement personnel on why such policies may not be ideal. Furthermore, the laws being drafted also have a political element that can't be overlooked and will be measured at the ballot box.

Generally, lawmakers expect a world-class, highly trained, professional police and corrections force that can also function on a shoestring budget. Such expectations are unrealistic given the volume and variation of duties required by law enforcement.

When laws are being debated, the legislature takes the brunt of the public's criticism. After the law is passed, however, law enforcement has to step up and take the public's criticism on laws they didn't create. It's convenient to have public servants who must, according to statute, enforce the laws made by legislators and then take the brunt of the public's dissatisfaction with their passage and enforcement.

INMATE PERCEPTIONS

A jailer's face and personality will be burned into the memory of the inmates in their housing areas. This memory will be especially strong if the jailer is seen as particularly callous or badge-heavy.

An arresting officer sees a citizen for a very short time in comparison to a jailer and is often not remembered as well. Street officers will be in direct contact with hundreds of citizens throughout the year, but few of these citizens will be particularly troublesome. The jailer, by contrast, will also have direct contact with hundreds of citizens, but these citizens are the people the street officers had trouble with.

If the jailer lives in the community they serve, it's unlikely that they'll be able to go anywhere without being recognized by those they've watched over. As a result, they may feel much less comfortable being out in the community. I myself can rarely go to a restaurant where I don't recognize at least two people from the jail. Seemingly overnight, there's no place where a jailer can relax other than home or other counties.

BREAKING THE FACADE

Acting with "authority" can seem enticing to the untrained or inexperienced eye. However, this authority comes with a level of responsibility and scrutiny that can break a person. Like law enforcement officers everywhere, jailers can suddenly become an instant villain. Your actions will be scrutinized by a public that is often too ignorant of what jailers are required to do and the sheer stress of the job to provide truly constructive criticism. Still, perception is king, and at the end of the day, facts might not be allowed to get in the way. The irony is that, once under scrutiny, a jailer's actions will often be viewed with more skepticism and criticism than those of the criminals they watch over.

Being a jailer means being put into nearly as much danger as a street officer but with much less recognition. Often, even within the law enforcement community itself, less credit is given to how difficult the job can be. For many people it is very much out of sight, out of mind.

Sometimes, in order to give themselves permission to act with authority, jailers will begin creating distance between their past poor decisions and their new law enforcement identity. Some jailers will reflect contempt for inmates and their decisions because they see those types of decisions mirrored in themselves. As law enforcement officers, they're expected to now make better decisions and hold themselves to a higher standard.

Like many professions, if you want to be truly good at the job, there's a steep learning curve. It's easy to overlook this learning curve when viewing the work from an outsider's point of view, especially when it seems like jailers just walk around, hand out toilet paper, and log unusual events. I've found that life experience can help with this learning curve, especially when it comes to communication and manipulation.

Many inmates use misdirection as a large part of their standard operating procedure. Many new jailers have to adjust their desire to trust others in order to better deal with such persons. No one likes being the person who was fooled. Therefore, jailers and those in law enforcement develop a hefty sense of skepticism in nearly all human interactions over time. A jailer must take this new identity, skills, and world view and then use them to manage the safety and security of individuals who are likely to be lying, exaggerating, omitting details, and observing their patterns in order to manipulate them.

THE JAILER IDENTITY

If being a jailer means having a badge, uniform, radio, and equipment, then anyone can do the job. In my experience, however, it's not that simple. Being a jailer is similar to all necessary but not socially desirable fields, like garbage collection and water sanitation . I have yet to hear kids say they want to do these jobs when they grow up, but trash removal and water treatment are vital in keeping cities sanitary and staving off disease, while salvagers recycle needed items and ease the burden on the environment.

Like trash and water sanitation workers, sometimes jailers are mired in smelly biological waste or working with individuals that haven't seen a shower in weeks. Like the salvager, we try to refocus individuals toward a more socially acceptable means of living while reducing the impact of their predatory decisions on the innocent, overly trusting, and most vulnerable in society. Like these other careers, jailers and corrections officers will also seldom be praised in public, and will be exposed to consistent emotional, psychological, or physical violence and stress.

The environment of a jail is at a natural state of elevated risk. You have people being brought to jail with all manner of disease, dysfunction, and elevated stress. Many people transfer their stress to others, and jailers are a main target because they represent the system. Jailers become very aware of the many communicable diseases that are brought into a facility and feel extra stress because they know they can bring this back to their families should they fail to decontaminate before they get home.

Because of this elevated exposure risk, many jailers become very concerned with how clean things are, sometimes resulting in taunting about being obsessive compulsive.

In times of emergency or crisis, jailers become counselors, case managers, emergency medical personnel, scientists, social workers, detectives, information technicians, and crisis communicators in addition to being law enforcement professionals.

Working in such an environment takes its toll on a person. Some jailers I've worked with have longed for another career but couldn't quite move on for one reason or another. Many try to stay in the field as long as possible because of money, retirement, a sense of accomplishment, or because they know the person next to them is having a similar experience. A core few love the career and the challenges it brings.

As a result of these challenges and the different personalities we bring to the field, a person working in a jail for long enough will begin to see trends in types of jailers.

JAILER ARCHETYPES

There are some general archetypes for the jailers you'll work with. Although I hate to admit it, at various times in my career, or during specific events, I've slipped into quite a few of the archetypes listed below. Although I've tailored these to the jail environment, I can imagine a version of them for almost every type of work or career out there. I guess people will react similarly no matter what job they may have.

The New Deputy

This person has just begun their career. Sometimes they're unsure of themselves in certain situations. Other times they're so sure of themselves that they throw caution and safe practices to the wind. As with a stone tossed into a river, time, pressure, and distance will make them smooth. They may also go through periods or moments, like I did, where they dip into one or more of the following archetypes.

The "Other" Deputy

When an inmate is caught doing something they aren't supposed to do, they often say, "The other deputy said I could." The "other" deputy is a seemingly mythical person who lets inmates do whatever they want, doesn't enforce the rules, and does favors for the inmates. However, like all myths, a tiny percentage of jailers may be doing one or more of these things, giving rise to the legend. If caught, these deputies' names often become a verb describing that particular style of management or a mistake that's been made.

The Caregiver, Cheerleader, or Counselor

This person tends to look after those around them. They always seem to be available to lend an ear, help motivate you, or ensure that you have the things you need to make it through your day. They tend to be more interested in helping their coworkers and maintaining a community than career advancement.

The Badge-Heavy Deputy

Because many inmates inherently resist and defy authority, some deputies respond by enforcing every rule to the max, especially if the inmate is being difficult. These deputies know the full extent of the disciplinary options available to them and will push the envelope of these when they feel slighted by a particular inmate. There will be frequent radio calls to their areas to remove difficult inmates and the deputy may openly brag at being able to lock down entire areas due to disciplinary issues. Supervisors may respond by moving these people to less troubled areas and some of their coworkers may accuse them of not being able to "run a pod."

The Hard-Ass

This deputy believes the book was written to be followed and that all good employees do what is outlined in policies and procedures. They're wary in making exceptions to policies even when a situation calls for it, and they like to run their areas in a particular way. They're generally fair and willing to help to the extent they're "allowed" to. Even though they appear to be unmovable they're usually just more cautious and conscientious.

The Desk Potato

This deputy is rarely seen away from their desk—so much so that some of the inmates will relax greatly knowing that the deputy doesn't want to leave it. Some inmates will hide, and others will then fill the "power vacuum" left by this deputy. The deputy will walk through the pods at the assigned times, call emergency codes when necessary, and enforce discipline when an action is so blatant that they know they have to address it. If your jail allows phones, they are sure to be on it rather than watching the inmates under their charge.

The Antagonizer

There are a few jailers who, by nature of their style, appear to antagonize the inmates under their care. Many times this isn't done purposefully, but because there isn't enough consideration given to the difficulty of the situation. However, some jailers cleverly do things to purposely agitate inmates: pretending not to hear them, ignoring requests, using names or unprofessional tones, or singling out one person for a particular rule violation are some examples of how this is done. This deputy relies on their position of authority to ensure their safety and control.

The Game Master

There are some jail deputies who have done the job for so long that they need to spice things up a bit. They'll set up elaborate plots to get an inmate to follow the rules (this usually includes isolating them by disrupting their social network). They'll often use terms like "fishing" when they allow an inmate to get away with a blatant minor rule violation because they want them to reveal the violations of other inmates.

The Gossip

The name is enough on this one. This person knows everyone and all of their business. Depending on the personality of this deputy, they can take care of everyone or sow seeds of rivalry and discontent.

The Brutus

This person combines gossip with politics. In an effort to distract others so they look better, they'll throw their coworkers under the bus.

Those in law enforcement are used to being held accountable for their decisions and actions. There are times when a better tactic or decision could have been made, but it was a learning experience. This learning experience, as brought forth through the chain of command, will involve defining the issue, examining the causes, coaching for a better future outcome, and counseling and support.

The Brutus will turn this learning experience into an inquisition. Instead of learning the lesson in a positive way, a very negative interaction happens, and those who experience it will feel like they're being attacked by both the inmates and their supervisors. The stress generated and transmitted to the entire staff can be tremendous.

The Born Critic

This jailer has a gift and a curse. In an near instant, they can see a situation or action and find the spot where it isn't optimal. These are the people you want working on space or aviation equipment: they can spot gaps, holes, shortfalls, bad designs, and flat-out bad ideas almost intuitively. However, this type of gift often comes with a price, which is that they can't shut it off.

Many times, this person also has either a limited or nonexistent filter. The result is that they can drive people away. I nearly always find the this deputy's observations insightful, but if they're chronically under-appreciated, marginalized, or focused on negatively, they could become a Burnout or a Cancer, which are further down on this list.

The Old-Timer

This person has quite possibly been around since before jails were invented. They've seen every style of management and have discovered a way to remain professional, adapt to constant change, and shed excess stress. They will often have well-run areas but may not be up to speed with the latest technologies.

The Insecure Badass

This person wants to help others and is generally a good person. However, they have significant social insecurities they make them seem over the top and overzealous. They often attempt to dominate conversations, and they over-emphasize their accomplishments in order to feel equal to those around them. The irony is that the more they behave this way, the more their coworkers become skeptical and begin to chip away at them.

The Burnout

In contrast to the Old-Timer, these jailers have often mastered their craft but haven't been able to deal with change, stress, or career-advancement setbacks. Over time, their productivity will drop, and they'll be less and less willing to take extra shifts or process disciplinary actions. Sometimes getting a slightly different assignment can help this person, but it's very difficult to get out of burnout when it occurs.

The Squirrel

This person has the energy and attention span of a squirrel: they're ready and willing to volunteer for just about everything. The downside is that they're unlikely to finish a project before taking on three or four new ones, thereby overloading themselves.

The Prepper

This jailer is prepared for every contingency. At the gun lockers, they spend several minutes off-loading their guns, ammo, several knives, two batons, and other items they have "just in case." They're also likely to have extra food and snacks with them, making them the person to go to if you forget your lunch. They like to go over "what if" scenarios that feature unlikely tools or solutions because the most likely scenarios are too easy.

The Cancer

This person has been in the organization long enough to criticize everything about it. It's rare if they don't point out how a new policy negatively impacts them and the whole organization. Unlike the Born Critic, they have many stories about how they were exploited or wronged by the agency. It isn't that some of this isn't true—in fact, more may be true than not. However, some of the truth is covered over by negativity and avoidance. Often this is the stage that follows being chronically burned out, or when a more grandiose facade has been broken.

The Inmate Whisperer

This deputy is a direct-supervision Jedi—they have the gift of gab and a sixth sense for knowing what inmates are going to do before they do it. This deputy will amaze you at their predictive capabilities and will often have a way to de-escalate nearly every agitated person. That being said, they also sense when words are going to fail and are ready to use force while others are unsure of what's going to happen next. Their areas are generally run very well and they're often given challenging assignments.

The Storm Trooper

This person likes all things tactical: they'll have the appropriate response and tactical solution to almost every scenario. They'll likely be on some sort of emergency response team or arrest and control cadre and have really cool tactical gear to go with it. They're ready to get in on any enforcement action and often train others in regards to tactics and use of force.

The Surly-but-Caring Veteran

This person has had this career for several years. They've done a decent job at stress management but have developed a surly exterior, using a lot of quips, wisecracks, and sarcasm. However, the mere fact that they talk to and give (sarcastic) advice is proof of how they they caring about their coworkers. They truly want others around them to succeed, and they look after their tribe. Just don't expect them to be all cheery about it.

The Idea Monster

This is the person who always has new ways of doing things. They get bored with the status quo and look to new technologies, other agencies, and research in order to bring the latest and greatest. Their search to learn and grow never seems to diminish—the downside is that those who've been there, done that may feel like this person is stirring a pot that's already been stirred enough.

The Hidden Talent

They're "just a jailer," right? No. This person has a hidden talent like singing, woodworking, landscaping, contracting, building custom luxury homes, farming, or ranching. In their spare time, they might be a real estate agent, or an electrician, programmer, pilot, corporate manager, author, pen maker, astronomer, or flintworker. It's crazy how many jailers have other talents that can benefit their coworkers or their families.

The Leader

This person tends to naturally generate confidence in their decisions and trust from their colleagues. They're often the person who's bombarded with questions by line staff and supervisors alike because of their competence and approachability.

The FTO

Field training officers (FTOs) are your teachers and unofficial leaders. They provide guidance, support, and training, and they build the confidence of newer staff members. They're the backbone of a professional operation in that they're better than your average deputy. However, this comes at a price: the average FTO makes it about three to six years before getting burned out or wanting to step down as a trainer.

The work is hard because FTOs have to maintain their areas, supervise new deputies, and document both operations in detail. They often have to stay late to complete their work and are usually not exempt from mandatory overtime. They genuinely care about those they train, which means they can also sometimes talk a bit too much about practices, methods, or policies.

CHAPTER 8 PREP

A newly hired jail deputy doesn't know what he or she doesn't know—this is where the jail mini-academy and the field training program come in. These programs teach the very basics of the profession before letting the new deputy join the front line and further their education through real-life experience. The next chapter will talk about these programs, what they include, and how a new deputy learns to be a jailer.

Chapter 8: Learning to Be a Jailer

When I was first hired at the jail, I knew without a shadow of a doubt that it would be one of the bigger challenges of my life. It wasn't the skills I would learn or the general requirements of the job—I was concerned about how I would perform knowing that I didn't like violent and predatory people. Growing up, I'd directly experienced the mentality of such individuals firsthand, and I knew it would be very challenging to deal with them day in and day out, especially when I'd sought to leave those things behind as I became an adult.

LEARNING TO BE A JAILER

The process of becoming a jailer can be long, arduous, and stressful. In general, the more life experience you have, the easier the training will be. I've heard of a time (hopefully long since passed) in some jails where a person would be handed the keys, given a policy manual, and then turned loose to do the work. Hopefully, your agency wants to set you up for success while keeping you safe, and therefore will provide some level of training. Some states have a central corrections academy that certifies staff for these types of positions statewide. Others leave this to the agencies to handle themselves.

The rest of this chapter is an overview of how my agency prepares new deputies for jail operations. Every agency has different ways to train, and if your jail uses a different process, it doesn't mean you're getting below-par training. Agencies have different levels and types of resources, goals, and cultures. It's usually their mission to provide superior public safety and service with the limited resources given to them.

Since Colorado doesn't have a central corrections academy, the first step in my training was our jail's mini-academy—a very condensed version of specific specialties necessary to the safe and secure operation of a jail.

First, we went through staff introductions and education regarding "officer-involved protocols" that explained the level of liability we were taking on and how we should expect to be viewed as suspects should something happen.

Next, we took a jail tour to see where everything was. Then we were trained on radio procedures, gang studies, direct supervision, verbal de-escalation, safety and security awareness, emergency procedures, drug recognition, medical unit operations, inmate discipline, arrest control techniques, body scanners, court services operations, and suicide prevention.

Additionally, we covered the Prison Rape Elimination Act of 2003, criminal investigations, cell searches, domestic terrorism, computer database training, report writing, excited delirium recognition, inmate rights, cultural diversity, the special emergency response team (SERT), less-lethal weapons, and Tasers.

Finally, we also learned about emotional survival for law enforcement and how to successfully get through the field training program itself.

After I finished the mini-academy, I was ready to enter the field training program.

The Field Training Program

A good field training program is designed to bring a person from their academy-level education and transition them to the field. In general, their trainer is their coach, mentor, and evaluator. Depending on your base model (Reno or San Jose), there may be varying levels of checklists, homework, tests, and either a larger focus on specific skills or a philosophy.

The program I went through was inspired by the San Jose model. The program originally focused on standard guidelines, which were evaluated area by area inside the jail through the use of a checklist. After training in one housing area for a certain amount of time, the trainee was signed off in that area and could work it alone. The training wasn't complete until you were signed off in every area. As a result, when short on FTOs, the supervisor could have a trainee work an area they were signed off on. However, in time it became recognized that a trainee may not have all the necessary skills to run an area independently.

The current field training program looks much different in that it's skills-based, not area-based. It uses a five-point scale that's guided by checklists, and trains for core competencies that adhere to standard evaluation guidelines. The training is broken into four phases, which I've outlined in detail below. I worked with the field training team within the agency to create this new model, and we're constantly reevaluating the program in an effort to chase excellence.

The current field training program consists of four general phases:

- Phase 1: Learning database and computer operation, emergency procedures, and policies and procedures
- Phase 2: Gaining skills such as direct supervision, inmate interaction, cell searches, status checks, inmate discipline, general awareness, and basic officer safety and security

- Phase 3: Putting phases 1 and 2 together and then adding the specifics of each housing area and any special needs (this phase consists of both a day- and a night-shift component)
- Phase 4: The trainee runs their housing areas without any assistance from their FTO

If the trainee passes every phase, they graduate the field training program and become a jail deputy on a probationary year.

Phase 1: Information Overload

As outlined above, the first phase of training in the field training program consists of database and computer operation, emergency procedures, and select policies and procedures.

First, the trainee is expected to learn how to operate the computer and enter codes into the database regarding area activities as well as individual inmate events. In essence, they have to log every time they walk the area, along with area visitors, area movement, individual movement, individual visitors, individual disciplinary records, and then incident or criminal reports. In addition to this, they have to be able to navigate through informational resources such as the policy and procedures database, inmate handbooks, maintenance requests, court reports, inmate behavioral reports, visitation schedules, and emergency procedures. The emergency procedures in particular are gone over again and again to ensure that the trainee has an idea of what to do when they're running their area and something happens.

This phase ends with a policy test and computer tests. If the trainee passes these, he or she is cleared to move to phase 2.

Phase 2: Direct Supervision

The second phase of training consists of learning more about direct supervision, inmate interaction, cell searches, status checks, inmate discipline, general awareness, and basic safety and security. If the trainee has difficulty with strong personalities, threats, conflict, physical action, security practices, or the enforcement of discipline, then a strategy can be developed to help them. If they are still unable to adapt to the work, their scores will reflect this.

The trainee is expected to conduct "status checks" in their area to check on the condition of the inmates as well as the building. They will be taught how to conduct a cell search and what to watch out for as far as safety. Serving meals, enforcing discipline, conflictual communication, de-escalation, and basic area operation are taught. Just like in phase 1, emergency procedures are gone over again and again.

Trainees in this phase need to learn to be aware of their surroundings, body language, and little changes throughout the day. This is a skill that takes years to get good at but pays dividends in a jailer's dealings with people in general.

Phase 3: Putting It All Together

The third phase of training consists of putting the material from the first two phases together and then adding the specifics of each housing area for both day and night shifts. This is also the stage where the trainee is given more responsibility for their decisions and is held more accountable for their impact on their housing area.

Here, our jailers learn more about dealing specifically with intake areas, general population, mental health populations, and segregation for both female and male pods. Often, new jailers will be in what is known as "conscious incompetence." In other words, they now have an idea of what they don't know about the job, which can make them hesitant to take action. As a result, some of them will have great difficulty making independent decisions. The weight of the liability for their decisions begins to weigh heavily on them and the stress is often visible.

The ability to quickly shift between tasks, manage your time, manage inmates, and make decisions are built up during this phase. By the time a person finishes phase 3 they're expected to be consistently making good decisions based on experience and knowledge. From here they go to phase 4 to see how they operate independently.

Phase 4: Checkouts

Phase 4 is a quality-control phase that takes place over a couple of weeks. The trainee is expected to operate without the interference of the FTO and to show good judgment. They should be asking for help when they need it from the sources available to them. This phase is the last step before they're expected to take on the full liability of their decisions and join the rest of the staff on the line. The real learning begins once they're on their own, as it will still be the better part of a year before they feel comfortable that they have the basics of the job down.

ANECDOTES FROM THE JAIL

"Intimidated"

While training a new jailer in a male general population area, I noticed that a particular inmate appeared to be intimidating the trainee. I then began to notice that the trainee appeared to be avoiding inmate contact and conflict. He would seldom speak with inmates directly and would avoid inmates that had strong personalities. I later asked him about that inmate and he admitted to being a little intimidated by him. This isn't unusual for someone new to the field who isn't used to individuals who use psychological threats and physical intimidation as their normal mode of operation.

We moved to the women's intake pod in an effort to reduce his stress and work another angle of conflict. Although there are serious assaults in the women's area, most conflicts are loud verbal altercations. After he conducted a cell search, a female inmate began yelling at him from across the pod. She yelled, "You better be leaving my shit alone! Stay out of my cell!"

The entire pod stopped what they were doing to see what would happen next. They first looked at the trainee to see his response. He had put his head down, shoulders forward and hunched, and he avoided eye contact and speaking to her. He appeared to scurry back to the mini-control where I was.

I could see genuine surprise and looks of satisfaction on some inmate's faces, and some laughed. The deputy was so uncomfortable with conflict that his body language made him a target for predatory personalities that are very comfortable with conflict and psychological intimidation.

"Firm, Fair, and Consistent"

One skill needed to maintain authority and credibility in a housing area is to be firm with your decisions, fair in their application, and consistent with previous decisions. This is particularly important when addressing rule violations, as some inmates see the lack of enforcement as permission to break any and all rules. Once others see a lack of response, more respond by also breaking more rules. A housing area can quickly become difficult to manage as a result. During training, we look at how the trainee will enforce the rules while remaining firm, fair, consistent, and professional.

One morning, I asked a trainee to search a room that had a lot of contraband visible from the cell doorway. I also asked that he decide what disciplinary approaches to use should he discover any contraband in the cell. The inmate had several oranges that were peeled and placed into a peanut butter jar in preparation for making alcohol. The inmate had additional peanut butter jars, other containers, many extra pencils, modified pencils, and saved food. He also had extra and altered items in his cell, including a torn washcloth. There were many extra books in the cell and other items that could be used to make a weapon when placed into a pillowcase. The trainee made no effort to speak with the inmate or hold him accountable despite repeated reminders to deal with the situation.

Later in the day, after another cell search, the trainee discovered property that had been transferred to the pod worker from at least two other inmates. In our facility, inmates aren't allowed to share things. The trainee didn't address these violations with any of the inmates involved except by speaking to the person whose cell he searched. That inmate told him that he'd picked up the items from the common areas. The trainee was suddenly not sure if inmates could share these items or not, so I encouraged him to again look up the information.

Having observed him not address these issues, I again demonstrated enforcement of rules and approaches to addressing violations. I also provided one or two isolated examples of how to deal with other disciplinary issues. Having given demonstrations and verbal guidance, I put him into a position where he had to decide what to do with the next violation.

An inmate put coffee in a piece of paper and was going to share it with his cellmate right in front of the trainee. I pointed out the violation and asked him what he was going to do about it. He decided that he was going to seize the coffee. This showed me that he could make decisions regarding disciplinary actions, but that I had to force him into action by putting him on the spot. The trainee was having difficulty addressing any rule violations—let alone those in areas he was responsible for—in a firm, fair, and consistent manner.

"Fire Response and Evacuation"

Sometimes trainees try to reinvent the wheel when it comes to fire and evacuation drills. We teach order and controlled movement to the point that, when tested, the new deputy tends to overthink a fire and evacuation drill. They know what the policy states; we've gone over it in verbal scenarios. However, their responses in the verbal scenario tend to not work in real life. After I have them go over this particular scenario several times in a day, I unleash an actual fire and evacuation drill.

Before I pose the scenario that the area is starting to get smoke coming in from another part of the building or a specific cell, I quietly notify the inmates that we will be doing the drill. I even enlist one of them to not respond to calls to stand outside of the cells or to evacuate because they're "sleeping" on their bunk.

With the stage set, I give the trainee the scenario and tell them to simulate the radio traffic but physically do everything else. Generally, this request is met with a look of horror.

Some deputies initially lock their inmates down, ensuring that they would suffocate in their cells due to smoke inhalation. Others stand the inmates down but then think they have all the time in the world to do a facial recognition while "smoke" fills up the housing area. Other deputies begin evacuation immediately but then stop each inmate at the door to get a facial recognition. This slows down the evacuation, and they also have no hope of remembering who they saw or didn't see when it comes to making sure that all the inmates were evacuated. Some deputies evacuate the inmates without bringing anything to verify which inmates they have (or don't have). These responses tend to happen because they're thinking about the required procedures as they're trying to make them work.

Once at the primary evacuation point, trainees tend to stand right next to inmates with their heads down, attempting to see the faces on the tags and compare them, exposing themselves to possible attack while doing so. Once they've conducted a facial recognition as required by policy, I ask them if they have everyone. They almost always say yes, despite the fact that they used a method that guaranteed that they didn't know for sure. And of course, there's still the inmate who was "sleeping" in their cell.

Once the trainee is made aware that they don't have all their people, they often return to "the smoke-filled area" without any protective gear on. This leads to discussions about smoke inhalation, how to ensure that their inmates are supervised, and how to evacuate to the next area should the need arise.

Most of the time, the issues I see are a result of reinventing the wheel, test anxiety, and the fact that it's an imagined scenario rather than a real one. We all remember how it was done in grade school: collect your roster, calmly get everyone out of the affected area, have them sit, and then conduct a roll call. This is still the most efficient means out there, and it's so simple that it doesn't need improved upon.

CHAPTER 9 PREP

The field training program provides a strong base for the new jailer to be able to take their place on the line and be trusted to generally make good decisions and know when to ask for help. Still, learning to manage those citizens who find themselves in jail takes some work and skill. Inmate management is an area that we train for and evaluate throughout the entirety of our training program, and throughout a person's career.

Chapter 9: Inmate Management

ALTHOUGH SOME GENERAL MANAGEMENT SKILLS are very useful when working in a jail, due to the distinct aspects of jail operations and the similarities of the people who frequent them, there is a decidedly unique flavor to managing inmates.

Before we look into ways to influence and manage incarcerated citizens, we first need to examine the two main kinds of inmates: those serving short-term sentences for misdemeanor offenses and those who are pre-trial for more serious offenses that could land them in prison.

THE SHORT-TERM INMATE

These inmates are released back into the community after serving relatively short sentences. A few will return after their next petty offense, misdemeanor, or probations violation, or because they failed to comply with their sentencing conditions. (In fact, I've seen inmates released out the front door only to be brought back in a few minutes later for committing a crime in the parking lot.) The short-term nature of the incarceration means that habitually jailed citizens get to know the jail's operating procedures and staff members. Inmates who aren't regularly jailed, on the other hand, will remember the deputies, but the deputies probably won't remember them.

As a jailer, the opportunity for rapport-building, in general, is shorter because of time constraints and the stress of the job. Because of all the tasks that must be accomplished during a shift, many jailers may not utilize each interaction as a chance to build rapport with inmates. For some jailers, the constant turnover of inmates increases their stress because they have to continually teach new inmates the operating procedures and deal with the inevitable dissatisfaction when the citizen finds out that jail isn't like a hotel and the deputies aren't concierges.

Managing inmates with many relatively low-level offenses also means having to stabilize people while they're withdrawing from drugs, alcohol, internet or phone addictions, and sometimes a profound sense of entitlement to special treatment. Many aren't at their best and are dealing with identity issues, dissatisfaction with a system that doesn't treat them as individually as they would like, and feeling stonewalled because the jailer in front of them doesn't have all the information they feel they should have. Often, the inmate transfers that stress and frustration to the symbol of the system in front of them. These challenges aren't usually experienced to the same degree in the department of corrections, where longer sentences are the norm.

THE PRE-TRIAL INMATE

For inmates in pre-trial status, special attention must be paid to the Fifth and Fourteenth Amendments:

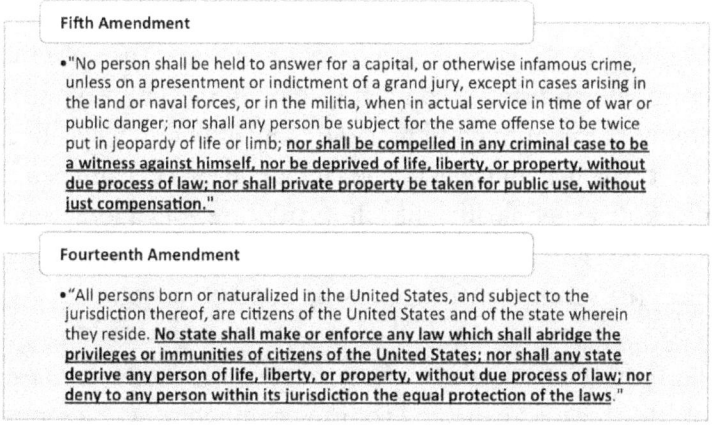

Fifth Amendment

- "No person shall be held to answer for a capital, or otherwise infamous crime, unless on a presentment or indictment of a grand jury, except in cases arising in the land or naval forces, or in the militia, when in actual service in time of war or public danger; nor shall any person be subject for the same offense to be twice put in jeopardy of life or limb; <u>nor shall be compelled in any criminal case to be a witness against himself, nor be deprived of life, liberty, or property, without due process of law; nor shall private property be taken for public use, without just compensation.</u>"

Fourteenth Amendment

- "All persons born or naturalized in the United States, and subject to the jurisdiction thereof, are citizens of the United States and of the state wherein they reside. <u>No state shall make or enforce any law which shall abridge the privileges or immunities of citizens of the United States; nor shall any state deprive any person of life, liberty, or property, without due process of law; nor deny to any person within its jurisdiction the equal protection of the laws.</u>"

When a person has been convicted of a crime and is sent to the department of corrections, their status changes. As far as the Constitution goes, this means that the person now has enhanced protections under the Eighth Amendment against cruel and unusual punishment (through sentencing or as a by-product of sentencing) because of their conviction status.

Other than this constitutional enhancement of protections, once a person is convicted of a crime, there are really no appreciable differences in the constitutional protections of pre-trial detainees and convicted inmates. However, there are some differences between states and even counties on what is allowed when it comes to enforcing law, order, and discipline inside jails.

When a person is still presumed innocent because they have not yet been convicted of a crime, there's a general expectation that they should be treated differently or with more care than a county-sentenced inmate or a prison convict. However, many jails don't have enough resources to separate pre-trial detainees and those convicted of crimes. Also, those in pre-trial status tend to outnumber those who are serving sentences inside a jail.

DIRECT-SUPERVISION PHILOSOPHY

Jails that use a direct-supervision philosophy design their areas to enable more prolonged and direct contact between the inmates and staff. The idea is to decrease behavioral issues and increase safety by upping inmate and staff contact through jail design, program availability, reinforcement of good behavior, and active supervision. In my experience, you generally get the behavior you expect from people, and in a jail, treating people like the adults they are goes a long way. If you expect bad behavior, it shows in your body language, facial expressions, and tone. The same goes for expecting good behavior.

In order to have effective inmate management, you have to establish control. This means hiring and training competent staff, empowering them to be capable supervisors of their housing areas, and making good communication an agency standard. Coupled with appropriate inmate classification, orientation, and a fair and just disciplinary system, the likelihood that jail operations will be manageable, cost effective, and safe for everyone increases greatly.

Although my jail was an early adopter of the direct-supervision philosophy, we've endeavored to get better, which requires a lot of hard work. Staff attrition and changing norms of inmate behavior make it a very challenging aspiration to be a model agency for direct supervision. Still, it's well worth the effort!

INFLUENCING INCARCERATED CITIZENS (INMATES)

How do you get someone to do something they don't want to do? How do you convince an angry person that it's in their best interest not to act on impulse even though they think they have no future? How do you satisfy the needs of eighty people when you're their only point of contact? Inmate management is one of the more difficult skills to learn because of the sheer volume and variation of requests and the limited time you have to assist people.

Each person's individual situation is important to them, and their freedom to get things done on their own in jail is severely restricted. Their only option is to use the methods available to them through those who can assist in those methods. However, how many requests can a housing officer get to in a day while also facilitating meals, medical attention, recreation time, visits, safety, and telephone calls, and also documenting inmate activity and enforcing discipline?

Each deputy has a finite amount of physical, mental, and emotional energy that gets depleted at variable rates depending on the situation and behavior of the person(s) involved. As a result of these variables, deputies may give some inmates more attention (who don't deserve it) in order to minimize their impact on this energy reserve. Meanwhile, more deserving inmates may not get the attention they need. Either way, communication is vital to influencing inmates to act in their own best interest. In fact, it's so important that communication is specifically covered in more detail in chapter 12. Here are some basic ways to effectively influence inmates.

Discipline Fairly and Predictably

Discipline is often the start of a conversation and an opportunity for the inmate to learn. The conversation is usually about regulation and structure, and how these can lead to predictable consequences (both good and bad). If consequences are predictable, individuals can see how their decisions influence the outcome. The idea is that they choose to do the right thing, or the thing that has a reward rather than a negative result. I discuss discipline more in chapter 15.

Be Consistent

Inconsistencies in the application of discipline, the enforcement of policies, and general operations provide a wide-open channel for manipulation and exploitation by inmates. If there are too many inconsistencies, jailers begin to doubt the professionalism of their coworkers, increasing inmates' ability to manipulate to their benefit.

Watch Out for Manipulation

Some people are very good at analyzing a system and getting the most out of it, or moving within it in a way that was never intended. There are no exceptions to this within jail walls, and whether you call it gaming the system or manipulation, you're in the right neighborhood. Inmates figure out what they want and how to get it. Sometimes the methods they use are illogical as they're detrimental overall, but some people are satisfied with a short-term "win."

It's common for an inmate to attempt to get a jailer to compromise themselves, usually in a small way at first, in order to manipulate something more from them. It's important to understand common manipulation techniques and where or when you, as a person, are more susceptible to this manipulation. It's also important to have a plan in place to deal with situations where you might find yourself tempted or in the first stages of compromising.

Avoid Arguing

Avoiding arguments doesn't mean avoiding conflict. Some people want to voice their frustration and dissatisfaction by yelling about how messed up it is and how it needs to change. Often, this takes place when an inmate is already escalating, and they're working themselves up some more. The logic in their arguments is often lacking, but it tends to be an emotional complaint by definition and will likely not be solved with any "reasoned" words.

Instead, I've found it much better to give the person a task that may actually help them or at least give them a reasonable outlet for their energy. Sometimes this is writing their grievance down or leaving them with a thought that you'll return to in a few minutes. In the end, these inmates often get the last word, and that's okay because we often get the last action.

Maintain Authority

In my experience, maintaining authority is easier when a person has a developed "officer presence," broad working knowledge, confident communication, and has built rapport with most of the inmates in their area. It takes time to develop some of these skills, but not as long as one might think. What you wear, how you act, and your body language become your officer presence. Having a strong working knowledge of your craft results in a reasonable chance for you to answer a inmate's question with the right information, building trust. Considering how many people aren't up to speed with how the system works, this is huge. Communicating confidently includes being able to tell someone what they don't want to hear, not getting pulled into arguments, and demonstrating empathy with active listening skills.

Building rapport can be difficult, but it generally takes place when you help someone in some way. Rapport is often built when we listen to someone who's having challenges in their lives and then provide guidance that eases their concerns. Other times it's built because we've answered someone's questions directly so they know they aren't getting the runaround. It can also be gained when we hold people accountable for their actions and decisions in a way that is respectful and empathetic. Just asking about their day and stopping to listen can go a long way.

Custer and the Battle of the Greasy Grass (Little Bighorn)

When Custer decided to attack at Greasy Grass, he took a gamble that the shock and speed of the Seventh Cavalry would disorganize the defenders and send them running in panic and fear. Having disorganized them, his troops would then dominate despite their smaller numbers. He knew he was outnumbered; he knew where the defenders were. However, he didn't know that the Native Americans had a technological edge over his troopers and a strong will to fight. His soldiers were carrying breech-loading, single-shot long-range rifles. In addition, his troops were taught to dismount, with one out of every four troopers holding the horses for the other three. Furthermore, the troops he had were not the seasoned veterans of the Civil War, but relatively newer soldiers.

Although most of the Native Americans (who were defending their families that day) had lesser weaponry than the Cavalry, they had sufficient numbers of Henry repeating rifles to tilt the balance of firepower to them. These rifles allowed them to fire multiple shots at the Cavalry for each one fired in return. Once the Cavalry had been weakened and their mobility taken away, the attack stalled and the Native Americans overwhelmed the remnants of the Cavalry.

So what does this lesson have to do with jailers? In jails, the ratio can be one hundred twenty inmates to one jailer. Where I work, we sometimes have a eighty-eight-to-one ratio in the housing areas. Clearly, as far as sheer brute physical force goes, the inmates have the advantage.

Even a ten-to-one ratio could be problematic depending on the inmates, the policies of the jail, and the skill level of the jailer. Not many people can simultaneously engage physically with more than one or two people at a time. This means that we should look at the reality of the situation when addressing how to best prepare ourselves and our coworkers for the possibility that we find ourselves cut off from help, outnumbered, and fighting for our lives.

Know Fact from Fiction

The Seventh Cavalry built up a reputation for speed, good-quality horses, superior distance rifles, good training, and firm leadership. Effective troops and flashy uniforms are what Custer brought to the fight. However, he overestimated the abilities of his newer soldiers and underestimated the combat power of the Native Americans he was up against. He believed in the facade of invincibility that he'd created for the Seventh Cavalry rather than appreciating the reality of the situation. That being said, there's sometimes no greater defense than a forcefully projected facade to those you're trying to influence. A great example of this is the Spartans: they were few in number, but their training and reputation did so much to intimidate their enemies that many wars were avoided based on their reputation alone.

Law enforcement operates within a similar framework. Officers are given specialized training, information, equipment, and the authority to use all three in order to maintain order and rule of law and to investigate criminal activities. The purpose of the training and authority is to dissuade individuals or groups of individuals from enforcing their own versions of justice or challenging the authority of the state.

Somehow, it seems that the perception of the general public as of late has been that officers are highly trained special-forces types that use the authority entrusted to them in a haphazard or biased way. The reality is that the vast majority of officers are trained to a basic proficiency level with firearms and demonstrate average skill with this level of training.

I think it's somewhat naive to expect special-forces levels of ability at the pay grade of a rural community police officer whose department has even less money devoted to training.

If the average officer were as highly educated and superhuman as they're made out to be, then why are there simple mistakes made in logic, evidence collection, and the use of force? The seemingly haphazard or biased actions that police are accused of may, in fact, be an indicator of the natural variation in abilities within communities. This is especially true in regard to the wildly varied ability of communities to provide funding for training, attract talented officers, and retain officers that meet the quite substantial public expectation.

There isn't a central law enforcement academy in the United States where all police get trained. In fact, many of these training centers are either state- or community-based and vary from city to city. Each policing agency also has its own culture. A good way to put this issue into perspective is to look at firefighters. They study fire science, use the same types of tools, and discuss how to achieve the best results with others in the field, and yet they have different approaches when it comes to their individual communities. I would find it brow-raising if people protested their local fire department for the actions of another city's fire department.

Like firefighters, each law enforcement agency utilizes similar basic education, discusses tips and tactics, and tries to use similar tools. However, there are sometimes drastic differences in culture from one department to another, which is often exacerbated by deep-rooted historical precedent. Each county has at least a sheriff's department, any cities within that county could have their own police departments, and the state usually has a highway patrol or some equivalent. Although these departments may work with one another, the cultures between them will be different.

The fact is, like the communities from which they come, law enforcement agencies have a minority of high performers who exemplify excellence and professionalism. They also have a minority of low performers who seem to make many errors and exemplify what most people dislike about police. The majority of officers will be proficient enough to be professional, but they're not without a bad day here and there. This is why the agency's culture becomes very important: a toxic culture is reflected in the performance of their officers. A culture that is always looking for excellence will actively seek to learn from each incident to improve itself, and will likely retain the trust of the community in the process.

HOW THIS APPLIES TO JAILS

Why don't the inmates use their superior numbers to assault jailers, take over the jail, and escape? Inmates and jailers are just people from the community. People have many personal issues to deal with, and, in general, act in their own self-interest unless given a reason to band together. Jailers need to project competence, authority, and concern for those under their care in order to effectively influence them. Furthermore, jailers have to show that they're able to deliver fast and decisive force to any given situation in order to maintain the monopoly of force inside the jail walls.

If jailers ended their training once they had flashy tactical uniforms, equipment, and techniques in the use of force, they would likely lose the majority of their influence over time as well as play into media stereotypes about badge-heavy jailers. Jailers get training in force projection to help rapidly deploy and sustain forces in a crisis, but most of the time, jailers operate in ones and twos when watching an area and rely much more heavily on relationship- and rapport-building.

A good jailer recognizes that building rapport inside the walls will pay great dividends in gathering information and influencing the housing area. In fact, the ability to talk to people and build rapport is the single most effective tool a jailer brings with them to work.

CHAPTER 10 PREP

Some people have a conflictual communication style, which can lead to a disproportionate level of clashes, altercations, and disagreements within a jail. However, despite this conflict, you will be working constantly to solve problems while attempting to optimize the operation of your housing area given the many demands on your attention and time. This isn't easy, and your decisions can have results that last anywhere from several hours to several months.

The next chapter will outline the problem-solving and decision-making methods I use when dealing with these types of operational issues and questions.

Chapter 10:
Problem Solving and Decision Making

I WAS FORTUNATE TO BEGIN working a jail after having spent time in the military and completing some higher education. It isn't that these are requirements, but they can help a person learn the problem-solving and decision-making skills needed to work in a jail. As a jail deputy, you need to be able to recognize a problem, think critically about the options for addressing it, decide the best approach, and respond quickly.

PAID TO OBSERVE AND LISTEN

Before a person can solve problems or make decisions, they must first see or hear that there's an issue. Even if you recognize an issue, it's useful to discover whether or not you're seeing the root of the problem or just a symptom of it. In a jail, a deputy will have to learn when to use their ears and eyes to recognize critical clues of any issues developing in their housing area. This task is very difficult at first because it can cause information and sensory overload. Jailers have multiple individuals speaking, moving, and communicating with body language in their pods. This doesn't count the communication the jailer receives via radio and other information devices such as computer databases.

It takes time to learn when to relax your eyes in order to see more and how to focus your hearing without blocking out too many other sounds. These skills can be difficult to master for some and second nature to others. Beyond being observant and listening, you have to be able to recognize some things as being unusual or peculiar while having the mental discipline to not dismiss them out of habit.

PAID TO THINK

As outlined earlier, the criminal justice system is imperfect in the sense that it requires people (not robots or machines) in order to function. As a result, the jailer must be able to critically think about the policies and procedures in regard to a specific person or circumstance and decide to either keep strictly to the policy or make adjustments. Problem solving and troubleshooting issues will be a frequent part of the work, along with the anticipating events and planning effectively.

PAID TO DECIDE

Having thought about an issue and developed possible solutions, the jailer must then decide which solution will be used. The safe thing to do is to follow policy, as it outlines the expectations of the agency and standardizes the response to questions or problems so that expectations regarding due process, regardless of circumstance, are preserved. However, there are situations where a policy may be more of a barrier to fair treatment or was not designed to work in a particular situation.

If the jailer decides to alter a standardized practice in order to accommodate a special situation or help someone who has more barriers or difficulties than the average person, then they have to be prepared to articulate the reasons for this. Furthermore, they must be prepared for the consequences of their decision. Ignoring or adjusting policy on the fly shifts liability from the agency to the jailer. As a result, the jailer must articulate that a reasonable jailer with the same level of training and experience would've made a similar decision given the information available at the time. In addition to this, the jailer has to articulate why, given the situation, they did or did not consult others or their supervisors. It's with these types of decisions that the liability and stress can be the highest, but the rewards can also be great, especially when the outcome works in the best interest of both the agency and the individual.

PAID TO RESPOND

Deputies and jailers train so they can properly perceive an issue and respond appropriately. These responses require training, thought, and good judgment. As a result, individuals should work through various scenarios in their minds so they can train a response instead of having a half-baked reaction. A jailer who is over- or underreacting is likely not training themselves to "respond." As a result, it isn't enough that a jailer can see that there's an issue and know the related policy. They must decide on a course of action and respond. Inside a jail, a decision to wait can be a valuable response. However, being unresponsive because of an inability to recognize an issue or decide on a course of action is unacceptable.

RESPONDING WELL

Challenge, Objective, Planning, Preparing, and Action (COPPA)

Unlike the open streets of a community, the jail environment is pretty well controlled. We have limited places to hide and acquire weapons. We control the doors, temperature, access to phones, food, and other services. As a result, we can, far more often than not, choose the time of action. There are times when immediate action is necessary, but the vast majority of incidents have some leeway with the response time. As a result, we have many opportunities to think about the challenges facing us before we act.

I have, on many occasions, seen a newer jail deputy jump straight into an action without knowing what they want the outcome to be. Not only did they not know what they wanted to accomplish, but they also leapt into action with no preparation. Therefore, it's no surprise that many of these actions often result in even more challenges, stressors, and negative outcomes. As an FTO, when I could see them about to leap into action, I would ask them the following questions:

What Is the Nature of the Challenge?

Sometimes people react emotionally and viscerally to a problem or challenge without knowing the origin of the issue. Sometimes the origin is irrelevant, but many times it's part of how they got to the point where they are now. Newer jailers know they should react when there's a situation, and they can feel it. They're trained to jump in and assist instantly when it comes to use of force, so they want to move quickly. However, the jailer will usually have time to consider the larger picture and formulate a response rather than rushing in. Rushing can end with injuries to both the inmate and deputy. Sometimes the challenge and the solution may be obscured because of mental health issues or because of poor communication skills.

It is worth asking, is the challenge or problem an emergent medical need or physical assault in progress? Is it behavioral in nature thus making an emergent response unnecessary? Is the issue close enough to your sphere of influence that you can resolve it quickly, or will it involve multiple people, sections, or outside resources?

What Is Your Objective?

Once you have an idea of the challenge facing you, it's time to forge an objective (purpose) for your chosen resolution. With newer jailers, objectives tend to be much narrower in scope than with experienced jailers. I mean, often, there is a need to consider more than the desired immediate action for a larger end goal.

For example, a newer jailer's objective may be to notify an inmate of a rule violation when it's discovered. An experienced deputy may want to find out why the violation was made or if there were any other factors involved, build rapport with the inmate, avoid escalation or de-escalate the offender, and generate voluntary compliance.

Once you have an objective or possible solution to the challenge, it is time to SPELL it out. SPELL is another decision-making system that greatly assists a person in determining if the proposed objective or solution is a good one. Developed by Mr. Seth Graham, it is designed to help a Law Enforcement Officer (LEO) quickly evaluate the solution while there is still time to make a better choice.

The SPELL (Safe, Policy, Ethical, Legal, Liability) System

Graham's system of evaluating an objective or goal is designed to assist the LEO by asking five questions. These questions will help the officer determine if the objective or goal is solid or is likely to have a poor outcome. Graham's system asks:

1. Is it Safe?
2. Is it within Policy?
3. Is it Ethical?
4. Is it Legal?
5. What is the Liability?

What Is Your Plan to Achieve Your Objective?

After you've decided what your objectives are, it's time to start planning how to achieve them. I strongly urge this planning phase for all deputies because it slows down the pace of things so they can think before acting. If it helps, write it down and make a checklist.

After I have trainees outline a basic plan for an objective, I will then add a layer of difficulty by asking "what if" questions. For example, what if, while you're giving the inmate their discipline, they become angry, stand up, and begin pumping their fists? Newer jailers must be prepared for everything to go both smoothly and sideways on them. I will often hear good responses about policies and procedures from them, but by the time I'm done asking questions, their perspective on possible events broadens greatly and they can see how multiple areas of training can suddenly become relevant or necessary at nearly the same time.

How Can You Prepare for the Action?

After you've planned things out a bit, it's time to prepare for the action. By preparing, you can reduce the number of demands on your attention during the critical moments of the action. Knowing how you'll position yourself and if and when you'll call for assistance, setting the stage for the action, preparing good documentation and recording devices, ensuring that your equipment is functional, and having a backup plan are all necessary considerations.

I often speak of a pilot on a landing approach to show why this step is very important. If a pilot waits until they're on final approach to check with the tower, make sure their landing gear is functional, check their flaps and spoilers, examine wind directions and speed, and look for other aircraft in the landing pattern or any obstacles on the runway, then they'll likely be overwhelmed by too many tasks on final approach. As a result, a crash is much more likely.

ACTION PHASE

If all the previous steps were followed, then it's time to make things happen. You'll also be far more likely to achieve your desired outcome because you took the time to think things through. That being said, there are times when immediate action is necessary, especially when it comes to situations where the preservation of life is required. For those situations, you have emergency procedures that should be honed to second nature. Often in those situations, understanding John Boyd's concept of the observe, orient, act, decide (OODA) loop may be of great benefit until you've gotten control of the situation.

The OODA (Observe, Orient, Act, Decide) Loop

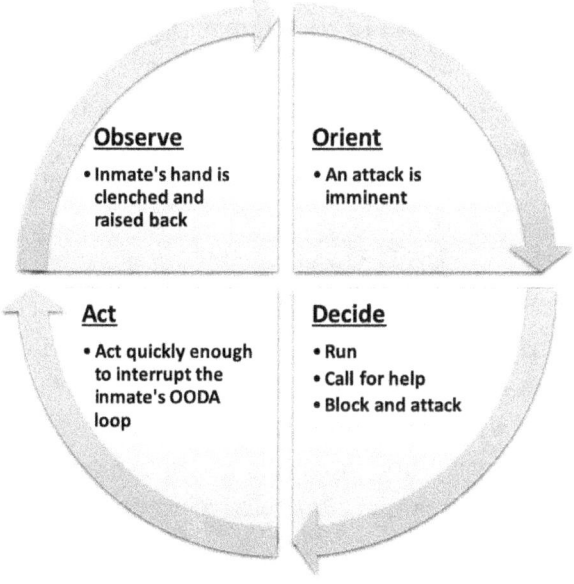

If you have time to follow the steps in the OODA loop, you will have prepared yourself for alternate scenarios and will be able to respond to those more quickly should they, or a similar scenario, occur. Preparing builds confidence because the possibilities are carefully thought out in advance and the deputy is ready for any attempted deflections or manipulations by the person(s) in question. The OODA process also allows the jailer to use time itself as a tool to appropriately prepare themselves and put things into perspective.

Good Judgment

Most who have good judgment are able to apply past knowledge to a new or slightly different situation and reason out a good course of action. However, many have to first build that reservoir of knowledge through experience, study, and watching others succeed and fail. Experience takes a great deal of time, as does watching others. However, self-directed study can be a great help, especially if you take the time to reason out the "why" of things.

A great way to do this is to take a policy you've read or learned about and ask yourself how and why it deals with the safety and security of the individuals in the jail. Sometimes the answers are obvious, but other times they're unclear or rooted in a forgotten event in the agency's history. In any case, reasoning out the "why" will empower you to stand firm on those policies when necessary and articulate why you deviated from policy when it doesn't fit the situation.

Anticipation and Initiative

What can make good judgment seem like magic is the ability to anticipate a future event. Experience really helps with this, and so does learning about and memorizing the timing of certain events and procedures and then coupling this with your knowledge of inmates' individual behaviors. Good judgment and anticipation can be the difference between an area that runs relatively smoothly and one where inmates are more agitated.

Taking the initiative to prepare for events—whether or not they actually occur—will pay off in the long run. New policies and procedures are created this way, and old policies are refined or modified. The name of the game is safety, and it's through anticipation and initiative that a jailer can be prepared for anything.

Frequency Hopping

The jail environment has a lot of information, activity, challenges, and tasks to complete, which means that the ability to "frequency hop" is a must. Many people use the term multitasking to describe juggling multiple demands at one time. I call it frequency hopping because it's improbable that a person can actually do more than one thing at a time. Instead, I often observe a person pausing of one event or activity in order to focus on another, then resuming the first event when the second is completed.

In order to become efficient in problem solving and decision making, a jailer should factor in the ability to pause the current task, switch gears and focus on another task, and then resume the first task as if there were no delay. This takes the ability to keep track of multiple events and their states of completion. Some people have excellent short-term memories and are able to juggle in and out of each task as the situation requires. Others may need to keep written lists or notes so they can move between tasks.

Some people have a hard time switching their focus on short notice, ignoring the new task or information until they've completed the task they're on. This often results in some sort of backlash or consequence for ignoring a higher-priority task. I've also seen newer jailers who couldn't control the flow of new tasks, resulting in an overload that leads to many of the tasks being left incomplete or poorly completed. This brings us to the next component of decision making: the prioritization of multiple tasks.

PRIORITIZING TASKS

Setting priorities for tasks in a high-stress, high-volume environment is like doing triage in a hospital emergency room. Experience and knowledge play heavily into it, but so too does critical thinking. There are enough varied tasks and challenges in a jail that the possibilities for task order are numerous. However, there are some basic strategies for prioritizing tasks in a jail that may be of use to a new deputy. Here is a basic prioritization model:

1. Safety

It's always recommended that a jailer complete the task or challenge that directly impacts the safety of those under your charge. Whether a person is having a medical issue or is rumored to be thinking of self-harm, or a non-security-minded visitor is in your area, their safety comes first. This safety aspect includes status checks of the housing area and your inmates. Sometimes you'll have competing safety interests and you'll need to influence events in your area to assist in dealing with these in a safe and controlled manner.

2. Preservation of Evidence

After the safety of everyone in your charge is seen to, focus on preserving the evidence or the crime scene. This step is only necessary if the event requires it, and many times it won't be needed. However, it's an often-overlooked element, and deprioritizing this step results in the unnecessary destruction of good evidence.

3. Facility Movement

A jailer should control the flow and movement in their areas to maintain influence over the number of tasks, challenges, and questions dealt with at any one time. However, preparing inmates for movement to court, medical services, counseling services, visitations, and meetings with their legal counsel are a higher priority than individual requests.

4. Housing Area Operation and Documentation

Inmates need access to the dayrooms, recreation yard, programs, and supplies. Documentation is a huge part of housing area operation, as keeping track of many individuals and their behavior is very challenging. As a result, a jailer will have to remember, note, and record incidents and behaviors that are happening in the area. This also requires dealing with disciplinary issues.

5. Inmate Requests and Questions

The citizens in a jail will have many questions regarding their individual cases, facility rules, and personal requests. Although these individual requests are important, their priority is lower than area operation and the documentation of behavioral incidents.

Competing Priorities

Competing priorities are a frequent issue. You'll have to decide whether an attorney has more priority than a nurse or a counselor wanting to check up on a patient. You may have to ask an inmate to wait on their important request because another inmate is behaving badly and requiring more attention. Sometimes you may wonder if a nurse giving medication to an inmate has priority or if you should pause this activity so you can walk the entire pod to ensure the safety of more than just one person. There will be many competing challenges, priorities, plans, resources, and requests for the jailer's time and attention. This challenge alone can make a person mentally exhausted by the end of a twelve-hour shift. Still, time and experience will make these types of decisions much easier.

ANECDOTES FROM THE JAIL

"Inconvenient Fingerprint Collection"

I was training a deputy in the booking area of the jail. His responsibilities in this area were security, searches of arriving inmates, iris scans, photographs, fingerprints, and the occasional DNA collection. We also dressed people for and moved them to housing. Because he seemed to be having trouble knowing what to do next, I asked him to fingerprint someone and prepare him for housing. The person had a splint on his right arm due to an injury, but the fingers were uninjured and mobile.

The deputy spent thirty minutes fingerprinting one hand and then elected to stop. I asked him why he didn't attempt to get the prints from the hand that was in a splint and he said that the collection of the prints wasn't worth the chance of injuring the person further. Although I understood why he was hesitant to attempt to get these fingerprints, I saw him make no attempt get these prints. I also observed that he didn't ask me (his training officer) or anyone with more experience if it was even possible. In our line of work, it's important to recognize when you need help and ask for it.

Instead of guiding him verbally, I demonstrated how he could still get those fingerprints. My objective was to get the fingerprints without causing further injury, and to demonstrate this to my trainee. I began my planning phase by looking over the person's injury and asking some questions regarding his capabilities. I prepared for taking these fingerprints by asking the inmate for his help and adjusting the equipment to accommodate him. I then initiated the action phase and solved the challenge of getting the fingerprints without further injury to the inmate.

Instead of using problem-solving and decision-making skills to resolve the challenge, the new deputy decided to avoid the situation entirely. Although the stated intention of not causing further injury was the correct one, it wasn't an excuse to avoid thinking critically about the challenge or passing a difficult job off to others in an effort to avoid responsibility. In our line of work, making decisions that appear to be an avoidance of responsibility is a trait that fosters distrust. It will make colleagues view you through a more critical lens.

"I Took His Time for Making Noise in His Cell"

Part of decision making revolves around the disciplinary process. In general, as long as an infraction is addressed either through a verbal warning or lockdown, the policy is satisfied. However, one also has to take into account the severity or string of actions or decisions. I was training one deputy in the segregation area when an inmate presented this type of decision-making challenge. The deputy, after a bit of time following an incident with the inmate, had begun to work on a behavioral report (BR).

This report documents an interaction that is outside of the norm. It isn't a disciplinary form, but it can be used to initiate disciplinary actions. The deputy was writing this BR because the inmate was pounding on things in his cell, including the cell door. The other inmates in the area were getting agitated with this, so he thought he may have to act.

As he was writing the report, he asked me if I thought that revoking the inmate's time out of his cell for the afternoon was an adequate solution to his dilemma. I told him that I needed more information on his thought process before I could answer. Of course, I already had an answer, but I wanted to see what his thought process was and how he was making his decisions. Furthermore, he was nearing the end of his training program and he appeared to be waiting for me to give him an answer rather than reasoning it out for himself.

I asked him to tell me more, and his thinking was based solely on the noise the inmate was making and not the many behavior-based rule violations that led up to the inmate making incredible noise from his cell. The deputy simply didn't see the entire situation and was making his decision based upon the agitation of other inmates, not the behavior of the inmate in question, which constituted multiple rule violations:

Minor Rule Violation	• He was out without proper clothing before being told to lock down
Minor Rule Violation	• He did not have his identification band on
Minor Rule Violation	• He initially refused multiple orders to lock down
Minor Rule Violation	• He made obscene gestures and used profanity toward staff
Minor Rule Violation	• He had banged inside his cell for more than twenty minutes
Major Rule Violation	• He was already on ad seg status, showing a pattern of rule violation

Despite our discussion of the above violations, the deputy wasn't able to link all of these violations together to present a full picture of the very bad behavior of the inmate. Instead of articulating that the inmate's behavior was bad enough to take away his time out for the day, he said that the simple pounding on a cell—and the agitation at this by other inmates—was enough to justify the taking of this time.

Furthermore, he didn't give the inmate written discipline for any of his actions or behavior, leaving a simple question to be answered: if the inmate's behavior was bad enough to remove his constitutionally allowed time out of his cell, would it not also require some sort of disciplinary record illustrating the need for it? Even after I brought up all of these concerns and asked him this question, he waited for me to tell him what to do rather than make the appropriate decision and action based on the facts.

A deputy must be able to make reasonable decisions based on articulable facts, not instinct. Although the decision to take the inmate's time was the correct one, he didn't understand why it was right despite a lengthy conversation about it. The reason he gave about the noise and other inmate agitation was not enough to make the taking of the inmate's time out reasonable.

CHAPTER 11 PREP

If you want to work in a jail, you have to be able to deal with conflict. That being said, you also have to be able to quickly determine what conflicts are worth the energy and stress and which aren't—not everything needs to be a "war" or a "battle," and knowing when and where to stand your ground during everyday operations can be difficult at first. In the next chapter, I introduce the types of conflicts one will deal with while working in a jail. I also provide some examples of how these conflicts are expressed in the housing area.

Chapter 11: Conflict

Most everyone can deal with some level of conflict for a limited amount of time. However, the intensity and, more importantly, duration of conflict can begin to erode a person's stress-mitigation strategies, resulting in consequences that can be career-ending. Some people develop an aversion to the job itself because of the repetitive nature and high intensity of conflicts created by citizens in the jail. Many retired jail deputies have told me how much happier they are after they have a few months to recover and reduce the frequency and intensity of these types of conflictual interactions.

Not everyone is affected by conflict in the same way. My colleagues and I have similar reactions to repetitive psychological conflicts in that if there are too many in too short of a time, our general mood and energy levels are significantly affected. I, too, have had moments where I didn't fully enforce a minor rule because the cost of doing it exceeded my energy or psychological reserves at that particular time. In addition to these conflicts, there are also the general dangers of working in a jail.

When I walk through a housing area and someone displays aggressive body language, I think, "Is today the day I'll have to fight for my life?" The dangers inside jails are unique because the mental and physical states of newly arrested people vary, as do the extent of their crimes, which are still being investigated. I've heard that mental health professionals in the department of corrections have fewer issues than we do in jails because jails, by and large, do the work of stabilizing people.

Whether it happens right away or not, conflict will happen and you must be ready. Many conflicts come from difficult inmates, while others will come from coworkers or citizens. Some conflicts will originate from within yourself about things you may have seen, heard, done, or not done.

VERBAL CONFLICTS

As a deputy, you will hear many negative comments and verbally abusive words or phrases. You'll encounter people who want to argue and others who speak in an aggressive way just because that's their standard communication style. Some of the best wordsmiths I've had the privilege of working with will take the negative comments, wait for and isolate an opening, and then send back an affirmative statement along with a reasonable request.

For example, an inmate could be yelling insults at one of these deputies only to be met with a calm voice, an acknowledgment of the difficulties the person is going through, and a request for a thoughtful response from this "reasonable person" going through a hard time. I've even seen some jailers derail an inmate's clearly thought-out plan to escalate staff by redirecting their focus on the real issue involved and asking for their cooperation and help in order to resolve it.

One of the most common of these types of scenarios is when an uncooperative inmate is threatening the deputy (or their family) and telling them to open the cell door (the threat of direct violence). In this situation, the deputy can redirect by saying something like, "I know you aren't feeling well, and I would like to let the nurse help you. But

I need you to help me out by acting right so the nurse will feel and be safe enough to help you. Will you help me with that?"

Passive Verbal Conflicts

I've seen inmates refuse to participate in a simple conversation. They're clearly uncomfortable, in pain, or have another issue, but they refuse to talk about it, as if their silence is a tool that works in their favor. It's as if they think that refusing to voice these things is as beneficial as pleading the Fifth Amendment.

However, when it comes to being heard or understood, an inmate's use of silence as a tool in a conflict is ineffective because jailers love silence, and one tool that jailers use effectively is time itself. Jailers have so little time and so many inmates to deal with that the "silent treatment" backfires. Another inmate will gladly take that time to express themselves. There's an element of truth to the old saying, "the squeaky wheel gets the grease."

Active Verbal Conflicts

Some inmates actively use their words as weapons. This onslaught of words is largely designed to be psychological in nature. However, such verbal attacks can simply be a demonstration that only the inmate can control the inmate. Experienced jailers know this very well and have developed tools to deal with this type of conflict. However, it's difficult to prepare for because this form of active verbal conflict is as variable as the personalities of the jailer and the inmate.

PSYCHOLOGICAL CONFLICTS

Words may be the tools of a verbal conflict, but the mind is the battlefield. Most of the time, words are used to increase situational tension and tax a deputy's stress-management system. However, the longer one works in a jail, the less powerful the words themselves are and the more powerful tone, body language, and physical actions become.

I've heard inmates threaten to do horrible things to deputies, their spouses, and even their children over relatively small things. It isn't the words themselves that are the true weapons, but the damaging effect these threats have on an individual's psyche. These types of psychological conflicts and assaults are common but certainly not sought after by jailers. It's a challenge to weather the storm and redirect this negative energy. In my opinion, this type of conflict is the hardest to mitigate and redirect.

Passive Psychological Conflicts

Some inmates use simple noncompliance as a tool for passive conflict. Jailers will find themselves thinking, "I've told that person five times already!" The point, again, of this interaction is simply showing the jailer that he or she doesn't control the inmate. Instead of using words, the lack of action on behalf of the inmate may create a psychological or emotional response that is unprofessional or seems heavy-handed.

It's best to try and bring this type of conflict into the verbal realm in order to build understanding. If that isn't possible, following disciplinary procedures and not visibly caring may be your best bet. Keep in mind, however, that giving consequences based solely on an inmate's attitude means the inmate was successful in their efforts to get you to remain focused on their behavior.

Active Psychological Conflicts

Active psychological conflicts happen when an inmate repeatedly attempts to cause psychological stress. This is most often achieved by visual and audio displays that can be heard by everyone. Banging on metal objects, making loud sounds, screaming constantly, refusing to return items, threatening to "go off," and threatening the jailer or their family are signs of an active psychological conflict. Sometimes a citizen of the jail will obviously break a rule right at the end of your shift to keep you later or challenge your authority and willingness to hold them accountable. These conflicts can be short in duration, but they often take place over long periods of time.

These types of conflicts are among the most common and psychologically demanding within the jail. There have been times in my jail that staff had to be rapidly rotated out of an area due to the frequent and intense psychological conflicts initiated by a particular inmate or several inmates. Some inmates do this because, in their own words, they're bored.

PHYSICAL CONFLICTS

Some physical conflicts start as verbal conflicts, escalate to psychological ones, and finally become physical. With the increasing number of inmates with mental health issues, sometimes there is little to no warning that a physical conflict is imminent. Like the other conflicts, you must prepare for them, meaning that you have to have a good working knowledge of arrest control and some physical conditioning. It's more important to be psychologically prepared for these types of assaults and the impact they may have on you and your family.

Passive Physical Conflicts

Most of the time, this type of conflict is demonstrated by a person who just flops onto the floor when you ask them to move from one location to another. However, sometimes these types of conflicts are more sophisticated. Some inmates will place their biological waste in locations they know you will walk or search through, intending for you to come into contact with it. Just because they aren't throwing feces or blood at you doesn't mean they aren't trying to get it on you or contaminate you. The same goes for faking medical emergencies: a faked seizure can result in an opportunity for a punch or a kick, so you should be prepared for this. Inmates know that even faked seizures will be treated as real until a medical professional says otherwise, so it's important to remain vigilant and keep civilian staff members safe.

Active Physical Conflicts

Usually there's some indication that direct violence is imminent. Clenching jaws, pumping fists, and shifting feet are the most common. However, sometimes there's no apparent or recognized warning other than a feeling that something isn't right.

You have to first be mentally prepared for an active physical assault. What I mean by this is that you need to understand and accept that it could happen so that you don't waste precious seconds telling yourself "I can't believe this is happening." You then have to recognize the type of threat and the appropriate force to respond with. At first this is seems easy: when someone is trying to injure you, you can defend yourself as needed. However, once you have the advantage, you must transition to a controlled use of force. Otherwise, you'll find yourself using excessive force.

Transitioning the use of force from a fight for your life to securing the aggressor is what really challenges the law enforcement officer. As a result, the jailer needs to fully understand the use of force policies for their agency and state, and then be able to recognize when to use them. There is no substitute for good training and scenario-based discussions.

So, make sure that you make time to go over the possibilities in your mind. I've seen physical conflicts begin in numerous situations: when trying to give someone food or medical attention, in court, upon arrest, and when issuing discipline. I've even seen active physical conflicts happen for no apparent reason because an inmate heard voices telling them to do it.

STAFF CONFLICTS

Like all professions, there are conflicts within the ranks at times. Sometimes it's a simple personality conflict. Other times, a feud-like state exists and those involved try and rally supporters. Intra-staff conflicts are among the most challenging because you're all on the same side.

Quite simply, you want to trust the person who may be the one who helps you get home to your family alive.

Like any workplace, there are those who act mostly in their own self-interest and forget about their colleagues. There are also those who, through lack of training or errors in judgment, make mistakes and then expect colleagues to help keep these mistakes "in the dark" despite the obvious issues this raises about integrity. Ask yourself: if they hid this mistake, what else are they hiding? Bringing the mistakes from the shadows to the light can be uncomfortable, but it's necessary in our work. The trick is to build a culture where mistakes are normalized and shaming isn't tolerated.

In the end, as law enforcement, you'll be expected to work past your differences for the common good and keep things professional. This is much easier said than done, but it will be expected by your supervisors, coworkers, and the general public.

CONFLICTS WITH YOURSELF

When you're at war with yourself, you can't protect your relationships by pretending that somehow your loved ones don't notice. Your personal relationships will absolutely suffer, not because of the stress in and of itself, but because of how it's dealt with or ignored. It's hard to speak about things you have or haven't seen, heard, or done. You may be judging yourself very harshly, increasing the fear of disappointing others. You shouldn't ignore these conflicts, cover them up, or take things out on those you love—that path will likely lead to personal ruin. Instead, reach out to someone. If your agency has some sort of peer support program, utilize it!

What You See and Hear

As a representative of the law, a jailer is one of the first people to bear the brunt of a person's anger, frustration, violence, depression, and any negative emotion they wish to unleash. Expect to hear "fuck you," "punk-ass bitch," "pussy," and any other profane word to the point where you'll seldom remember exactly which one was used toward you. The sounds, natural and seemingly unnatural, will definitely affect you. You'll hear groans of pain, howls of psychological despair, shrieks of anger, and repeated banging, singing, threats, stories, and verbal nonsense.

There are many things a person can't unsee. How frequently this happens in a jail is an issue. You'll see people doing the most unbelievable things: moving in contorted ways, spreading feces and sculpting it, masturbating, inflicting injuries on themselves, and much more. Fortunately, the dark humor that jailers are known to employ will make this somewhat more tolerable.

Your Choices and Decisions

You're likely to miss birthdays, holidays, and important events with your family due to staff shortages and the types of schedules utilized by your agency. Some jailers may also start avoiding crowds and public events they would've gone to before working in a jail. Because of these changes in preferences, those closest to you may begin to feel left out or avoided. This distance develops slowly but surely. Over time, a jailer may question their bonds with those who were once very close. This self-imposed isolation is something that has to be guarded against and worked on. Some people may put their families on hold while working toward promotion or some other goal, but the effects of this—despite the positive reason—can be negative. A person must consider these types of consequences.

You may develop other internal conflicts as well. Sometimes you may wonder if you're doing things right and if those "right" things are the "smart" things. In my experience, most people who begin a career in law enforcement aren't looking to gain power as much as to embark on the challenging road it presents. Each person must reconcile the responsibility of the work and the authority entrusted in them with the difficulties encountered in trying to make their community a better place.

If you're a conscientious person, it may be difficult to feel confident that every decision you make is the right one. Sometimes you may find yourself wondering if you should go the extra mile to help someone because some people will still accuse you of not doing your job or of showing favoritism. As a public servant, we want to help people, but we also have limited time and resources. Also, once one person gets this "extra-mile" treatment, others will expect the same.

ANECDOTES FROM THE JAIL

Below are two stories that began as verbal conflicts and escalated into psychological conflicts, but were successfully de-escalated before they became physical.

"Skewed Perception"

In the facility I work in, meals are served at the pod (module) doors. While there, we observe the food to ensure roughly the same portion sizes, confirm that the inmates are wearing their appropriate outfits, and mentally note their general condition. In one instance, while my trainee was doing this a few feet away, I began working on documenting his training progress. A couple of minutes later, I heard an inmate raising his voice at the trainee.

I rose to observe the interaction. The inmate, who was a very tall and large individual, was upset about his portion size. The trainee held firm that the portion size was not different than the others. The inmate threatened to throw his tray on the floor several times and demanded to speak with a supervisor. The trainee held firm and I could now see that there was an escalation in progress.

First, the inmate, in his skewed perception, believed that he had a smaller portion size. The staff member held firm in order to demonstrate that he was correct about his observation of portion size, not afraid, and not going to bend to threats. The inmate had not eaten anything off the tray issued. Although the trainee was clearly in the right, to people who perceive an injustice, no reasoning will change their minds. The choices were: bend to the inmate's will and order a new tray, ignore the inmate and risk a physical altercation or escalation over the tray, or find some other solution. I asked the trainee if he would be okay if I stepped in and demonstrated one way to deal with a person with a skewed perception.

I stepped in and offered for the inmate to look over the uncovered meals on the cart. He saw one and swore it had a larger portion size to the one in his hands. They looked the same to me, and I'm sure they looked the same to the trainee. I told the inmate that he could switch his tray out with the other one. He did so happily, and he was no longer yelling or escalating. This allowed for the de-escalation of the situation in the moment. We later pulled the inmate out and discussed his behavior and the disciplinary consequences of his threats. I discussed this strategy in more depth with the trainee later to demonstrate an alternative to a black-and-white approach to these types of scenarios.

The point is that the "skewed perception" inmate sees a difference in portion size when we don't. They see something, in that moment, that is reliant upon a distorted perspective, and they're ready to fight over it. In their minds, they're the ones who are right, whereas everyone else is trying to trick them or pull something over on them. This can easily lead to a disproportionate escalation that can turn a small disagreement into a physical confrontation.

"Food Inspector"

One morning, an inmate came out of the pod with his meal tray. His sharp movements and confrontational body language informed me that this person was about to attempt to start an argument. He then showed me his tray and informed me that his bread was moldy. I looked at the bread and didn't see any mold on it. I did see that there was a discoloration on the underside of the bread where it had been exposed to heat. As a result, we had two different conclusions.

When I started to express that I thought it might possibly be due to the cooking process, he spoke over me and categorically stated that it was mold. Seeing there was no point to this discussion as he was not going to be open to any other viewpoints, I ended the conversation and continued to walk through his pod to check on the status of other inmates. He waited a few minutes and then requested a grievance form. I gave him the form, thinking he might grieve the kitchen for their preparation or the perceived mold. A few minutes later, he returned to the control center wanting to turn in his grievance.

I asked him where he wanted it routed to, and he said he had previously submitted a request to medical on the subject. I scanned through the grievance, and he was claiming that he was being subjected to a viral and bacterial environment without adequate access to medical care.

He was verbally saying the same thing to me. His tone, body language, and words were aggressive and argumentative. He projected his feelings like an artillery barrage and seemed to strongly believe what he was saying was true and that his health was at risk. However, I thought it was equally probable that he was attempting to get some reaction from me that would enable him to bring a lawsuit. As I continued to look at him, I observed that his arms were full of tattoos (both jail and regular tattoos) and couldn't help but be amused by the irony.

A person who gets a tattoo runs the risk of catching any number of blood-borne pathogens and diseases. They also run the risk of staph infections, MRSA, skin irritation, and scarring. Here was this inmate, in jail facing serious and violent sex-offense charges, acting like he was afraid of being killed by two miniscule discolorations on the bottom of his breakfast roll. Either his perception was completely skewed, or he was intentionally attempting to start a conflict and litigation.

I urged him to bring his intensity down a notch. It wasn't that he didn't have an issue; he just needed to present himself differently so he would be better listened to. I tried to help him understand that once a person is already argumentative, it's difficult to have a two-way conversation regarding any issue. Furthermore, he needed to decide on who the grievance should go to, as I couldn't make that decision for him. It seemed to work, as his body posture relaxed some and he held onto his grievance in order to submit it to medical staff.

CHAPTER 12 PREP

In the next chapter, we will go over communication—one of the most important skills a person can bring with them into a jail. Keeping people safe inside a jail means being able to hear them out, de-escalate those you can, and provide both guidance and consequences for their decisions. There are many facets to communication, and a jailer must be able to communicate effectively while also following up with the use of force should it become necessary.

Chapter 12: Communication

As you can imagine, working in a jail means working with people who use both their hands and their words as weapons. I've been fortunate to receive additional training in de-escalation and verbal deflection. I've also been lucky enough to get training that aims to provide guidance on communicating with individuals who have mental health challenges or are in crisis.

There are resources and teachers out there who specialize in verbal techniques and how to use these effectively in a law enforcement environment. However, if your agency doesn't offer them, you should strongly consider learning de-escalation and verbal deflection skills on your own. If you have interest, you can check out "Verbal Judo: The Gentle Art of Persuasion" by George Thompson. This chapter will outline why you should take the extra time to develop these skills and give some limited guidance on communicating with inmates.

A CHALLENGE OF MEANING

When I'm at home or with friends, I tend to avoid conversations about things that aren't engaging or that don't hold my interest. For me, this generally means avoiding conversations about the weather, sports, and television shows. However, I can be interested in those things when

I'm trying to learn about someone and what they enjoy. Do they like to fish? What sports do they like? What things appear to be important to them? What subjects do they know a lot about or enjoy talking about? Professionally, I've found strategic and tactical value in these types of conversations because of how they reveal a person's personality.

I've found communication to be the most valuable tool available to me: I've used it effectively to de-escalate groups of people in a housing area. I must confess, however, that verbal communication doesn't come easily for me. There are days and times when my word choices are a disaster. I often see things in pictures, and I find that words don't quite convey what I'm thinking. I mean, you can describe a picture, but it isn't the same as seeing that picture. I continually strive to develop my communication skills, and I think I'll always be working on improving.

People, in general, telegraph some thoughts through body language and some through tone. Inflection and speed provide yet more information. However, the spoken word—absent of these—still has some valuable information to be gathered. Sometimes, the use of particular phrasing can be of great help when it comes to communication.

SAYING NO BY SAYING YES

Deputies often must inform individuals of what they can't do. However, hearing "no" all the time is likely to lead to some frustration. I've seen people go from hopeful to downright defeated when told no. At some point, people get fed up and, like a geyser, anger erupts—usually when you least expect it. In my experience, saying no by saying yes often diffuses the frustration because you're also providing guidance on when the "no" can become a "yes."

For example, if an inmate requests to go outside in the recreation yard but it isn't time for this type of activity, a deputy can simply say no. However, giving a "no" answer without context won't build rapport with the inmate. Stating, "No, the appropriate time for this is ..." is a better approach as it provides context for the "no" answer. However, depending on the tone, this may be just as frustrating as a straight "no."

This is why I believe it's better to say, "Yes. At 1:30 p.m. we will be opening the door for the yard and you can go then." You're telling the inmate that they can go to the recreation yard (just not now), providing a time when it can be achieved, educating them that there are allotted times for this activity, and increasing the chances of building trust and rapport.

WORD CHOICE, VOCABULARY, AND STATE OF MIND

Word choice and vocabulary can provide clues to an individual's expectations and state of mind, even without inflection and tone. Here's an example:

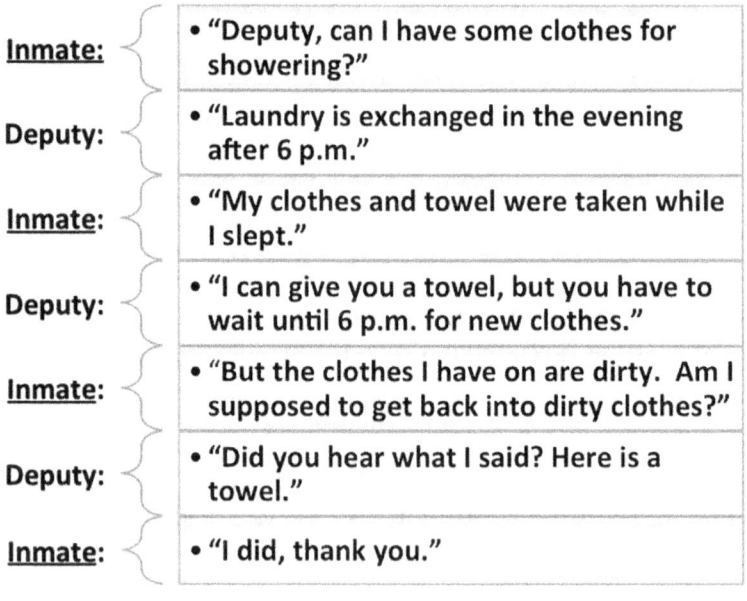

Inmate:	• "Deputy, can I have some clothes for showering?"
Deputy:	• "Laundry is exchanged in the evening after 6 p.m."
Inmate:	• "My clothes and towel were taken while I slept."
Deputy:	• "I can give you a towel, but you have to wait until 6 p.m. for new clothes."
Inmate:	• "But the clothes I have on are dirty. Am I supposed to get back into dirty clothes?"
Deputy:	• "Did you hear what I said? Here is a towel."
Inmate:	• "I did, thank you."

Void of any body language, inflection, tone, or tempo, there's still information on the state of mind of both the inmate and the deputy in this scenario. There was a simple request made for clothing. Rather than stating yes or no, the deputy responded with the policy regarding the exchange of laundry. We could speculate on the reasons for this, but let's assume that the answer was a "no, and here's why."

It's likely that this deputy wanted to do two things at once: notify that the request was denied and let the inmate know when they could expect to get clothing. This also informs us that the laundry is exchanged every evening.

The inmate then responds, "My clothes and towel were taken while I slept." Again, there can be much speculation on the reasons for the inmate stating this. However, let's assume the reason was to provide a good reason why the policy shouldn't be followed in this case.

The deputy counters this by offering to give the inmate a towel but doesn't budge on the issuing of new clothes. The deputy may be thinking of a way to enable a shower but not violate the policy on the issuing of laundry. The inmate, having already gained a partial concession, mentions that they would have to get back into the "dirty" clothes they're currently wearing.

The deputy probably sees the inmate's mention of dirty clothes as an attempted manipulation. As a result, the deputy questions whether or not the inmate heard them.

Even with just text, one can imagine that the tone of the deputy was curt. Still, the inquiry was about if the inmate understood when the exchange was to take place and also that the deputy was not going to budge on the matter. However, the deputy did offer a towel to the inmate, who accepted it and thanked him for it.

CONTEXT IS A MUST

Many times, agitation can be avoided by providing some context within the communication. We have televisions that are turned on for the housing areas so the inmates can keep up with the news. They can also watch a movie now and then in order to occupy them for a time. On one such afternoon, while I was training a newer deputy, the absence of context increased some tension.

On this day, inmates in the housing area had not cleaned the area. The area was a mess and really needed cleaning. The deputy working the area wanted those in the area to clean up before he would turn on the television. Having decided this, he then made the following announcement: "Gentlemen! Sweep the floor, sweep the bathroom floor, and make your beds!"

I then heard some verbal pushback from the inmates because the words and tone were more of a direct order than a request. It became clear to those in the area that the deputy intended to keep the television off until they complied, so they did as he said.

Sensing a learning opportunity, I spoke with him at a later time about this. I asked him why he announced it the way he did. He angled his head, raised an eyebrow, and, instead of answering my question, asked me what he could have said differently. Using his words, I made a few additions that changed both the tone and provided context for them to evaluate.

My suggestion was: "Gentlemen, the floor in the dayroom and bathroom needs sweeping. I will get the TVs on again when the cleaning is complete and your beds are made."

I demonstrated how the tone was less order-like, more informative (by giving the condition of the floors), and provided guidance as to how the TVs could be turned back on quickly.

There are times when direct orders need to be given, but sometimes providing more context can reduce pushback, diffuse tension, generate voluntary compliance, and increase rapport.

NONVERBALS ARE KING

There are times when a person gives very little indication about what they're going to do. Most of the time, nonverbals will still be there even if they're somewhat hidden. There are all sorts of expectations or thoughts displayed by nonverbal behavior that may indicate state of mind, intended action, or action. I've seen experienced jail deputies give an inmate a look followed by a slight head movement, and the inmate will change their behavior or come into compliance with a rule without one word.

Other times, an inmate can telegraph when they're about to physically resist or attack. There can be the removal of footwear, the lowering of the center of gravity, the angling of their core, the focus on a target, the clenching of fists, or the positioning of hands or arms in a way to speed up the attack. You must be aware of these signs and be proactive or suffer an assault.

There are many people out there who have done years of research on nonverbals. Conduct an internet search and find a book or resource on this that works for you. Having at least one such work on your shelf is a good idea if you're going to be working in a jail.

COMMUNICATING STATE OF MIND

Most people can pick up on an altered state of mind: aberrant behavior and physical tics are some of the most obvious of these. However, a change in physical mobility, communication, or freedom status—or simply being subjected to the workings of the justice system—can easily lead to a deviation from normal behavior for individuals.

Individuals' choices and actions often communicate their state of mind, giving you a clue as to where your focus needs to be. Avoiding food, covering up their body in the dayroom, turning toward a phone and blocking your view of their face, suddenly talking back, and staring out into space are nonverbal indicators that indicate a high level of stress.

This level of stress tends to reveal itself nonverbally before it becomes a verbal behavioral issue. However, once it becomes verbal, the person will need to be dealt with quickly in order to reduce the chances that he or she negatively impacts your housing area.

COMMUNICATING INTENDED ACTION

For safety reasons, we teach new staff about things like inmates pumping or clenching their fists as an indication of intended action. Inmates who are giving nonverbals that demonstrate an intention to attack also tend to stare or focus on a target area, delay or avoid compliance with orders to move, and try to turn or move when told to stay still during the application of restraints. The best defense is to know the previous behavior of the inmate (an indicator of future behavior), plan and prepare for the negative behavior, assemble a team to ensure monopoly of force, give clean and firm direction, and act decisively when the inmate shows any nonverbals that indicate a potential attack.

I've seen inmates kick off their shoes in advance of an inmate-on-inmate fight. I've also seen them prepare a room for cleaning before a fight takes place in that cell—they're then able to clean the blood off quickly to erase the evidence of the crime. Fights that happen without some sort of preparation usually take place in front of staff rather than in a cell or under a stairway.

COMMUNICATING POSSIBLE ACTION

When jail deputies think there may be an altercation with an inmate, they put on protective equipment. At the minimum, this consists of eye protection and gloves. At the most, it means putting on body armor, helmets, and other less-lethal tools. Sometimes, however, a special emergency response team (SERT) or corrections special operations group (CSOG) will bring even more equipment and tools when a more forceful response is required to ensure the safety of others in the facility.

When deputies begin putting on gloves or eye protection, the inmates take notice. If the inmate in question sees one or multiple deputies putting on gear, that signals possible or intended action. In almost all cases, deputies will prepare based on current or past displays of behavior. If an inmate has shown high volatility, the deputy will bring protective gear and other deputies. Seeing this preparation, an inmate might feel pushed into action. This also works the other way as well.

When inmates begin putting soap on the floor, storing biological waste in containers, throwing feces on the wall, flooding their floor, and intentionally covering their cell-door window, it's an obvious display of preparing the "battleground." Covering the window shows an intention to force staff to make a cell entry. Then, having prepared for battle, the inmate could assault staff with biological material or ensure that they make physical contact with the biological contaminants spread throughout the cell. Their nonverbal preparation is very valuable in determining where things have a higher likelihood of going.

BEING ON STAGE

When I speak with newer deputies on the topic of communication, I let them know that the interactions they have don't take place in a vacuum. Even if a conversation was in a private conference room, the inmate will deliver their version of this interaction to the rest of the pod. If the conversation happens in a dayroom or cell, the person you're speaking to hears it, and so does everyone within earshot.

As a result, nearly every communication should be thought of as a public announcement. It's sort of like being on stage, playing a part with everyone watching. This is very important to remember during disciplinary interactions as well as during emergencies and area disturbances.

ANECDOTES FROM THE JAIL

"Restroom, Please"

One morning I was taking over a female housing area from the night-shift deputy. I saw that there was a female inmate in a conference room who was yelling and being very loud while pounding on the glass. I asked the deputy about the situation and he said he didn't really know what was going on, but she started being overly loud just before I arrived, so he had her go to the conference room to wait while we went through the shift change.

A few minutes later, I released the night-shift deputy and entered the conference room to find out what was going on. The woman was upset, and she seemed to be under the influence of some sort of substance or having some mental health issues. After a few minutes of observing her yelling loudly and having erratic body language, I picked up on the message she was sending. In essence, she really needed to use the bathroom and was upset because she felt like she couldn't go.

I was able to stop the behavior by asking her if she wanted to go to the restroom now. She said yes, and I said, "Well, go and then get some rest." After that she went to the restroom and then went to sleep. Despite the shouts and the erratic body language that displayed physical aggression, she was still trying to communicate her discomfort and, in a strange way, was asking for help to deal with it.

"A Guiding Voice"

It was toward the end of a day shift and the inmates had just been given their evening meal. I was training a new deputy in the area and I wanted to catch up on my documentation. I asked him to remain alert while I put my head down for a minute or two to focus on his training record. After about five minutes, I heard a commotion in the dayroom.

I looked up and saw an inmate sitting at a table and moving in a way that looked like they were choking. I looked at my trainee and he was just looking at the inmate. I again looked at the inmate and now other inmates were calling out for assistance. I looked at the trainee and again he stood motionless, looking toward them.

I got up and moved toward them and asked if the inmate was choking as I prepared to facilitate lifesaving measures. The inmates answered back that the distressed inmate was not choking; the inmate was having what appeared to be a panic attack. I went back toward my trainee and had him get out into the dayroom to deal with the situation. The other inmates in the immediate area were beginning to show signs of distress and panic.

The trainee went out into the pod as I asked, but he seemed lost. After moving around the area instead of going to the inmate in question, he looked back at me with his eyes wide, a sign that he needed additional guidance. This is when I used my voice to loudly, slowly, and calmly direct him and the inmates at the same time.

I said, "First you have to lock down your area." The inmates, hearing this, began to move on their own, and then he announced it.

He then tried to leave the area and return back to me, so I gave him more guidance. "Then you need to stand by them [the affected inmate] to make sure they don't pass out and hit their head."

He then went to the inmate and stood in a way to prevent accidental injury and again looked at me wide-eyed. The other inmates, who were a little nervous about the incident, were becoming visibly calmer by my directives as they continued to lock down.

"Then use your radio to ask a nurse to come to your area," I said.

He made what sounded like a stressed, but fast, call for medical assistance that was sure to bring all available staff to the area. They soon came and the inmate was seen by medical, calmed down, and allowed to remain in the area.

Even from a distance, tone of voice, command presence, and decisive directives can be used to great effect.

CHAPTER 13 PREP

A person arrested doesn't totally leave society. Instead, they're relocated to a society within a society, which has its own version of ethics. The culture inside a jail can be difficult to adjust to for citizens who don't generally run with career criminals or repeat offenders. Although not comprehensive by any means, the following chapter will delve into the society within a jail and outline some general inmate ethics.

Chapter 13: Inmate Ethics

When citizens are incarcerated, they're thrust into a new social structure with different values and codes of conduct. These codes, or rules, depend on a level of voluntary and involuntary cooperation by those within the society. For the sake of simplicity, I'll discuss the three general types of inmates I see in the jail: career criminals, one-and-done citizens, and repeat offenders.

THE CAREER CRIMINALS

Career criminals have established themselves within the shadow economy, have often spent time in prison, and will generally speak directly about it. They'll be honest in meaning but evasive in words when speaking about their future and what they do. For example, if you ask what they might do after they get out of jail, you may hear something like, "I've gotta do what I've gotta do, just a little smarter."

Career criminals know how to work the system. They know where the cameras are and how to put on a performance. I've seen these guys put their hands up to make it look on camera like they don't want to fight, yet goad another inmate verbally to fight. On a camera with no sound, it looks like they're being non-confrontational. In reality, they're being the aggressor because if the person they're goading doesn't respond, they'll soon be seen as prey.

Career criminals often have other inmates do their "dirty work"—you rarely see them fight themselves, but they have influence over others who will do their bidding. They're good at using lies and deception for the purposes of manipulation.

Career criminals will tell you that they've chosen this life and that they'll live and die by their own rules. They can be polite and accommodating one minute and trying to kill you the next. These inmates can make the jail environment very difficult and dangerous to work in.

ONE-AND-DONE CITIZENS

Those who fought, trespassed, became belligerent, didn't pay a traffic ticket, or drank a little too much and drove may find themselves in jail. Many of these citizens made a mistake, and jail isn't where they want to be. As a result, they get through their incarceration and make every effort to stay out.

Such individuals have to deal with the jail environment and their new identity, but they're likely still good people who prefer not to make the same mistakes twice. These citizens are the "easy" inmates to watch and they generally follow the rules given to them. In my area, they quickly find themselves in alternative sentencing programs and leave the jail in short order. As a result, we mostly have career criminals and other repeat offenders remaining in the jail.

REPEAT OFFENDERS

Although career criminals are technically part of this group as well, I separate these inmates into their own class. These individuals would love to stay out of jail but just can't seem to do so. Most repeat offenders return to jail because of a substance abuse problem, mental health issues, incomplete education, disabilities, or difficulties in maintaining employment. Many of these individuals have difficult personalities and behavioral issues in general, making their management very challenging. As much as you try to help and influence them for the better, many don't have the support mechanisms, resources, motivation, or capacity to make lasting changes. These are the hard cases that very few communities have the resources or political will to address.

EFFECTS OF CAREER CRIMINALS ON THE HOUSING AREAS

Career criminals can increase tension or require additional attention because of the unique challenges they pose. As a result, the ethics of the career criminals have a larger impact inside the jail, and this gives rise to interesting social dynamics. This dynamic seems more akin to a feudal system that anything else, but it's also more basic than that. A predator-and-prey mindset would better explain the dynamic.

When a predator doesn't want to be prey to others, they develop strategies and tactics to suit. Mutually assured destruction is one such strategy where a predator maintains a balance of power by making it clear that if he goes down, the other person will too. This makes for a tension-filled housing area. Another strategy is where one predator consolidates power and becomes a clear leader. This emerging leader then uses violence and the threat of violence to keep other inmates toeing the line. It comes down to who is influential enough to claim to be the leader, and if sufficient numbers will choose to follow them.

It's important for deputies to set the tone, rules, and avenues for witnesses to come forward. We have no issues relocating career criminals and eroding their influence over others in housing areas. We make it a point that we, the jailers, are responsible for the running of the housing areas, not the career criminals. This doesn't mean that the system created by career criminals isn't present, but it is driven into the shadows.

INMATE ETHICS

Personality

Branding is important to the career criminal because there is a type of criminal hierarchy. Criminal leadership is often carefully cultivated by navigating in the narrow space of what is "acceptable" criminal behavior and what isn't. The stronger the personality, the more influence they have.

When a career criminal with a strong, brazen personality joins forces with someone who can measure and walk the fine line of the jail and legal systems, their "following" tends to grow. Depending on their intention, they can either become a major problem or they can work in the shadows. Those who become a major problem are usually separated, and their influence is systematically dismantled if possible.

Loyalty

Career criminals make much of loyalty, but it's more like swearing fealty to whoever is most influential at that moment. There are usually pledges to one another or to "the strongest" about loyalty. As a result, the person who has the allegiance of others has greater influence in the pod, and over the behavior of those who have pledged loyalty.

However, this loyalty is contingent on perceived strength and continued political influence. Like all political activities, loyalty moves with the wind and betrayal is waiting in the shadows. I find it wantonly ignorant that many criminals expect loyalty when a predatory or opportunistic mindset doesn't really allow for it.

Expected Silence

Another paradoxical behavior I've observed is that career criminals expect lawyer-like confidentiality when speaking with other criminals. Professional criminals can make or break themselves on this behavior alone. The more "confidential" a criminal is with another criminal's secrets, the more they're trusted. Being able to brag about their predatory exploits is how they measure one another and cultivate their influence. However, as with all things regarding politics and persona, if loyalty switches or the information can be traded for a sweet deal, then this confidentiality may evaporate quicker than ice in the Sahara.

Honor Among Thieves

Although it can be very difficult to prove or substantiate at times, career criminals playing cards are most certainly gambling. With gambling comes bluffing, debt, and ruin. It never ceases to amaze me that these professional liars and thieves expect one of their own to suddenly be an upright citizen and pay their debts. Yet the coercive influence that career criminals have with one another is sufficient enough that not paying a debt often results in staff intervention and the removal of an inmate from the housing area in order to preserve their safety.

Child Predators

Despite the hype around inmates assaulting child molesters, I've very rarely seen any assaults happen in practice. This may be because we separate people by classification. There may also be a deterrent in the fact that housing officers file criminal charges for crimes committed in their areas. However, inside the jail, many people clearly dislike child predators, and none are more vocal about this than convicted child predators trying to deflect suspicion.

There's a lot of tough talk from career criminals regarding child predators, but most inmates are more worried about their own circumstances to risk additional charges for assaulting one. However, this doesn't remove the possibility that the child predator is being made to "pay" for his protection. This can be monetary or through food or actions. We try to prevent such things from happening through thoughtful housing assignments and paying attention to issues in the housing areas.

Your Word

Career criminals may give you "their word." For most of them, this really means something. Still, you have to exercise caution, as they'll let you assume the meaning of a statement and then hide in the semantics of it. You should also expect them to break their word now and then when it's beneficial for them or when they think it will be most difficult for you.

However, if you give your word to them, you should stick by it. For the career criminal, not keeping your word tends to be an excuse for particularly bad behavior. If you lie, then any "word" they give you afterward will likely be a ruse. Since your word means nothing to you, why should it mean something to them? You set the tone.

Predator or Prey

Victims aren't victims to predators—they're prey. As prey, their job is to evade and elude the predator. Those who aren't quick enough, smart enough, or who show low physical prowess are considered "deserving" of the victimization they get. This, in general, is how career criminals view the world: they see to their own needs by taking from those who are unable to protect themselves. They believe that this is ethically okay because the prey "let them" do it.

Because of this mindset, they're always trying to avoid being prey themselves. Any challenges that label them as prey, physical actions that demonstrate "weakness," or damaging criminal politics are likely to be fiercely resisted because it will mean their "blood" is in the water.

Manipulating Deputies

No one likes to feel like they've been duped, but misdirection—particularly emotional misdirection—is a main element in manipulation. For a jailer, the most dangerous types of manipulation are built upon the facade of trust.

Inmates have a great deal of time to observe each jailer, and they can tell whether you're having a good or bad day. They'll use other inmates in the housing area to "throw under the bus" in order to start building rapport and trust with you. For some predators, much of the "fun" comes from the stalking, fooling, and manipulation of "prey" (in this case, you) before the strike.

The manipulations often begin with very small things. One very small favor or an overlooking of a rule violation indicates that trust is building. Some will use this to advance their influence in the housing area. Others will attempt to cultivate an emotional bond with a jailer. Once an emotional bond is forged (pun intended), the requests or violations become bigger. The excellent manipulators will make you think they care, thus luring you into giving more and more trust or information for yet a stronger "bond."

Every now and then, the manipulation is so successful that it will end a jailer's otherwise good career. We tell jailers to empathize a little in order to help with successful communication and de-escalation, but we also encourage jailers to maintain a healthy detachment from those who are inside because of how likely they are to attempt to use your empathy to "hack" your judgment.

"Allegedly"

I've taught many a new deputy this nifty conversational trick. I had noticed, over the years, that career criminals would rarely talk straight about anything unless I used the code word "allegedly." Remember, the game is for them to be able to brag about their criminal activities while denying it at the same time. I've had many career criminals and repeat offenders tell me everything they did because I asked, "What did you 'allegedly' do this time?" Almost every time, their eyes lit up, they smiled, and they told me their story in great detail, prefaced with the "Well, I *allegedly* ..."

Deputy Shopping

Some inmates operate with this basic principle: if at first you don't succeed, try another deputy. It seems standard among inmates to try and play deputies off of one another. Often you'll hear the phrasing, "The other deputy lets me . . ."

If an agency's leadership routinely enters housing areas and then tries to "assist" their housing deputy in general operations, they're more likely erode the authority of their staff than help. This happens because inmates will learn to bypass housing deputies in order to speak to leadership to get what they want. They'll also wait for anyone to walk into the area who might do something for them. This is why it's always best to refer any requests back to the inmate's housing officer.

Snitches, Witnesses, or Confidential Informants?

Unlike a department of corrections (DOC) facility, the majority of inmates in a jail are pre-trial. That means that career criminals looking at long DOC sentences are mixed in with other inmates who are more willing to trade or give information. In general, this trading of information is better for "the people's" legal case and bad for the accused. This giving of information to law enforcement is called "snitching" by criminals and "being a witness" to the rest of us.

Calling someone a "snitch" implies that the person witnessing this information is of lowly character. (Well, lowly when compared to the other criminals inside the facility.) For me, the criminal attitude toward this type of information-gathering is paradoxical, hypocritical, and a blatant attempt to turn someone who may want to do the right thing into the "bad guy."

In order to establish credibility, many career criminals speak of their exploits. Their aim is to become "known" in order to build their criminal credibility. In order to be known they have to brag about their crime and expose their villainy, yet they still demand a level of confidentiality usually reserved for priests and lawyers.

The accused will often confess elements of their crime to some other criminal who will likely use this information, should it be necessary, for their own self-interest. Some inmates hearing the confession will keep quiet unless sharing the information will benefit them. Other people, like the one-and-done inmate, may find the confessed criminal repulsive and pass on the information to law enforcement because it's the right thing to do.

Once the information is handed over to prosecutors, it will be brought to trial or used to encourage a plea deal. Sometimes the information is used to secure a conviction at trial. Either way, the confessed criminal feels betrayed by both the system and the person(s) they trusted when they bragged about their crimes.

I think it's strange that a criminal would freely give out a confession in order to build their criminal standing inside a facility and yet not expect that information to be used against them in court. It's hypocritical for these inmates to victimize people and still expect to be protected by other predators. Sometimes, these criminal "top dogs" are also informants, particularly against those who could threaten their position of strength.

If you're fortunate enough to develop a working informational rapport with a few inmates, then you should treat them as confidential informants (CIs). As far as CIs go, it's important to protect their identity and follow up on the information they provide. You'll quickly figure out who's trustworthy, who isn't, and who has mental health issues. It takes time to develop a CI who is relatively ethical in their approach to dealing with information. They'll leave out some information at times and reveal some other information with a targeted purpose.

Still, once in a while you'll have the opportunity to work with a "one-and-done" citizen who feels it's their duty to inform you about the criminal predators in their pod. It's important to protect their identity by leaving them out of reports, if possible, because your reports are discoverable by the defense. Once the defense attorney knows about your CI, they'll either tell their client or their client will read your informant's words in discovery. As a result, your CI will be labeled a snitch and will be at much greater risk of being harmed.

ANECDOTES FROM THE JAIL

"Predator versus Prey"

For some people, taking advantage of a situation or others is just the way they operate. On the street it's a distraction followed by a theft. The point is, these people don't see anything wrong with what they're doing. In fact, they're likely to blame the victim as being stupid, naive, gullible, and deserving of such treatment. To be taken advantage of is the fault of the victim, as these criminals believe that most of society is like them: predatorial. Below is one example of such behavior.

While inmates were out eating in a large, open bay, the deputy had to leave his mini-control in order to check every cell to ensure safety. Just after he passed inmates who were eating, an inmate sitting at a far corner table turned and started punching another one. That other inmate rose and began to fight back, and he was more of a competent fighter. He punched the inmate into a more open area of the pod.

The deputy then noticed the fight and moved toward them after calling for assistance to the area. As soon as he was between the inmates fighting and those at the tables still eating, other inmates got up and stole food from the trays of the inmates fighting. Others began to trade food very quickly while the deputy was occupied with putting the fighting inmates on the ground at Taser-point. Soon, the other deputies arrived in the area and both the trading and the fight were ended.

"The Alleged Molester"

During a full facility lockdown, inmate A hit his intercom. He told the deputy that he was being threatened due to his charges and that if he didn't give coffee to "those who are in charge" by Friday, he would get beaten up. When asked to clarify, he said that the gang members who run the pod were forcing him to give up commissary.

Inmate A was cleared to move to a different housing area. He packed his stuff, and while he was talking to supervisors, inmates all over the pod were yelling "chomo" (slang for child molester), "molester," and "you better move."

The inmate in question was in for charges of theft. The lie (that he was a child molester) was being used to create a hostile environment and coerce his property from him by creating a situation where he would have to "pay" for protection.

"The Bragging Gambler"

While scanning an outgoing letter from an inmate, a jailer noticed how the inmate specifically described gambling with other inmates in the pod. The letter stated that he was always on the poker table and that he bet every week on football. He also wrote, "I play pinochle a lot too, but only for money."

During a later shift, a deputy confiscated playing cards being used as poker chips from a different inmate. The inmate who wrote the letter was involved in that game. He became upset and challenged the deputy in the pod. The result was the confiscation of his "winnings" and the cards, plus discipline.

INMATE ARCHETYPES

Just like for deputies, if you work long enough in the field, definite inmate archetypes appear. Sometimes inmates will fall into multiple archetypes, which is a testament to how complex each person is. The following are some inmate archetypes that those who work in the field will recognize. Although I put a humorous spin on many of these, the fact is that they represent the real and unique challenges that these types of individuals bring to the work of a deputy.

The Ignorant Inmate

It's this inmate's first stint in the jail, and they were a bit out of sorts when they came in. Therefore, they didn't understand the video or handbook that outlined expectations. Quite often, they don't want to be in violation and will comply if given the opportunity. These inmates are just ignorant of the rules.

The Conveniently Ignorant Inmate

This type of inmate has been in and out of the jail at least five times—they know the rules, but when they're caught breaking one, they say, "I didn't know." They try this strategy on newer staff members in particular because these deputies tend to not recognize them. However, there are some inmates that use "I didn't know" as their standard reply for just about every situation.

These inmates can be somewhat entertaining to deal with, especially when you bring up their last eight incarcerations and previous disciplinary history. Most of the time, these inmates accept their issued discipline if you catch them. Occasionally they become highly irritated, as if that will change the fact that they committed a rule violation.

The Direct-Threat Inmate

This person tells you directly that they're going to assault you, find you on the "outs," hunt down your family, or cause you to stay late doing paperwork because they're going to break sprinkler heads or other jail property. They'll do all of this because you're giving them a written warning for violating some minor rule. They tend to be over the top, and they're counting on their loudness and size to influence you.

Most jail staff don't want to have a long day dealing with such people, but there are direct-threat inmates in every jail. They tend to find their way into some sort of segregation due to their behavior. At first they can be very difficult to adapt to, but it gets easier when you realize that they tend to act like a very large three-year-old throwing a tantrum in the fact that they yell, act out, threaten, and then demand your respect. Still, never underestimate a person's ability and willingness to cause you harm for a real or imagined offense.

The Indirect-Threat Inmate

This person may attempt to come off as trying to help staff by helping them navigate a threatening environment. I've seen them tell newer female staff members that they [the inmate] were ensuring their safety in the pod (module). This inmate also suggests that they know information about threats to your safety but then won't reveal them. They can also do things like look you up in the phone book or have a friend find you using an internet-based background checker, and then tell you about your life. Again, this inmate attempts to influence the staff in order to avoid discipline or increase stress on individual staff members.

The TV Nutritionist

These "nutritionists" have zero training and no experience working in a kitchen, yet they know how all food should and shouldn't be prepared and have a calibrated eye for the calories and nutritional facts of food placed on a tray. In nearly every case I remember, these inmates complain about the quantity and quality of the mass-produced food under the guise of being nutritional experts, where those with actual training or knowledge know exactly what diets to get on for the benefits they seek.

The Litigator

This person attempts to get staff to make an error in judgment that's litigation-worthy. I've experienced inmates using threats and inflammatory comments in order to goad staff into assaulting them or denying them their rights without a true security threat. I've also had these inmates attempt to get me into an argument over policies I didn't write. I don't mean that the person was venting; I mean they were trying to escalate me into defending a position that didn't need defending.

The Podly Defender

This is your unqualified jailhouse "lawyer" who provides "legal assistance" to other inmates. Sometimes this person was able to get off on a technicality while representing themselves on some previous case. Often, this emboldens them to continue representing themselves and touting their victory as a reason for others to listen to them. Other Podly Defenders haven't had this success, but they still provide advice to others about how to "get off" on technicalities. Most of the time, the advice these inmates give ends in disaster.

The Ignorant Constitutionalist

A conversation with one of these individuals usually results in them quoting, "We the People," and then making a grievance about how their incarceration is a violation of the U.S. Code, the Articles of Confederation, the Uniform Commercial Code, or the Constitution pre-Fourteenth Amendment. Although some have solid historical education behind their views, most have a stunningly ignorant understanding of the historical reasoning and intention of those who drafted these documents. In the end, their argument is that you can't hold them accountable because said document doesn't allow it, even if the document was never envisioned or designed for their particular circumstance.

The Grifter

These types of individuals manipulate others simply because they love it. Many are sociopathic or sadistic, or they think that conning others is a legitimate strategy for life. They don't believe anyone, they have multiple plots in order to attain some sort of goal, they see their targets as gullible or deserving of the con, they think they're smarter than those around them, and they're generally not honest with themselves. They're likely to try and manipulate for the smallest of things, as even a small advantage is a "victory."

The Deputy Shopper

This inmate is like a child asking different family members for something until someone gives them the answer they want to hear. They don't take no for an answer. They'll ask any new deputy who walks into the area—often right in front of a deputy they just asked—in an attempt to get an affirmative response. They'll ask corporals, sergeants, and even a lieutenant if they see one.

The Kibitzing Manipulator

For whatever reason, this inmate watches what takes place in the pods and then offers seemingly helpful advice to the jailer. This person doesn't generally cause trouble, but trouble never seems far from them. They have enough influence to be a player in pod politics, but they deal in information and influence. They often try to make it seem like they're helping you in order to gain favor or other information from you later on. These inmates can, if you aren't careful, get a jailer to compromise themselves in the smallest of ways, which can lead to bigger problems later.

The Suddenly Concerned Hygienist

These inmates sometimes appear utterly ridiculous. They complain about how dirty things are, yet they make very few efforts to clean.

They may also suddenly claim that their cell mate is dirty or doesn't shower in order for you to move them out of the cell or be placed with a "friend." This inmate can also be a meth addict who, after being incarcerated, complains that the food isn't healthy enough or that their body is a temple that shouldn't be desecrated with jail-provided vitamins.

The Smelly Celly

This really does happen. There are some people who never bother to shower or clean up after themselves. They can make a whole housing area miserable, and if not taken care of in a reasonable time, they can cause problems.

The Eye Batter

This female inmate thinks she can manipulate you by batting her eyelashes. When this happens to me I find it mildly amusing that they think it would work. I then look at the inmates standing behind her, who are usually already laughing at the attempt, before I ask if she has a medical condition that affects her eyes. However, if this tactic never worked, she wouldn't do it.

The Shirtless Wonder

This is the male inmate who takes his shirt off every chance he gets when females are in the area. These females can be deputies, medical or counseling staff, program leaders, or volunteers. He will have his shirt on all day, but he'll suddenly be by his door shirtless, attempting to show off his physique, when females arrive.

The Skewed-Perspective Inmate

I find this type of inmate one of the most challenging. This person suddenly become inflexible and skewed in their perspective. Their over-the-top tantrums are entertaining after the fact, but they can easily lead to a physical altercation over a perceived injustice, real or imagined.

The Doctor Who Went to CNA School

Sometimes we get people who had a short time as a certified nursing assistant (CNA), and now they magically have nursing degrees and "offer" or shout medical advice at the nursing staff during a medical emergency. Their comments toward security and medical staff during an emergency are distracting, but they protest that they're trying to help. If they're particularly divisive, they attempt to unite the pod by declaring the medical staff inept and saying that more emergent action is needed. Either way, they have to be spoken with, when it's prudent, in an attempt to avoid future incidents.

The Tattooed Macho Man Who's Afraid of Blood and Needles

Imagine the biggest, baddest tattooed macho man who works out every day and uses the direct-threat methodology to get what he wants. Suddenly, this man takes ill and demands to see a doctor. He's eventually granted the opportunity, and the doctor requests blood samples. Suddenly the inmate can't function. He is hyper-afraid of the needles despite his tattoos, and the most supportive nurse of the nursing staff has to convince him that it's for his own good. However, he declines the help in the end. Later that day he complains about substandard medical care, states that he was personally injured by malpractice, and screams at the staff to take him to the hospital or else.

The Shot-Caller or Pod Father

For whatever reason, this inmate has enough influence that many other inmates will defer to them. Sometimes it's gang rank, sometimes the person is physically very big, other times they're very politically savvy. When this person wants the pod to be quiet, it will be quiet. If they want the pod clean, it will get clean. For some deputies, it's tempting to utilize this dynamic in order to deal with troublesome inmates. However, allowing this gives the inmate legitimacy and reinforces the idea that the inmates—not the staff—are in charge. I don't recommend letting such events occur in your jail, as it creates an overall unsafe environment for staff.

The Musclehead

These guys are your typical gym muscleheads who have committed crimes. They're worried about bulking up, they compete with others on physical prowess, and they strut around the jail like birds. They're usually physically and socially secure and generally don't cause issues.

The Chihuahua

You know the personality of this type of person: small, loud, full of confidence, mean, and hard-headed. It's difficult to take them seriously because they're physically unimposing and they mostly just yell. Jailers (and other inmates) find them annoying and tiresome. They demand respect just like the Shot-Caller or Musclehead without the means to physically intimidate.

The Old Man

There are two types of Old Man in a jail—the career criminal of advanced years and the older inmate who finally did something crazy or got caught after years of getting away with crimes. Sometimes these guys are looked after by the younger inmates. Sometimes they become victimized because of their weakened condition.

The Young Kid

Similar to the Old Man archetype, there are generally two types of Young Kids. There's the timid, first-time-in-jail type who just made a mistake. Many times these guys complain about various things that the older inmates find tiresome, aggravating, and a touch whiney. Then there are the Young Kids who have chosen this path and feel they have something to prove. They will prey upon others in an effort to gain respect and power. They're also quicker to use violence to achieve their objectives.

The Not Crazy Inmate

This person does everything to convince the counseling and medical staff that they have a mental health problem, but in reality, they're acting. Despite the wild antics they exhibit, the counselors will eventually inform you that the person does not have mental health issues but doesn't want to seem in control their own behavior. Sometimes they'll shorten the explanation and just say that the individuals are "behavioral."

The Mental Health Inmate

These inmates come to the jail in bad shape. Often, they've stopped taking their medications and have extreme difficulty managing even the smallest tasks required of them. Most of them want to be left alone and isolate themselves in a cell. Sometimes they can become violent in a moment's notice, other times they're just very confused and clearly having the hardest time doing the easiest of tasks. Unlike the inmates who pretend to have mental health issues, these individuals clearly march to the beat of their own drum.

The Foreign National

Sometimes jailed individuals from different countries are just afraid and confused, and helping them get ahold of their consulate can help reduce their anxieties. Other times, this person doesn't care in the least about what they do until they're prepared for deportation. Some countries inflict further punishments beyond our sentencing and can impose additional consequences up to and including execution for embarrassing the country.

The "Poocasso"

There are a few inmates, mostly upon entry into the jail, who remove feces from the floor or directly from their rear and place it on their windows. Not stopping there, they decide to draw pictures and artwork on the glass or the wall with it. Sometimes it's just a written message to all who must weather the stench to ensure that they're still alive and well. Every once in a while, someone has that artistic flare that, other than the smell and obvious biohazard, would be a great work of art.

CHAPTER 14 PREP

Discipline can be the start of a conversation that can quickly become mired with omissions, half-truths, challenges, and outright lies. There are certain occasions in which you, as a law enforcement officer, can lie to the suspect or inmate as part of an interrogation strategy. However, the rest of the time you'll either be required to tell the truth or strongly encouraged to be as honest as possible when dealing with inmates who run afoul of the rules inside the facility.

Chapter 14: Lies and Excuses

IF YOU WANT TO LEARN about lies in depth, there are any number of books, magazines, seminars, and classes that offer the chance to learn more about the signs of deception. These are very useful during interrogations, when narrowing down suspects, and when attempting to gain a confession. This section isn't about acquiring that level of skill when it comes to detecting deception—rather, it will focus on the basics of deception, how lies affect law enforcement, and common phrases and actions that inmates will use.

LIES, HUMAN NATURE, AND LAW ENFORCEMENT

Avoiding the Truth

For some people, fantasy is more palatable than reality, and they learn to believe their own lies. Other people run from the truth and then make up details to justify their conduct. You'll also find that some people use lies as weapons against others for entertainment, personal gain, or to create "reasonable doubt."

Even in the best circumstances, and with the best intentions, our memories can be inaccurate. This can result in small deviations from the truth as we fill in memory gaps with what seems reasonable or logical.

Fortunately, most situations are mundane enough for memory to render a good representation of events.

Those in law enforcement are required to strive for the highest levels of integrity. If you remember, you remember; if you don't, then say so. If you did it, own it. If this isn't a challenge that you can take on, law enforcement is definitely not for you!

The Brady Rule

In 1963, the Supreme Court's decision on Brady v. Maryland made it clear that prosecutors must disclose any evidence that may be exculpatory. This includes evidence that casts doubt on guilt, could mitigate the severity of a sentence, or challenges the credibility of a witness. Depending on your agency and judicial district, policies that deal with this can be quite invasive for a person working as a law enforcement officer.

Without integrity, the law enforcement officer is ineffective. The community won't trust an agency that tolerates lying from its officers. Once that trust is broken, it takes an enormous amount of time and effort to recover. In addition to this, the repercussions of noncompliance are steep. Attorneys can lose their licenses or be censured or criminally charged if an officer fails to disclose this type of information, and cities and counties can lose a lot of money in lawsuits.

Any internal affairs or professional standards investigation into an officer's conduct that highlights issues with credibility is discoverable by the defense. Therefore, this question will be asked: if you lied on one official document, how many more did you lie on? As a result, even the smallest of lies on an official form or to your supervisor can result in immediate termination and a questioning of all the work you've done. As public servants, it's our duty to tell the truth. Lies on official documents are punishable under the criminal code.

Still, there are appropriate uses for lies within law enforcement. The most common and accepted time for law enforcement to intentionally use false information is during interviews and interrogations. In this case, the officer will lie about the clarity of evidence or about how a certain act was "okay" in order to make it easier for the person to confess their crime. Lies may also be used in dealing with tactical situations, such as a hostage rescue, in order to give the officers an advantage.

In a jail, however, I've found it to be bad practice to lie to inmates. In fact, the more transparent one is, the easier it can be to deal with strong personalities. Noncommittal and half answers are sometimes seen as a lack of knowledge, purposeful antagonism, or a sign of a manipulatable personality.

Blame versus Responsibility

Some people lie to avoid blame, which they see as a form of rejection (and most people fear being rejected). Some lie so they don't have to take responsibility for their actions. Some shift the blame to someone or something else. If you go to work in law enforcement, you'll have to be able to accept responsibility for your choices and be prepared for the harsh judgments and shaming that those who lack experience and training will often throw your way.

Just remember that blame and responsibility aren't the same thing: the word "blame" tends to carry the social judgment of fault, or intentional misconduct. A person should be able to make a minor mistake and learn from it without being forced to carry shame around like some sort of scar. To take responsibility, on the other hand, is to simply accept that you made choices and had responses, and acknowledge that you have an obligation to own the consequences of these choices and responses. If your response to a situation wasn't ideal and the consequences were negative, then it's the right thing to do to accept your role in the resulting chaos. The trick to learning from it is to drop the shame.

Some people seem to thrive off of finding someone to blame and shame. Maybe this is because it's easier to pass judgment and villainize one person, or a few people, rather than acknowledge an overall lack of support, training, and leadership, or the shirking of obligations by others who may have also played a role in a particular event.

People in general don't like to be vilified, blamed, misunderstood, or caricatured, so it's easy to understand why someone would want to avoid blame by sidestepping their responsibilities. It isn't easy to stand by your decisions and actions in the face of potential social shaming, but sometimes it's empowering to do so: the vast majority of your mistakes aren't so disastrous that villagers will rise up and come at you with pitchforks and torches. People, in general, also seem to respect people who can accept responsibility despite their fears.

HOW INMATES USE LIES

Housing Area Politics and Sabotage

Some inmates use lies to great effect on other inmates and select staff members. I've known inmates to complain about inappropriate touching from jailers who were never near him or her, only because that deputy held them accountable for a rule violation. The resulting investigations on the deputies were extensive and uncomfortable for them, but they were exonerated in the end. There were no criminal consequences on the inmates for the false accusations.

Similar to this, some inmates will also attempt to exploit knee-jerk reactions from jailers by accusing them of wrongdoing. This can cause a jailer a great deal of stress while the accusations are investigated by the professional standards unit. Once in a great while, a jailer has been manipulated and compromised to the point where it results in their termination, litigation, and a loss of some public trust.

Inmates will use these kinds of lies on each other as well. Some inmates will lie about another inmate's charges in order to create a very hostile housing environment. Usually this means circulating rumors that the person is a child rapist. Suddenly, the majority of inmates in the housing area will make life very hard for that inmate and put them under threat. Often, the person is actually in on a charge that is more like robbery or motor vehicle theft.

I've seen some male inmates—who have a longer sentence or are facing prison—increase the housing-area tension for someone else in order to manipulate them to fight. That person, usually, is almost finished with their sentence. The predator, sensing the short-sentence inmate avoiding additional jail time, attempts to victimize or "punk out" that inmate, leaving them with the choice of either fending off the predator or encouraging other predators to move in. This harassment can result in a fight in a cell, injuries, and additional charges for the person who would've otherwise been released in a few days.

I've seen some female inmates be very persistent in getting another inmate caught in the act of some minor rule violation so they can see a disciplinary response, removal from the area, or the termination of that inmate from some sort of work program.

Common Lies and Excuses

When you were a kid, did you ever lie to avoid getting in trouble? As we mature, we tend to own our short-sighted mistakes and acknowledge them. Still, there are some people who believe the only way to avoid trouble is to deny their role in it and blame others for their decisions.

People don't learn these strategies overnight. Like all things, they take time to develop, and, more importantly, a reason. This may be where the broken home and broken bones come into play during a person's development. There are many sociological and psychological theories as to how these strategies develop and how they're incorporated into a person's personality. I've met quite a few people in jail with responsibility-averse personalities—they tend to exhibit chronic lying. Whatever the reason (accident, birth, or survival strategy), these individuals can be found in a critical mass in jails.

Below are some of the most common phrases I've heard used by inmates to avoid being held accountable for their decisions.

"I Didn't Know!"

At some point in your career, and mostly when you first start, you'll inform someone of their rule violation and they'll say, "I didn't know. Sorry, Dep." Once in a while, the person is telling the truth—they genuinely appear alarmed and worried that your verbal correction will bring more consequences. Wide eyes, hunched body posture, turning slightly to deflect, and rapid speech usually indicate this type of interaction.

The vast majority of time, however, you'll find that the person says, "I didn't know. Sorry, Dep," in a clear, unworried manner, and then turns to resume whatever it was they were doing. Check your database, records, or other means of determining past incarcerations and you'll likely find that such people have been in jail multiple times within the past year and likely many more times over the last ten years.

The point of this type of deception is to provide the deputy with a "reasonable" lie in order to avoid further disciplinary action and investigation. A new deputy is more likely to fall for this because they want to believe the inmate, they don't want to be the "bad guy," and they may not feel confident enough to call them out on their charade.

I've responded to this type of lie in many different ways, but one of my favorites is to say, "You didn't know? So, when I check for how many times you've been here, this will be your first time, right? I won't find that you've been here several times and have to lock you down for lying, will I?"

Sensing that the consequences of their lie are about to increase, most inmates will attempt to "get real" for a minute or two, allowing you to reinforce the verbal warning you'd already planned to give and let them know that this behavior won't be tolerated.

"The Other Deputy"

Let's say that you see an inmate doing something that strikes you as not right or a clear violation while you're walking your housing area. This could be having multiple mattresses, artwork pasted to the walls, more than the allowed amounts of books, art, photos, etc. As a result, you may decide to talk to the person about these violations, and they might say, "The other deputy allowed it." (Another variation of this is, "The corporal [or sergeant] walked by my cell and didn't say anything!")

The objective of this lie is to create doubt within the jailer and play on their inclination to not contradict other staff, therefore letting the violation continue despite the strong sense that it should be corrected. This usually works best on newer staff. If the inmate is particularly difficult and violent, they'll appear to become agitated (or pretend to be agitated) in order to "sweeten" the reason to not pick this particular battle and ensure their compliance with the rules.

When addressing this particular lie, my response is to ask directly who said it was okay. Ninety-nine percent of the time, the inmate won't be able to tell me a name but will attempt to still retain some legitimacy by stating that it was a deputy on the opposite shift from a couple of days ago. I then let the inmate know that anyone not doing their job needs to be corrected and that I need to know which deputy is doing this so I can get it resolved. At this point, the inmate stops attempting to win this particular battle but may still act out.

If the inmate becomes highly agitated (their attempt to get me to drop it), I conduct an assessment based on the condition of the facility in order to determine further action. What I mean by this is that I weigh the possibility of this inmate becoming uncooperative or combative at that particular moment with what has been happening in other areas of the jail. The vast majority of the time, I carry on with questioning the inmate and let them decide to do what they're going to do (continue to argue or drop the subject). Rarely, there are other more emergent events taking place in the facility and I will put further conversation on the back burner.

"You're the Only Deputy"

This is a variation of the "other deputy" excuse or lie. The inmate will say that you're "the only deputy" to enforce a certain rule or policy in the area. The goal here is to make the jailer feel as if they're breaking from the norm of the other deputies and change the likelihood of their enforcing discipline or policy. We jailers try and be as consistent with each other and policy as possible, but we accept that there will be variation. This variation most often works to the inmate's benefit because there's room to get different things done at different times.

Even if you're one of the few deputies to enforce a particular rule, chances are that you don't enforce something else to the degree another deputy does, so it balances out. On the rare occasion that an inmate states this to me, I tell them how the inconsistency already benefits them and how much harder jail time would be if we all enforced the rules all the time like robots.

"Check the Cameras"

Another phrase the inmates often use is "check the cameras." Not every facility has cameras, but my jail has a fair amount of them. However, getting and viewing the video footage takes time. Banking on the deputy not being able to get the footage before the end of their shift, or knowing that the deputy would have to stay late in order to get the footage, some inmates will break a rule right in front of you and then demand that you check the video footage before you enforce discipline.

The reasoning behind this type of excuse and lie is to use law enforcement's training and ethos regarding evidence collection to avoid being held accountable, and to create a condition where the inmate can argue and look reasonable. Deputies are trained to gather information, attempt to preserve the evidence, and secure such evidence to back up statements and witness testimony. As a result, there's a strong urge for the deputy to reinforce and secure the evidence when their observations are questioned. A jailer may then feel like they have to have a "bulletproof case" in order to hold the inmate accountable.

In this situation, the inmate is hoping that the effort of evidence collection would take too long for the deputy to verify, or for a more emergent disciplinary action to redirect or distract the housing deputy, thereby letting them slip through. If this tactic succeeds, they look like a genius to the other inmates who will also use this tactic. However, the burden of proof for internal disciplinary measures is reasonable suspicion, not "beyond a reasonable doubt." As a layer of protection, inmates usually have access to an appeals process should the jailer happen to be wrong.

In addition to attempting to influence deputies to treat minor disciplinary actions like a homicide investigation, the inmate is likely trying to prove to the housing area that they can openly argue with the staff without consequences. This is done by putting the deputy on the defensive in front of the housing area by accusing them of not following proper criminal processes. Because jailers generally want to do the right thing, there's a chance that the jailer may delay the disciplinary action, forgetting that the inmate was arguing with them in the housing area. Admittedly, this is a problem that mostly newer deputies face when dealing with experienced inmates.

In my experience, the best way to deal with this type of situation is head on, with confidence, and by using humor if you can. I've responded by saying things like, "Let me get this straight. You think that this [insert minor violation] is worth establishing a special task force? How about you just own what you did, learn from it, and stop doing it?"

Usually, the inmate sees that you're giving them an opportunity to reverse course and take responsibility. Of course, some inmates will double down on their tactic and insist that you check the cameras.

Now, if you didn't actually see the violation or it took place during a busy time, the inmate could be telling the truth. But the majority of the time, the inmate is just trying to get you to drop it by insisting that you're wrong. However, I believe in trust with verification. I tell them that I believe them, but that I will check the cameras. I then notify them that since I'm going through the effort of reviewing video, every infraction I see during the timeframe reviewed will be addressed. This means that every rule violation I missed will now have consequences, and those inmates will likely not be happy with this. If they did it, the inmate usually stops pushing for me to check the cameras at this point. If they didn't do it, I'll verify it and let them know that I was wrong!

ANECDOTES FROM THE JAIL

A note about food in the jail: people can't select their own portion sizes, so there are many complaints about the quantity of food available or given. As a result, inmates begin to intimidate one another for food. Every once in a while, a person willingly gives their food to another person. However, the sharing of food is a rule violation because the sharing or stealing of it could result in assaults or threaten the orderly operation of the facility and the safety of those inside. Commissary items have a similar effect and are not allowed to be shared, bartered, gambled, or forced to be exchanged between inmates.

"Lying and Stealing"

I had observed an inmate with extra food on his tray. This was not a little bit of extra food, but an entire tray on top of his issued amount. I was one tray short and had to order another, so it was likely that the inmate grabbed two trays and dumped one on top of the other. In our facility, sharing food or taking extra food is against the rules as it fosters adversarial relationships inside the jail. I took him into a conference room where I asked him further about the food on his tray.

He stated that he got the extra food but didn't steal the tray. I told him I would take him at his word and issue a written reprimand for his conduct as he was honest with me. I also told him that I would likely check the cameras to confirm this, and he urged me to do so.

The camera footage showed him go through the lunch line twice. Following my review of the video footage, I issued him a forty-eight-hour lockdown for lying to me. When I served him both disciplinary forms at the same time, he was confused. I informed him that the first reprimand was what I'd promised when I took him at his word. Discovering that his word was a lie earned a forty-eight-hour lockdown. I further let him know that he'd burned any trust that he could've developed with me by lying about something so minor. As a result, the inmate didn't protest the lockdown and later apologized for lying to me.

"A 'New' Veteran Inmate"

I was walking through the pod and noticed that an inmate seemed to be sharing his commissary purchases with another at his cell door. As a general rule, we believe that sharing is done to settle a debt or to establish a favor on the receiver for later use, not out of the kindness of their hearts. This type of trading and sharing usually sows discord in the inmate populations and occasionally ends in assaults and criminal charges.

I stepped near and asked the inmate at the door to leave. I then cautioned the other inmate, who had been in and out of the jail several times, against sharing his commissary. He said that he wasn't going to share his stuff anymore and that he didn't know the rules. His tone was matter of fact, non-conciliatory, and robotic.

I've heard this excuse many times from inmates who've been in and out of the jail for the last decade. Some of them have multiple arrests each year. That was the case with this inmate, who seemed to have forgotten that we'd met many times before.

I then advised him that when I hear an inmate say "I didn't know" so nonchalantly, I'm inclined to think they've been here before, and I double check to see if I'm right. If the person has been previously incarcerated, I will then have confirmed that the person lied to me. I then have to discipline that person with two violations: one for attempting to transfer personal property and one for lying to staff.

I then said to the inmate, "A person could, instead, take the advice I'm giving them, without excuses, and not give their property to others." The inmate agreed and no further action was needed.

CHAPTER 15 PREP

When it comes to disciplinary action, many people are unsure of themselves. Many inmates think the rules are "petty" and pay them no mind, believing you should do the same. Some people learning to be deputies have a hard time saying no. In the end, you teach by what you do and don't do. Inmates will learn your patterns, likes and dislikes, and what you will and will not enforce. You can help set them up for success as the adults they are by respecting their decisions to break the rules and providing them with consequences and guidance.

Chapter 15: Discipline

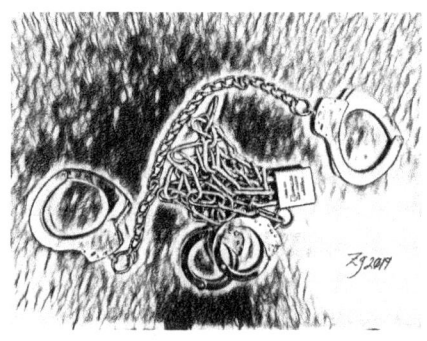

What is discipline? In Latin, *disciplina* means to give instruction, learning, and knowledge. Today, discipline generally means to train self-control or obedience using rules enforced through consequences, the ability to control mental or physical activity, or an area of study. Jails are holding areas for citizens who are awaiting trial to determine innocence or guilt, but they don't have to wait until the result of trial to change their path.

Inside the jail where I work, disciplinary processes have multiple objectives. Discipline can provide structure, order, and predictable consequences for people's decisions or actions. However, it can also teach humility and promote responsibility, self-control, and the importance of taking a moment to conduct a cost-benefit analysis.

For me, discipline is the start of a conversation. Whatever the desired outcome, the goal is to communicate expectations, consequences for not meeting those expectations, and strategies for meeting the expectations. It also promotes good decision-making skills.

STRUCTURE AND ORDER

Due process is a central part of the U.S. judicial process, and as such, it should be administered equally. Order and structure inside a jail seek to satisfy this requirement while attempting to greatly increase the safety and security of the inmates going through due process. As a result, people will find themselves in a heavily restricted and structured environment that is geared for safety and security while preserving due process.

It's desirable to remain as consistent as possible with these processes because it's important that individuals aren't singled out for special treatment (positively or negatively). Special treatment could be considered preferential or prejudicial depending on who is being treated differently, who observes this treatment, and the background of the inmate, citizen, or jailer. Needless to say, a jailer should endeavor to be firm, fair, and consistent.

PREDICTABLE CONSEQUENCES

Rules or codes of conduct that reinforce structure and order for safety and security purposes should have fairly predictable consequences. The idea is that an informed inmate who disrupts the safety, structure, and order should be aware of the consequences for doing so. Having predictable consequences is further evidence that a jail is providing all under its charge with due process and allowing individuals to conduct a cost-benefit analysis regarding their actions.

HUMILITY

Some people are so used to doing what they want, when they want, without consequences, that suddenly having consequences is difficult to accept. Whatever the reason—nonexistent parenting, bad parenting, or personality—they've developed a life strategy that somehow led them to expect little to no consequences for their actions. A structured and consistent disciplinary response can help them learn an important lesson; namely, that consequences for their decisions can come with little to no warning whether they believe they should or not.

I've seen some inmates have a violent reaction to this lesson. I've also seen many of these inmates, over time, replace this violent reaction with humility and understanding. One can never predict who will learn this lesson and who won't.

RESPONSIBILITY

Before a person can influence what happens in their life, they have to accept responsibility for their actions and choices. In a jail, structure, order, and predictable consequences are key to providing a person with a clear example of cause and effect. The structure, order, and consequences on their own aren't likely to change a person's mind—the critical component is that the inmate recognize that they can influence their circumstances through behavior. Often, working with the system—rather than against it—leads to better results, thus reinforcing responsible behavior.

An agency's culture can either greatly help or greatly hinder this process. For example, if your supervisors don't support your disciplinary decisions or constantly give inmates support when they behave badly, then the inmates won't learn this lesson. Instead, they'll learn that their bad behavior gets results. Should your agency's culture support disciplinary actions and only provide inmates with support when they demonstrate good behavior, then the inmates will learn that bad behavior will get them nothing.

Helping repeat offenders learn to take responsibility empowers them to make better life decisions. Your job is to help them to learn this by holding them accountable for their decisions like the adults they are. Don't treat them like children!

SELF-CONTROL AND A COST-BENEFIT ANALYSIS

Once an inmate buys into the concepts of humility and responsibility, then the greater challenge of reinforcing the benefits of this begins. Maintaining a humble and responsible attitude is a very difficult challenge for anyone, let alone a person who may have had a difficult upbringing. Learning techniques in the art of self-control and discipline can be greatly beneficial.

Each person is different enough that they'll likely have their own solution or method that works for them. Fortunately, my jail provides quite a few programs that give inmates more ideas on how to achieve the mental and emotional resilience necessary for this kind of personal growth. I wish it worked for everyone, but like most things, people can be pointed in the right direction, but they must make those changes, take advice, and walk the walk.

I've seen quite a few people in the jail have difficulty with impulse control. When given tools and strategies that worked for them, they were able to pause before acting. The simple act of pausing allowed them to look at what they wanted to do and weigh it against the likely consequences of their actions. Often, having paused to make a cost-benefit analysis, they made different and better choices.

THE START OF A CONVERSATION

A housing area can be a very busy place. When you have sixty to one hundred twenty inmates in your area, you don't always get a chance to speak with someone before they commit a minor rule violation.

As a jailer, you're responsible for making sure policies and procedures are followed in order to ensure safety and security. Inmates are to be held accountable for disruptions to the structure and order that make everyone less safe. But you can't make everyone safe by simply issuing "tickets"—just giving someone written discipline and then locking them down without an attempt at conversation increases area tension and erodes the chance to build rapport. Instead, every observed infraction is a chance to have a conversation.

Most of the time, reminding inmates of the rule is enough. Sometimes you have to pull them aside and have a longer conversation, however, as there can be events in their lives outside the jail that are impacting them significantly. A bad day at court, losing a relative, or the loss of a relationship is very likely to have a great impact on stress levels, so such events should be considered a starting point for their sudden disregard of the rules. However, even if these events are recognized as issues, it doesn't absolve the person of their responsibility to follow the rules of the jail that are there to keep them safe and secure.

A good jailer will have a conversation with the inmates after they commit an infraction, when giving disciplinary consequences, and after the violation has been addressed or resolved.

ESTABLISHING A REPUTATION

Having created an environment where structure and order are enforced, the inmates will then expect some level of consistency from the staff. They'll also quickly exploit inconsistency. Establishing a reputation for consistently enforcing discipline is extremely important for the jailer: demonstrating that you can see a violation, address it firmly, fairly, and consistently, yet maintain an authoritative cool is critical to longevity in the field.

I often advise newer deputies to maintain a higher level of written disciplinary practices until they're about a year in. After they've established themselves as being firm, fair, and consistent, while maintaining an authoritative cool, they can more easily move on to more varied disciplinary methods that are likely to be even more effective. The trick is to establish their reputation first.

An important aspect of reputation is realizing that inmates learn from what you do, but also—and sometimes more importantly—from what you don't do. If you enforce contraband rules but are lax with horseplay, then inmates will limit their contraband but get out of control with horseplay. If they know you don't enforce rules close to shift change, you'll get brazen violations close to shift change. Inmates will learn your habits very quickly, so it's important to evaluate yourself and ask coworkers to call you out on your routines.

FAILING TO ESTABLISH A STRONG DISCIPLINARY REPUTATION

Establishing a lax reputation regarding discipline almost always comes back to bite you as a jailer. On more than a few occasions, I've witnessed a new deputy entering service having seldom used the disciplinary process and never becoming comfortable with it. Some of these new jailers have difficulty saying no, while others seem to feel like the "bad guy" for holding other adults accountable for their decisions.

Many times, these new jailers attempt to use methods they saw their FTO use, but this doesn't have the effect they desire because the FTO is already established. Inmates will see the avoidance of disciplinary action by the deputy as a weakness, or laziness. Therefore, if one inmate consistently bends the rules and gets away with it, more inmates will try it. Slowly, the level of infractions will get worse and the jailer will begin to feel their authority slipping from them.

In this way, these deputies will eventually be pushed to their absolute limit by the inmates. Usually, by then, both their coworkers and supervisors are also pushing the jailer to get in line with the rest of the agency. This means there will be pressure from above, from coworkers, and from the inmates. Often, inmates will say things like, "You were cool—what happened to you?" or "Are you trying to get promoted now?" Because the jailer had already established a lax approach, the pushback by inmates is amplified, not dampened.

Often, this jailer will then jump from inaction to over-reaction in order to gain their authority and reputation back. However, this level of operation can be very tiring and stressful. Before you know it, this jailer may start calling for more assistance to their housing area than normal, often when they're stressed out. Coworkers may become unsympathetic to these emergency calls and attribute them to the jailer not being able to manage their area. Generally, I've seen these deputies leave within two years of service.

BEING BADGE-HEAVY

Some jailers who are sticklers for the rules are called "badge-heavy," but they aren't. These jailers are just trying to do their job to the best of their ability. After a time, you'll see that many of them often go above and beyond what your average jailer will attempt when it comes to the enforcement of rules. Inmates who recognize this may call this deputy a hard-ass, but they'll respect them.

However, even to other jailers, there are also those who seem to enjoy stretching their authority to the limit rather than being measured in its use. These individuals are actually badge-heavy, and both the staff and the inmates will have a difficult time respecting them.

These are the jailers who enter a housing area and begin hunting for rule violations. These deputies don't just walk through an area, but close the doors loudly and make a clear show of looking for rule breakers. Anyone who spends any length of time working a jail knows you don't have to look hard to a find rule violation. In fact, more often than not, you have to pick your battles because there are so many violations.

To consistently make a spectacle of searching for rule violations has a downside. First, it establishes a badge-heavy reputation for the deputy. Second, it puts the entire housing area in a state of heightened tension. Increased tension is generally not good, as tempers flare and incidents happen. Third, it alienates the jailer from the inmates they're watching, increases distrust, and is a barrier to communication. Should one or two inmates decide that they're okay with getting additional time for assaulting the badge-heavy jailer, the other inmates may not feel comfortable giving the deputy advance warning or stepping in to assist should an assault take place.

Being firm, fair, and consistent with the enforcement of discipline is necessary to build an appropriate level of trust, cooperation, and authority.

ALTERNATIVE DISCIPLINARY ACTIONS

Jails usually have a policy regarding the documentation of all rule violations on a form or in a database. However, if jailers did that literally, they would have little time to actually speak to anyone because they'd be constantly filling out forms. Most disciplinary corrections are made using a verbal warning, but sometimes something more than a verbal warning (but less than a full day's lockdown) may be more effective.

Alternative forms of discipline such as temporary lockdowns that last part of a shift, the removal of valued contraband (like a paper photo frame), and moving the inmate from one cell to another can be used as consequences rather than formal discipline. Using these methods can be very effective for minor violations once your reputation is established and you've built rapport with the inmates in that housing area. That being said, if you haven't established your reputation and you use an alternative disciplinary action, you'll be inviting more inmates to commit rule violations. In addition to this, it is also totally inappropriate to use these methods for any major rule violations. Major violations should always be documented according to policy.

WRITING DISCIPLINARY FORMS OR REPORTS

Some people have a difficult time wording their rule violations. When writing disciplinary forms, it can help to use a method that makes this process clearer. One such method, borrowed from law schools, is known as IRAC: issue, rule, application, and conclusion. Using this method can help you write your disciplinary forms in a more professional way while preparing you for more challenging tasks, such as writing reports for criminal investigations or use of force. Here's how to use IRAC when writing your own reports.

DISCIPLINE | 185

IRAC: Issue, Rule, Application, Conclusion

| **Issue** | *"Inmate Doe manufactured a rope by shredding his sheet."* |

- Was a certain rule violated?
- What happened, and does the action violate a rule, guideline, or law?

| **Rule** | *"The inmate handbook states under violation 1-L2-34 that destruction of jail property is a rule violation. It is also a level 2 major violation because a rope can be used as a weapon or for escape. This could threaten the safety and security operations of the jail."* |

- Where does the rule come from? Policy, handbook, case law?
- Inform where the rule is and what it states

| **Application** | *"Inmate Doe's destruction of jail-issued sheets for the manufacture of a rope could threaten the safety and security of the jail because it can be used as a weapon or a tool for escape from custody."* |

- Combine the rule with the facts of the case or issue
- Your arguments and facts should be listed here to support the conclusion

| **Conclusion** | *"Inmate Doe has violated rule 1-L2-34 of the inmate handbook by manufacturing a rope through the destruction of his issued sheet. He will be given a five-day lockdown for this violation."* |

- Write a sentence or summary of your solution to the issue
- Restate the issue and what should happen

PROGRESSIVE DISCIPLINARY PROCESS

Jails are likely to have variations in disciplinary approaches, consequences, and the specific rules they seek to enforce. This is because there are different jail sizes, types of populations, resource allocation, and agency philosophies. In my agency, we follow a progressive disciplinary model, meaning that each infraction or poor decision may result in progressively more or tougher consequences. Here's a diagram showing how this works:

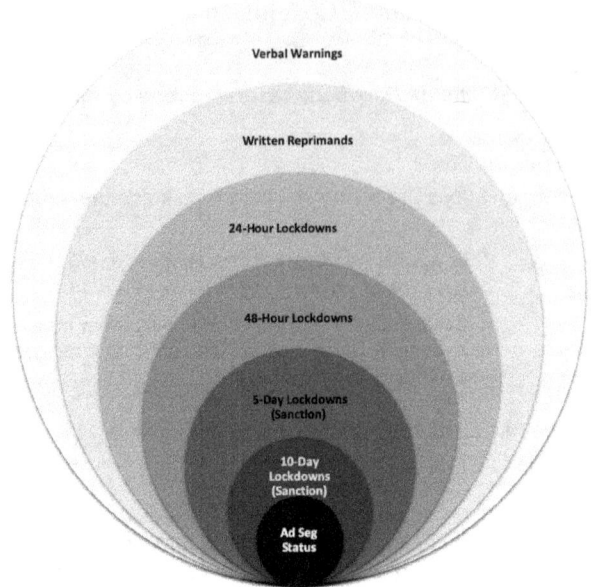

It's important for the inmate to make the connection between their decisions and the consequences of those decisions. It's also important to be consistent. However, it isn't possible to be everywhere all the time, so you should expect some pushback from inmates saying that another inmate didn't get written up for the same infraction.

When it comes to actual consequences, there isn't much more that a jailer can do other than locking a person down. However, these lockdowns can make things a little more uncomfortable for the inmate because it's hard to stay in a cell for a whole day. The level of discomfort is also related to the privileges extended to inmates—in our facility, these include program attendance, radio headsets, television time, commissary, and time out of their cell. The removal of privileges (not rights) is usually a by-product of a lockdown, but they can be lost one at a time due to behavior. In our facility, privileges may be temporarily restricted as a minor disciplinary consequence.

DISCIPLINE FOR MINOR RULE VIOLATIONS

Verbal Corrections

Most of our disciplinary work is verbal: what we really want is voluntary compliance and learning of expectations. Sometimes, simply asking an inmate to correct a violation and explaining why it's a violation is enough to generate voluntary compliance. Sometimes, it doesn't matter what you say—the inmate will do what they want.

Listening is perhaps the most important and overlooked skill in the field. You have to be able to separate the conflicting verbal and physical communication to get to the root of an issue before you can resolve it effectively. A jailer is expected to be able to listen and interpret a situation, then communicate expectations to inmates in a way that generates voluntary compliance and buy-in for the process. I wish this were easy, but it isn't.

Written Reprimands

This is a written document outlining that an infraction was found and discussed, and that the inmate understands the expectations. However, unlike a standard verbal enforcement, the record of this event sets into motion the progressive disciplinary process, allowing other jailers to hold the person accountable with tougher consequences.

Lockdowns

A lockdown means that the inmate is only given the minimum statutory time allowed out of their cell per day for the duration of that lockdown (although many jails, like mine, will offer more than the statutory minimum). Inmates are offered this time out, but they can decline it.

DISCIPLINE FOR MAJOR RULE VIOLATIONS

Administrative Segregation

When an inmate has committed a major violation, they'll likely be considered for administrative segregation, or ad seg, status. In general, ad seg status is given to an inmate if they've become a clear threat to others in the jail. It can also happen when the inmate has a significant amount of minor violations whose consequences were ineffective. Generally, inmates will have demonstrated a hostile unwillingness to follow orders and are dangerous to other inmates. If they're dangerous to staff, they'll also be classified as a high security inmate.

Ad seg is *not* solitary confinement, since the definition of solitary confinement is complete isolation from others. We have no area in our jail where this can happen—there are always other inmates in the area, along with access to staff. However, physical access to others while on ad seg status is heavily restricted. And since there's a process for being placed on ad seg, there's also a process for working one's way off of it.

APPEALS AND HEARINGS

Like the criminal process, the disciplinary process must follow guidelines. Allowing for some way of redressing an accusation or disciplinary consequence is part of this. However, this can be dependent on the level of violation. For a minor rule violation, an inmate might not be offered a hearing regarding the disciplinary action. However, they can appeal the disciplinary action or decision if they disagree with it. Furthermore, if they believe the jailer was malicious, they can also file a grievance against that deputy.

For a major rule violation, an inmate can ask for an investigative hearing. The disciplinary sergeant, or designee, will investigate and make a decision regarding the violation. The inmate can then appeal that ruling to the next level or file a grievance if there is a grievable issue.

ANECDOTES FROM THE JAIL

"Contraband"

(Note: Any items that are in excess of the allowed amount, are being used for other than their intended purpose, aren't in their original container, or have been acquired through unapproved methods are considered contraband.)

While conducting a cell search, a deputy found the following items:

- One sixteen-ounce bottle of Maxima Conditioning Cocoa Butter skin lotion with a clear gel in it (the original contents of this container are tan in color)
- Four extra AAA batteries hidden in a bowl under toilet paper
- Three plastic tortilla bags, one of which was being used to hold letters
- An adult coloring book that had been stamped as belonging to another inmate
- More than the five allowed photographs
- Approximately one and a half bundles of napkins
- A milk carton being used as a pencil box
- A soap box being used as a pencil box

When the deputy exited the cell, he gave the inmate a choice: because there was so much contraband in his cell, he could either forfeit the remainder of his time out for the day or get a forty-eight-hour lockdown. The inmate didn't respond verbally but went into his cell and slammed his door shut. The inmate then yelled that he wanted to see a supervisor. He was told that he could put in a request to do so.

The inmate proceeded to argue with the deputy about the items taken from the cell, and the deputy explained to him why each item was removed. The inmate was very upset and then stated, "I'm going to flood this place!" The deputy told the inmate that he should do what he felt he needed to do, and the situation would be handled appropriately.

The deputy then informed the inmate that he would be receiving a lockdown, and his time out was forfeited. Later that morning, the inmate apologized for his poor behavior.

"Contraband II"

One morning when leaving for court, an inmate informed the deputy and maintenance employee that she had covered her vent the previous evening. When told that she should uncover it, she said, "It's going to take a bit of doing." After going to court, her cell was searched. The vent was covered with paper and items glued to it and was going to take some time to uncover.

Also, during the cell search, the deputy found an excessive amount of contraband. The contraband included thirteen extra books (all in plain view), four extra combs (on the shelf with her hygiene items and in her tote), a commissary bowl full of approximately two dozen pencils, an envelope containing more than fifty photos, more than ten letters saved, and extra clothing (including two orange shirts, a pair of orange pants, three towels, an extra pair of underwear, an extra pair of socks and an extra bra), which were either in her tote, laundry bag, or on her bed.

All contraband items were removed, excluding the letters. The inmate was given the opportunity to choose which letters and photographs she wanted to retain in her possession while the excess was taken to her property storage area. She received a forty-eight-hour lockdown for not taking care of this by simply turning in extra items and requesting that extra letters and photographs be taken to her bulk property storage area.

"Kitchen Caper"

The kitchen supervisor notified a deputy that an inmate worker needed to be fired from the kitchen for attempting to take a plastic bag of brownie mix and smuggle it back to his housing area. The bag had fallen out of the inmate's pants directly in front of the kitchen supervisor.

The inmate then tried to convince the supervisor that he, the supervisor, didn't actually see the item fall from his pants. Security supervisors watched the video footage to make sure that the inmate had indeed taken the items, and, sure enough, it was as the kitchen supervisor had said. As a result, the inmate was fired and given a lockdown.

CHAPTER 16 PREP

In the next chapter, we'll go over the use of force. In general, communication is the first step for everything. When words and reason fail, however, the use of force is all but inevitable. Still, force isn't something a deputy should use haphazardly—a great deal of consideration must be made and a person has to be given plenty of opportunities to return to a reasonable state and avoid force. Furthermore, once force begins, it has to be as dynamic as the situation. In other words, force stops as soon as it's no longer necessary.

Chapter 16: Use of Force and Physical Assaults

IT'S USEFUL TO EXAMINE WHAT law enforcement considers an official "use of force" because it will likely differ from what the average citizen thinks is a use of force. Each agency will have their own policies, heavily guided by state statutes regarding the authorized use of force by law enforcement. As a result, agencies will have differing views and approaches to similar issues in regard to use of force.

I can only speak from the experience and training I've received at my agency. Since I consider my agency to be one of the best in the country, I have no doubts that the observations I have are, in general, a good representation of the challenges faced by jailers when it comes to use of force.

The following sections will outline what use of force means for my agency. It will also go over the guidelines on how a use of force is judged reasonable or not, and how this ties into decisions and preparation regarding officer safety.

RESPONSIBILITIES WITH THE MONOPOLY OF FORCE

Since U.S. citizens, through their elected representatives, give their government the monopoly of force through the rule of law and law enforcement, the least that those who have this responsibility can do is make sure this force is reasonable and appropriate. It isn't enough to dispense violent actions toward citizens because you're allowed to by law. More often than not, law enforcement officers have to think beyond the immediate and to what can happen next.

In my agency, one of our patrol deputies was approaching a man with a weapon (not a firearm) at a trailer park. The deputy approached the man from a safe distance and began giving him commands. The man stood up and began approaching the deputy. The deputy then pulled out his gun and trained it on the man while giving him commands to stop and drop his weapon. However, he had to think beyond the immediate. He looked to where his bullets would go should they passed through or missed the man. There were children's toys along the side of the trailer. Not knowing if there were children there or not, the deputy decided to act as if they were home. He holstered his weapon and began a fight for his life. Although he was injured, other deputies arrived in time to assist him in stopping the man and the assault.

Good character, good training, and good tactics play a huge part in ensuring that the public's trust isn't misplaced. As enforcers, officers have to be willing to both say no and use force. As protectors, officers have to be willing to sacrifice themselves for others.

USE OF FORCE IN STATE STATUTES

Law enforcement is created and governed by statute. Even the use of force is contained in state statutes that outline how force can be used and for what purpose. In Colorado, there are several statutes in regard to use of force. These include everything from the parental use of force, defense of property, and the use of deadly force. Some specific statutes address the use of force for law enforcement, jails, and corrections.

Some of these statutes for Colorado jails and corrections are outlined below:

Jails

- **C.R.S. 18.1.703 B**
  - "A superintendent or other authorized official of a jail, prison, or correctional institution may, in order to maintain order and discipline, use reasonable and appropriate physical force when and to the extent that he reasonably believes it necessary to maintain order and discipline, but he may use deadly physical force only when he reasonably believes it necessary to prevent death or serious bodily injury."

- **C.R.S. 18.1.707(8)**
  - "A guard or peace officer employed in a detention facility is justified in using deadly physical force when he reasonably believes it necessary to prevent the escape of a prisoner convicted of, charged with, or held for a felony or confined under the maximum security rules of any detention facility as such facility is defined in subsection (9) of this section; In using reasonable and appropriate physical force, but not deadly physical force, in all other circumstances when and to the extent that he reasonably believes it necessary to prevent what he reasonably believes to be the escape of a prisoner from a detention facility."
  - (9) "'Detention facility' as used in subsection (8) of this section means any place maintained for the confinement, pursuant to law, of persons charged with or convicted of an offense, held pursuant to the 'Colorado Children's Code,' held for extradition, or otherwise confined pursuant to an order of a court."

Corrections

- **C.R.S. 17-20-122**
  - "Justification of officer. If an inmate sentenced to any state correctional facility resists the authority of any officer or refuses to obey any officer's lawful commands, it is the duty of such officer immediately to enforce obedience by the use of such weapons or other aid as may be effectual. If in so doing any inmate thus resisting is wounded or killed by such officer or such officer's assistants, such use of force is justified and any officer using such force shall be held guiltless; but such officer shall not be excused for using greater force than the emergency of the case demands."

- **C.R.S. 17-20-123**
  - "Insurrection—duty of citizens. It is the duty of all the officers and other citizens of the state, by every means in their power, to suppress any insurrection among the inmates sentenced to any correctional facilities under the supervision of the executive director and to prevent the escape or rescue of any such inmate there from, or from any other legal confinement, or from any person in whose legal custody such inmate may be. If, in so doing or in arresting any inmate who may have escaped, such officer or other person wounds or kills such inmate or other person aiding or assisting such inmate, such officer or other person shall be justified and held guiltless; but such officer or other person shall not be excused for using greater force than the emergency of the case demands."

LEVELS OF FORCE

Some agencies have a continuum of authorized force depending on what the subject is doing. Our agency takes a different view on this because there is no way to know how much force is reasonable for every situation you may run across. Our training focuses on using good judgment to correctly identify when using force is reasonable. Furthermore, once force is used, the jailer has to know when that use of force is no longer necessary, and when to attempt other means of gaining compliance.

TYPES OF FORCE AND DEFINITIONS

Different jurisdictions will have slightly different wording, but generally, the definitions regarding force will be similar to those below:

Deadly Force

- Force that is intended to or likely to cause death or serious bodily injury

Physical Force

- Arrest control techniques, physical tactics, chemical agents, Tasers, impact weapons, less-than-lethal munitions or weapons employed properly, the emergency restraint chair, and using the Special Emergency Response Team

    (Use of escort holds and handcuffs aren't considered a significant use of force in our jail because they're standard for movement purposes and are done for safety)

Excessive Force

- Physical force that exceeds the levels allowed by law

WHAT IS REASONABLE?

What is reasonable force? This is the question at the center of all training regarding the use of force. Each use of force situation is dynamic and evolving, meaning that, in my opinion, "pre-packaged" responses usually result in either too little or too much force—especially when used by less-experienced jailers.

"Reasonable" is a moving target that changes according to the level of training a deputy has, precedents set in other areas of the country, changes in the law, and the facts of each individual situation. You should become familiar with the standards outlined by the Supreme Court for Graham v. Connor and for Kingsley v. Hendrickson.

Graham v. Connor

In 1989 the Supreme Court issued a decision on Graham v. Connor. The use of force will be evaluated by what is called the "objectively reasonable" standard and in conjunction with the 4th Amendment regarding Search and Seizure. In other words, the facts and circumstances surrounding the use of force instead of the motivation or intent of the officer. In general, when considering the use of force an officer will have to look at the following:

- The severity of the crime;
- If the suspect poses and immediate threat to the safety of others; and
- Whether or not the suspect is actively resisting or attempting to evade arrest

Kingsley v. Hendrickson

In 2015 the Supreme Court issued a decision on Kingsley v. Hendrickson. The use of force on pretrial detainees will also be evaluated on the objectively reasonable standard. However, it also expanded what would be expected of a reasonable officer working in a detention facility acting with a governmental interest. In general, when considering the use of force, a reasonable officer in a detention facility will have to look at the following:

- The severity and speed of the threat
- The proximity of weapons or improvised weapons
- The mental state of the subject (if known)
- The body language and conduct of the person at the time, as reasonably perceived
- Physical differences such as size, relative strength, skill level, sustained injuries, fatigue, and number of staff members
- The degree to which the subject is restrained and still demonstrating resistance
- Potential injuries to the subject, bystanders, or staff

- The level of resistance to staff, or an attack on deputies
- Whether or not immediate control or a prompt resolution of the situation is needed
- The extent to which the conduct of the subject poses a threat to others
- Any other emergent or exigent circumstances

Part of the equation in regard to the use of force (deadly force in particular) is the "priority of life" scale. In my agency, this scale orders the priority of life into four categories:

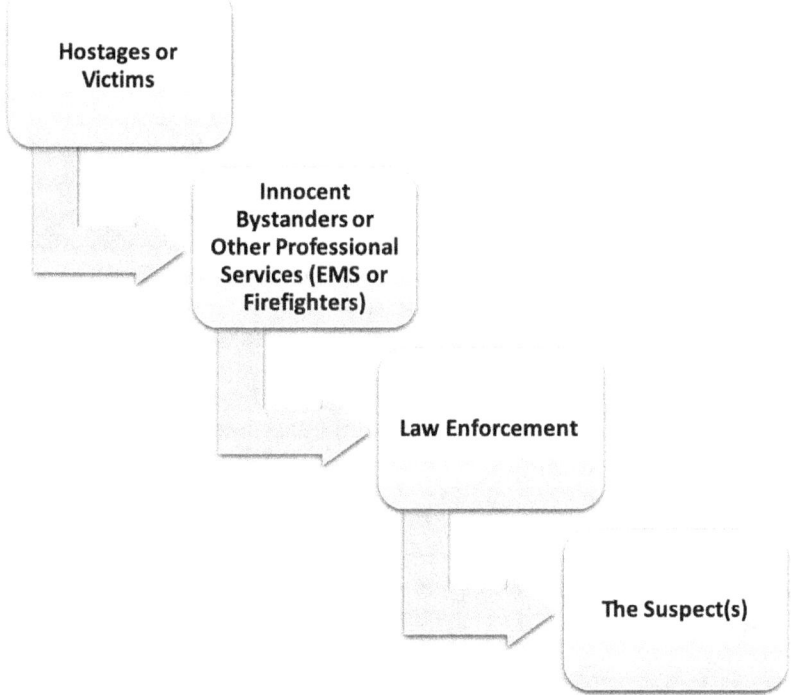

Report Writing

I could include an entire chapter on report writing—it's that important. If you've never taken the stand on a report you wrote months ago, let's just say that you can survive if you've written it well. If you've rushed through or left out details, however, you can go down in flames that no firefighter can put out.

Sometimes, imagining your potential report before taking action can help you remember to try de-escalation and other methods. It can also help you take the totality of the situation (including possible future litigation) into account before using force.

When writing your report, avoid catch-all wording like "passive resistance" or "combative." Instead, write that the inmate refused to stand, walk, talk, move, or was trying to strike, kick, or punch. Describe the body posture, tensing of muscles, and the like. If your report is used in a court proceeding, this "picture" helps the jury see what you saw.

While the IRAC method mentioned in the previous chapter is useful for writing reports on behavior, discipline, and the day's activities, you must also be able articulate why the use of force was reasonable. This is where the report format shown below (outlined by the Supreme Court in Kingsley v. Hendrickson) comes in. If you write all of your use of force reports considering addressing these points, you should be okay.

Standard Use of Force Report Format

<u>Threat Perceived</u>
Include a timeline of behavior and even past history if it played a part in the threat assessment.

<u>Immediate Threat</u>
Show how the immediate behavior threatened the safety of officers or others.

<u>Use of Force Was Necessary</u>
Document that a use of force was an appropriate response to the perceived threat.

<u>Legitimate Government Interest</u>
Explain why addressing the threat was in the interest of the facility, government, or community.

Severity of Issue
Assess the severity of the security issues resulting from the threat.

De-Escalation Attempts before Force
Document what attempts were made to de-escalate the situation or reduce the level of force necessary.

Level or Amount of Force
Demonstrate that the level of force used was appropriate in relation to the need for the use of force. This can change during the incident.

Resistance to Force
Was the inmate actively resisting? Describe this step by step.

Extent of Injuries
In addition to the injuries sustained by responding staff, be sure to document the injuries sustained by the inmate and any medical care that was given afterward.

USE OF FORCE IN JAIL

There are times when words fail and force must be used. If anything, we bend over backward to facilitate voluntary compliance in an attempt to avoid the injuries that come with the use of force. If the citizen is injured, we have to send staff to the hospital with them, thus leaving the building short. If staff are injured, the jail will be short on staff for the length of their recovery. Overall, unnecessary actions that lead to a significant increase in the probability of injuries are bad for business.

We train deputies to use verbal de-escalation skills and control holds to such a degree that sometimes our staff don't raise their levels of force quickly enough to meet the assaults by inmates. What I mean by this is that sometimes our jailers will attempt to place control holds on a person who is trying to seriously injure them, even when it's clearly appropriate to use strikes, kicks, and punches until the inmate ceases their attack, at which point the jailer can move to control holds. I guess you can say that those in my agency often go the extra mile when it comes to ensuring that inmates aren't injured, even when they have every justification for striking back.

LIABILITY WITH USE OF FORCE

One of the reasons that jailers hesitate to use force is lawsuits. I've seen inmates bait deputies into a cell by having contraband or refusing to return items. The inmates then assault the staff and claim they were the victims. A few months later, the staff involved in the aftermath are called into a lawsuit. Sometimes the inmates win. The reason for one win, cited by the jury, was that the reports were not as descriptive as they could be, and that the cell itself didn't have a camera to refute the inmate's statement that the jailers entered the cell for the express purpose of assaulting him.

As long as the use of force was reasonable, you're probably okay. That being said, even if you did everything right, you can be sued. Every movement, statement, and action might be gone over by attorneys and eventually put out for display in the public. At that point, it's no longer about the truth, but about what they think they can prove in court through selective legal maneuvers in regard to evidence and testimony.

TRAINING IN USE OF FORCE

Whatever training you're given by your specific agency is what you're supposed to apply when using force. The only exception to this is when deadly force is being employed against you—at that point you have the same right to life as anyone else, and you can defend your life by any means necessary. However, you still have to transition to control holds when the subject is no longer able to press their threat against you.

Generally, our trainers try to set up scenarios that require the use of verbal skills, physical skills, and tactics that challenge those going through them. Often, the scenarios are common events that occur in our facility, but there are also scenarios that have happened in other facilities throughout the country. This helps staff stay informed on the latest trends and actions by inmates while updating their training, methods, and tactics.

PHYSICAL ASSAULTS AND OFFICER SAFETY

There are some who believe that direct physical violence results from the combination of a system that maintains "structural violence" (which creates and sustains unequal social positions) and "cultural violence" (which normalizes and reinforces structural violence as a natural condition or necessity). Although I can see merit in this approach, sometimes a predator is just a predator.

Yes, predators can be "made," but there are many cases of serial killers, identity thieves, pimps, and human traffickers who are motivated by both money and the thrill of violent domination. Those who have psychosexual connections to their crimes, for example, are probably not motivated by the current social structures or culture. Instead, they appear to use these systems to hide themselves and their crimes.

Direct violence, regardless of the cause, is the tool of choice by many a person in custody.

Predictive Indicators of Violence

There are books about body language, verbal cues, and other factors that are supposed to be predictive of an impending violent encounter. Some of these resources are listed at the back of this book. In my experience, some of these can be indicators of heightened states of fight or flight, anger, or agitation, all of which can precede violence. However, these are far from being truly predictive. This is because, upon seeing these cues, we use verbal tactics and de-escalation strategies to help people bring their frustrations to a level where good decisions and actions can be made.

Despite not being 100 percent accurate, these indicators are predictive enough to make them valuable tools for the jailer, as they provide clues into the state of mind and possible intention of the person they're dealing with. However, some of the most violent attacks on jailers in my facility had almost no indication that the incarcerated citizen was about to become violent.

Body Language

In my experience, a few body-language cues do provide reliable information in general and can also help you describe why you felt fear or anxiousness when an inmate became loud or began to threaten you. Even if body language isn't 100 percent predictive, it's better to act with caution than suffer a violent attack.

The following body-language cues (either one or multiple) can indicate a possible imminent assault:

- Glaring at a target either directly or offset from them
- Clenching their jaw muscles
- Lowering their chins
- Furling their shoulders forward
- Clenching their fists
- Either raising or lowering both arms and stiffening them
- Loud and rapid speech or suddenly going quiet
- Kicking off or otherwise removing their shoes
- Shifting their legs and body into a fighting stance

Mental Preparedness

As an FTO, I encourage trainees to go over scenarios in their mind about what could happen. The reason for this isn't to make them paranoid or hyper-vigilant. Instead, it's to give their mind a framework to work from when they're faced with a similar situation. Many people, when faced with a sudden violent attack, go into fight, flight, or freeze reaction.

In our agency, we want people to respond rather than react. Instead of a person telling themselves, "I can't believe this is happening," I want them to think, "I thought this could happen, and this is how I will respond."

This mental preparedness can make the difference between a severe or fatal assault and going home at the end of the day. In addition, there's a possibility that you'll sustain an injury when you get into a physical altercation. Mentally preparing for scenarios where you could be injured is also important because you never know if an injury could end your career.

Physical Preparedness

It's physically exhausting to be in a one-on-one fight. However, you should be prepared to be in a one-to-three (or more) fight. I see inmates spend hours out of every day preparing for a physical confrontation. Mostly this is preparation for confronting or defending themselves from other inmates, but it's also to prepare to fight you.

Mental preparedness and toughness often make the difference when you're physically exhausted yet have to continue to fight. Fortunately, most jails will have responders there to assist within a minute or two once it's known that you need help. If an assailant is able to take your radio or attack you in a secluded lockable location (such as a cell), however, you may have to defend yourself for quite a bit longer than a minute or two. Your physical preparedness will help with this.

One aspect of physical preparedness is the status of your uniform. If your uniform is messy and not kept up, predators may see this as an indicator of your mental and tactical preparedness. As a result, you may find yourself an easy target, not because you're a particularly bothersome jailer, but because you're seen as easier prey than the one who looks "ready" to fight.

Predators in general try to avoid getting injured when taking down their prey. Make yourself tough and they may think twice or move on to an "easier" target. This doesn't always hold true as those with mental health issues aren't rational, though, so all bets are off.

Tactical Preparedness

It's important to know the most likely places that an assault could take place in your housing area. Inmates may hide in showers, other inmates' cells, or underneath a stairwell waiting for you to enter that location. We've had an inmate feign entry into a cell and hide behind a wall next to the mini-control room with the intent to seriously harm the deputy when they entered the area. However, the jailer felt that something was off, double-checked all angles from the mini-control, and saw the inmate crouching there. This likely saved the jailer's life.

Pay attention to the architecture of the building, average response times of staff, and radio protocol (if you have them) to get an idea of the realistic response times for both a good and a very bad day.

Your tactical preparedness should also include thinking about how you move through the housing area, how close you let inmates near you, your stance when they're within striking distance, techniques for pat-down searches and cell searches, and what cues will lead you to call for assistance.

Protecting Others

Since you're the primary person responsible for the safety of those in your housing areas, you may find that you have to think for others in regard to their security. This includes the counseling and medical teams, citizens working in programs or on tours, volunteers, attorneys, and the inmates. As a result, you'll have to think about the level of security knowledge demonstrated by these individuals and assist them in being tactically prepared.

You can't prepare them mentally or physically on the spot, so the best you can do is set them up for tactical success. This will include describing positions within the housing area, advising them on a number of tactical considerations in a professional manner, and explaining your reasoning so they understand why you would like things a certain way.

Educating those who don't work in this environment can be tough at times because they're out of their element, they forget easily, and sometimes they don't see the need to listen to you.

USE OF FORCE: AN INCIDENT BREAKDOWN

On Christmas day, an inmate became upset with the deputies in the segregation housing area and decided to raise a ruckus. The inmate was listed as Ad Seg level 1, which meant that his behavior was bad enough that he was not allowed out with other inmates.

He was also considered a threat to staff and was on two-to-one high security status, requiring two deputies to be in the housing area at all times while he was out of his cell. He had earned a reputation with the other inmates in segregation (they didn't like how his behavior impacted them), and he had also earned a reputation with the staff for active physical resistance and destruction of property.

The inmate had become upset because he claimed that he didn't have a towel despite being issued one. When the deputies called him on this attempted manipulation, he revealed his issued towel. He then wanted a new one. The deputies refused to switch out his towel, as his towel was issued the previous night and he could get another later in the evening. The inmate became angry and began acting out.

Taking the pod trash can in one hand and a towel and plastic spray bottle in another, he began smashing them on the housing area and mini-control windows. He was shouting at the deputies to enter the area and "see what happens" to them while calling them every name in the book. The deputies called for assistance to the area because he refused to lock himself down.

After I arrived in the area, I had almost convinced him to lock down. I told him I would switch out his towel if he locked down. He started to move, but then worked himself back up and began yelling again. The corporal then tried a similar strategy but was met with the inmate's refusal to lock down or drop the items. He was still swinging them like weapons, and it was clear he was intent on having this conflict.

He was now warned that, should he decide not to drop the items he was holding and return to his cell, force would be used against him. He was advised of this several times and was given considerable time to decide to do the right thing. In the end he made no attempts to move to his cell and continued to swing the items around like weapons.

The corporal now called for the mini-control to activate the handheld camera to document the inmate's activities. I was then asked to prepare for entry and informed that I was authorized to use a Taser if he was still in the doorway holding the trash can as a weapon.

Before the door opened, I informed the rest of the team that if he was moving toward his cell, I wouldn't deploy the Taser. However, if he didn't move or still had the weapons while standing in the doorway, I would deploy it and they would have to move quickly to hand cuff him while the Taser was still under power. This meant that we would try and handcuff him within the first five seconds of the activation of the Taser.

The door was opened at the corporal's command and the inmate still held the trash can in his right hand, ready to swing as a weapon. In his left hand he had a spray bottle and a towel. He was positioning the towel in a way that was meant to disrupt the deployment of the Taser probes. As the doorway opened, I gave him a second to drop the trash can and move toward his cell. Instead, he moved the towel in response to where he thought the Taser probes would go as a defense maneuver. In doing so, he opened up a perfect shot for me. I deployed the Taser and the probes landed as intended on his left lower abdomen and upper thigh.

The inmate bent at the waist and seemed to sit down while yelling "ow" and other choice words. We went through the doorway and cuffed him under power as we had intended. In the background, other inmates were laughing loudly and shouting, "Merry Christmas!" I also heard them shouting things like, "That's what you get, you dumbass!" The inmate stopped resisting after the cuffs were applied and he had no injuries. Medical responded to examine the inmate and remove the Taser probes. After the incident, we conducted a debrief. The reports were completed and the evidence (video, Taser probes, and statements) were preserved for a later review of force by the Professional Standards section.

Analyzing the Event

It's important to analyze each use of force and determine what could be done better. We all make mistakes, and each situation is dynamic. Sometimes we get lucky and other times gaps in planning, preparation, or actions result in a negative outcome. In this particular case, the force used was effective and the inmate was not injured and neither were any deputies.

To sum up, here are the steps we took throughout this process:

Getting the Inmate's History
- Inmate has behavioral issues (ad seg)
- Inmate has threatened staff before (high security status)
- Inmate will destroy jail property
- Inmate exhibits impulsive decision making

Observing Current Behavior
- Attempted to gain contraband (an additional towel for unknown purposes)

- Attempted destruction of jail property
- Hitting trash can against the glass
- Holding spray bottle (urine and feces mixture?)
- Threatening physical bodily harm to deputies
- Refusal to lock down and interfering with the orderly operation of a jail
- Other inmates in the pod could not get their time out due to his behavior
- His noise levels were agitating others in their cells and housing areas
- The facility had to shut down normal operation in order to assemble staff to deal with him

De-Escalation Efforts I
- Engage the inmate in a conversation to find the reason for the escalation
- Offer a reasonable solution to the issue at hand
- Provide a reasonable timeframe to make an informed decision

De-Escalation Efforts II
- Engage the inmate in a conversation to find the reason for the escalation
- Offer a reasonable solution to the issue at hand
- Notify the inmate of the impending use of force
- Provide a reasonable timeframe for the inmate to make an informed decision

Communication with the Team
- A focused team minimizes the chances of escalation of force
- Inmate has threatened staff before (high security status)
- Directs the force to be applied
- Sets expectations

Conclusion and Follow-Up
- The use of force was effective
- Inmate's resistance ceased

- Use of force did not escalate or go on longer than resistance to force
- Medical evaluated the individual for injuries
- Debrief staff involved in the action
- Document all activities and preserve evidence

Why Was the Use of the Taser Authorized?

The facility and segregation housing area, which were locked down to address this event, needed to return to normal operation. Other inmates have a right to time out of their cells, and delays increase the chances of not being out when it's a good time to call home. However, there are more ways that this can impact other inmates in the area. Here is a short list of how his continued behavior was impacting the facility and the other inmates on ad seg status:

- Constitutional rights to time out of cells were delayed
- Reasonable access to attorneys, medical care, etc. were delayed
- Maintaining of order and discipline facility-wide were impacted (leading to inmate frustration)

Here is a summary of the options available to the supervisor in this situation, along with the possible negative outcomes of each:

Verbal Request for Compliance
- Inmate may continue to ignore requests and orders

De-Escalation Attempts
- Attempt to resolve grievance
- Allow time to cool down
- Notify inmate of the imminent use of force
- Inmate may ignore these or work themselves back up

Arrest Control Techniques
- Is fast
- Inmate has a weapon and can injure staff

- It can be difficult to secure limbs of an uncooperative person
- Increases chances of injuries to inmate and deputies
- Can quickly move to a deadly-force situation because of the weapon

Deploy SERT
- Assembly of a team with equipment to force him into his cell
- Increases the chances of injuries to inmate
- Takes more time to assemble

Use of Less-Lethal Option: Pepper Spray or Pepperball
- Can be very effective if inmate is susceptible to it
- Must hit a narrow target area through a food chute or slit
- Takes time to set in
- May not be effective
- May be effective on responding staff
- Must decontaminate the inmate and responding staff
- Must decontaminate the housing area (impractical in a segregation area)

Use of Less-Lethal Option: Taser
- Can cause pain compliance and muscular incapacitation long enough to apply restraints
- Must hit a narrow area
- May miss or suffer a disconnect, rendering no effect
- Total body lockup can strain the inmate's muscles
- A fall while in total body lockup can cause further injury

Option Selected: A Taser

In this scenario, the Corporal chose to encourage use of a Taser. Here is the reasoning:

- The inmate was not in an elevated position
- A fall from total body lockup would not likely cause injury but would make it easier to gain control of the inmate's limbs

- No decontamination was required
- A higher level of force was needed to deal with the inmate's makeshift weapons
- The inmate was threatening physical bodily harm to deputies if they entered
- The inmate was not responding to de-escalation techniques
- The inmate's body language showed preparation for a physical confrontation
- Inmate had been given warnings on the use of force, the method to be used, and time to respond to the orders to lock down

CHAPTER 17 PREP

There are times, even in a jail, where special tactics and training are required to deal with a use of force scenario. Typically, if a jail is large enough, it has some version of a special emergency response team (SERT) or corrections special operations group (CSOG) that specialize in the use of force and unusual situations that require it. In my agency, the use of this team itself is considered a use of force.

Chapter 17: The Special Emergency Response Team (SERT)

Most people have heard of special weapons and tactics (SWAT) teams that work with law enforcement out on patrol. Jails and prisons also have situations that call for additional skills that go beyond de-escalation and arrest control, requiring a team with specialized knowledge and training.

Jails or prisons can become unsafe quickly (at any time and in any area), especially if a riot breaks out or an inmate arms themselves with a weapon. Sometimes inmates need to be protected from themselves but are highly dangerous to those around them, requiring special teams to deal with them. Other times, the facility itself needs to be protected from further damage. In rare cases, a simple order from a judge to collect DNA may require a use of force because the inmate is highly dangerous and refuses to give a sample.

For these reasons, a special team dedicated to using tools and tactics regarding the use of force is a great resource for an agency, and can:

- Provide protection from self
- Provide protection for others (staff)

- Stop criminal activity and facility damage
- Maintain facility order
- Facilitate a court order
- The Special Emergency Response Team (SERT)

On TV, riot police put on protective gear in order to deal with volatile crowds often armed with some kind of non-firearm weapons. In a jail, SERT members put on protective gear (which is almost always black) and specialize in extracting inmates from cells, dealing with individually armed inmates, or handling a riot in the pods. In the Department of Corrections, they are often called the Corrections Emergency Response Team (CERT).

There are several reasons that a cell extraction is necessary, the first being the safety of the inmate. The second is the safety of others and the facility. Third, sometimes it's necessary to deploy the team for a cell extraction when there's a need to maintain order or because the court orders that the inmate be brought to the courthouse despite their protests.

THE CORRECTIONS SPECIAL OPERATIONS GROUP (CSOG)

Many jails have an in-house SERT contingent, but others have gone to CSOG. CSOG is a non-governmental organization out of Virginia that attempts to enhance the use of force capabilities of a jail using tools, tactics, and training.

PRE-DEPLOYMENT OF SERT

Each team and agency will have some variation in their response due to the staff's level of training and the operational capability of the facility. Furthermore, it's very important for the entire team to know the objective before they move into the action phase of an operation. Most facilities have some sort of process that leads up to the deployment of a team. Generally, before a team is deployed to deal with a challenge, several things happen:

1. Staff observes the situation and attempts to resolve it with communication
2. Staff informs a supervisor, who reviews the situation and attempts to resolve it with communication
3. The supervisor activates SERT, the team commander gets a briefing, and the team assembles
4. SERT members stage outside the area, the team commander speaks to the inmate and attempts to resolve the problem through communication, and the inmate is notified of the imminent use of force
5. The inmate is still refusing orders, the team stages at the inmate's cell to prepare for entry and the commander repeats the request for compliance and notifies them again of the imminent use of force

DEPLOYMENT OF TEAM: THE CELL DOOR OPENS

At this point, if the inmate is still not complying with orders, the team will make entry. They're ready to meet a physically uncooperative inmate and use their force advantage in order to minimize the chances of injury to the inmate and staff.

There are several variations on team deployments, but two examples are:

Three-person team
If the inmate is complying, this is communicated to the team by the first member through the door and restraints are applied without force. If the inmate is not in a position required, then a less-than-lethal response may be employed.

Five-person team
The shield member is the first in the cell. If the inmate is complying, this is communicated to the team and restraints are applied without force. If the inmate is not in a position required, the shield pins them while the rest of the team controls a limb. The inmate is then secured in restraints and extracted from the cell.

Throughout the whole process, communication doesn't stop and compliance at any time will reduce the level of force.

ANECDOTES FROM THE JAIL

As outlined at the beginning of this section, special teams are usually deployed to: protect a person from themselves, protect others, prevent or stop criminal activity, facilitate orderly operations, or complete requirements from a court order. The anecdotes below illustrate some reasons why a team with special training in tactics and use of force may be of great benefit to a facility. Fortunately, most situations are resolved with communication and don't require this level of intervention or force.

For the Individual's Safety

"Shower and Cleaning Time"

Inmates sometimes have items restricted from them because of their past behavior. One such inmate was restricted from having a towel stored in his cell. He was allowed to have one when he needed to shower, but he had to return it as soon as he was done. However, this inmate decided to steal another inmate's towel instead of getting one from the jailers. He then refused to give it back and was using it to pound on items in his cell; he then began ripping it and tying it around his neck.

He was placed at Taser-point while SERT members entered his cell and retrieved the towel without incident. However, the inmate then covered his cell in feces, threw feces and trash, and urinated under his cell door into the dayroom. After this he began to bang on his cell door in an attempt to agitate the other inmates in the pod to also act out. SERT members returned to his cell, gave him directives at Taser-point to move to the shower, clean himself, and then move to another cell so the dayroom and his old cell could be bio-cleaned. The inmate showered, his cell was cleaned, and he was returned without anyone getting injured.

"*Spiders!*"

A SERT member was just outside of booking when an emergency call for help from booking was announced over the radio. Upon gaining entry into the booking lobby, the deputy observed an inmate (who was being booked) flailing his arms and running toward the staff at different sides of the booking counter. As the deputy got closer to him, he turned toward the deputy and moved to his left.

After the inmate moved to the deputy's left, the deputy became concerned for the safety of staff in the area. The inmate appeared to be seeing things that were not there. He was very muscular and appeared to be in a state of fight or flight as his eyes were open very wide and the man was tensing up as he attempted to get away from what he would later say were spiders. The deputy felt that when it came time to try and place him into control holds and escort him into a cell, the inmate would fight and cause injuries to staff because they would seem to be holding him down and whatever was chasing him would "get" him.

The deputy decided to deploy a Taser. He drew the Taser, activated the laser site, and placed the sight on the inmate's lower left torso with the objective for the first probe to be placed in the abdominal area and the other closer to his leg. The deputy pressed the trigger and the probes deployed roughly where anticipated, hitting on his torso.

After the inmate went to the ground, without striking his head, the deputy called for him to be turned over and handcuffed while still under power. After five seconds, the Taser quit cycling and after few more seconds he was handcuffed. After he was handcuffed, the inmate was sat upright and a nurse examined him for injuries and removed the probes. It was decided to move the inmate into a booking cell while he came off of whatever drug he was on.

For the Safety of Others or the Facility

"Touch My Feces"

One inmate decided to spread his feces on the floor and onto other articles from his toilet. He then broke a sprinkler head in his cell so the water would mix with the feces with the purpose of having the infected water infiltrate the dayroom, other cells, and of course onto the responding staff. SERT was activated to put on protective gear and extract, decontaminate, and watch over the inmate while the area was bio-cleaned.

The reason for this behavior was that the inmate didn't like how the deputy was running the pod. Often, this means that the deputy was doing their job and not allowing the inmate to manipulate them.

"Call This!"

An inmate broke both phones in a pod and was swinging them as weapons while refusing to lock down. He then attempted to break the glass in the mini-control, and SERT was activated. The team arrived in the area and he continued to yell and challenge them to fight. When the team opened the pod door, the inmate ran to his cell and shut the door. The inmate had destroyed the only phones in the pod for others to contact their families or for attorneys to call their clients.

SERT went to his cell, extracted him, and placed him into the emergency restraint chair while the whole pod was yelling, banging on their cell doors, and threatening to hurt that inmate when they had a chance. He was taken from the area for his safety and because he was threatening staff.

"Come in and Fight"

One inmate in the segregation area decided that he was not getting enough time out and refused to lock down. He began throwing the pod trash can and hitting the pod windows with it in an attempt to break them. He then told staff he was going to assault them with the can if they entered, while using the standard profanity that comes with such threats.

SERT responded to extract the inmate from the dayroom. Staging at the pod door with a shield and a Taser, they entered the pod and cornered him in a slow, methodical movement. He was escorted out of the pod without injury to him or staff.

"Lights Out"

Over the course of several weeks, SERT was repeatedly deployed to extract an inmate who was continually breaking the cell lights and creating sharp plastic shards that could be used to self-inflict a wound or as weapons against staff. He was off his medication and was having a hard time seeing any future for himself. He was removed from there and taken to a cell where it was much more difficult to damage equipment or harm himself. Of course, he was repeatedly seen by medical and counseling staff who kept trying to get him to take his medication, but you can't force someone to take something.

"Excited Delirium"

One inmate began to refuse to follow orders and was also removing his clothes, irritated by lights, and having guttural verbal responses. It was determined that he needed to be taken to the hospital due to signs of excited delirium, which can be fatal if not treated by medical professionals. It was then passed on to jail staff that a Taser was used three times during this inmate's arrest outside of the jail, and that the Taser was ineffective.

SERT members were used to gain control, restrain the inmate, and place him onto the EMS gurney. He was then taken to the hospital with three deputies as his escort. He did recover from this.

For the Order or Cessation of Illegal Activity

"Exhibitionist"

One inmate, while in a booking observation cell, was masturbating with one hand while inserting the other into his rectum. The observation cell has a very large piece of Plexiglas that allows staff to observe people who have been arrested, so all other arrestees could see him too. He was verbally asked to refrain from what he was doing, but he ignored repeated attempts to stop his behavior and notify him of his illegal activity. His behavior was erratic and generally violent, and as a result, SERT was called to put the individual in restraints.

The SERT member, using a shield for protection, entered the cell after it was opened and rushed to the inmate, pinning him with the shield so he couldn't move and assault anyone. However, since the inmate was still masturbating, his right leg became pinned by his forehead. The inmate then began to struggle to pull in his arms so the team couldn't secure him. The shield person activated the electrical pulse in the outer shield in order to distract and gain pain compliance from the inmate. The inmate screamed out, "Ow, my nutsack!" followed by, "That actually felt good! Do it again!" He was then secured in an alternate location in order to protect those in the booking area from becoming victims of his exhibitionism.

"Court-Ordered DNA"

A SERT supervisor for the day shift received a phone call from a booking officer that an investigator from the city police department had arrived to speak with an inmate, and that he would like to speak to a supervisor. The investigator wanted to meet with one of the inmates, so the supervisor arranged for this and the investigator went to a housing area where the inmate was. A short time later, a radio call from the housing officer asked for assistance in his area.

Upon arrival of staff to the area, the deputy explained that the inmate's behavior was beginning to escalate, and he was afraid he was going to become combative. At that moment, the investigator came out of the conference room and explained that he had a court order for non-testimonial identification authorizing the collection of DNA from the inmate, and that the inmate was refusing to comply with the DNA swab.

As the supervisor entered the conference room to speak to the inmate, the inmate began ripping pieces of paper in half and throwing them in the trash can. He stated that he didn't know what it said and didn't agree to anything. The investigator then told him that it was a copy of the court order that he had been trying to explain to him. The supervisor asked if this was his first time in custody, and the inmate said it was not. The supervisor then told him that we would appreciate his cooperation in getting a DNA swab as ordered by the court. He maintained that he was not going to cooperate, despite attempts to explain that it had already gone through the courts and was ordered by a judge, so they were required to gather his DNA.

He continued to argue, stating that he was not going to allow a DNA sample to be taken. At that time, the inmate's behavior began to escalate and his body language (tense muscles and balled-up fists) appeared as though he was going to become physically combative. The supervisor then ordered him to stand up and placed him in handcuffs, checking them for proper fit and double-locking them. The supervisor then escorted him to booking so he could cool down. It was determined that the inmate would be taken to the hospital to have a blood draw performed.

CHAPTER 18 PREP

Let's imagine that in one of the previous scenarios, the Taser didn't work and the inmate was able to use a trash can as a weapon to assault one of the deputies. In this case, a criminal investigation would begin. Evidence would be collected, a report written, the DA consulted, and charges filed. It turns out that this is quite an involved process, but not too complicated after you've done a few. The next chapter will provide a brief overview of the investigative process inside a jail.

Chapter 18: Jail Investigations

SOME PEOPLE FIND IT SURPRISING that I conduct criminal investigations in the jail. I do conduct investigations, and I feel the weight of knowing that my work will impact the lives of the victims as well as those I investigate.

In many jails, deputies will write a report and then send the case on to the investigations section. In contrast to this, my sheriff has pushed for each of the sworn deputies to learn how to conduct criminal investigations. This is a huge deal, as some jailers may not have a peace officer standards and training (POST) certification and some smaller departments might not be able to send jail staff to the academy.

It's important for those officers, who may be non-certified, to work criminal cases, as this speaks to the legitimacy of their position. In some states, even non-certified deputies can work criminal investigations should the limited authority to do so (inside the jail) be granted by the sheriff. This limitation usually has two requirements. First, the person is usually under the direction of someone who is POST-certified. Second, there are limitations, such as location or time. In my agency, this authority is granted only when the non-certified person is on shift, and that is usually at the jail. Here is the statute for the state of Colorado:

> ### C.R.S. 16.2.5-0103
>
> - 1. "A sheriff, an undersheriff, and a deputy sheriff are peace officers whose authority shall include the enforcement of all laws of the state of Colorado. A sheriff shall be certified by the P.O.S.T. board pursuant to section 30-10-501.6, C.R.S. An undersheriff and a deputy sheriff shall be certified by the P.O.S.T. board."
>
> - 2. "A non-certified deputy sheriff or detention officer is a peace officer employed by a county or city and county whose authority is limited to the duties assigned by and while working under the direction of the chief of police, sheriff, an official who has the duties of a sheriff in a city and county, or chief executive of the employing law enforcement agency."

Jail deputies are law enforcement officers who mainly work in the jail, but they need to be trained to conduct investigations in addition to their other duties. Just because an offender is incarcerated doesn't stop them from committing additional crimes. Among the crimes you'll typically find in jail are: inmate-on-inmate assaults, inmate-on-staff assaults, criminal mischief, harassment, violations of protection or restraining orders on victims, smuggling and selling of drugs, witness tampering, and attempting to influence public servants.

Because inmates know that additional charges will be forthcoming at our jail, we've seen reduced numbers of inmate-on-inmate and inmate-on-staff assaults. Having full investigatory responsibilities empowers jail deputies to enforce the law inside their little city, know that their efforts make a difference, and free up detectives and investigators to focus on those outside the facility.

A LEARNING CURVE

Although one would think it's a simple matter to collect evidence and pursue criminal charges, it really isn't. There are plenty of legal procedures and rules for evidence collection that are designed to ensure both the quality of the evidence and the preservation of due process for the accused. How an investigatory report is started and worded is important, and, just like spelling errors and grammar, will be under scrutiny.

The investigation and report are seen as a reflection of that officer and agency. Defense attorneys will analyze your words, structure, and evidence for the express purpose of attacking your credibility. These attorneys will attempt to make your work appear shoddy and untrustworthy at best, and, should your work be bad enough, seem like an attempt to frame an innocent person.

AGENCY AND COUNTY SUPPORT

Anyone who has the will and a bit of extra time can likely get help from other professionals working on investigations or for the courts. However, if you don't have extra time at work or you're unwilling to come in on your own time, reading guides written by staff or phoning a friend may be all the help you'll get. In this case, you'll learn by rising to meet the challenge and, of course, by your failures.

Still, you don't have to go it alone. I've found that a request for guidance, especially from your peers, almost always brings good results. I've requested help from the investigations, records, and evidence sections, jail deputies, and from the DA's office. Each person or section has their specialty and will help you polish up your investigation. Don't be afraid to ask for help!

BASIC JAIL INVESTIGATIONS

Each case you investigate is different, and your approach to the case may change depending on when you get involved, the support you have, or the challenges you face. There are many different ways to conduct a good investigation, but it's important to find a method that works for you and stick with it. There are also tricks of the trade that you'll learn from those with more experience.

JAIL INVESTIGATIONS | 225

Below is a very basic outline for a jail investigation. I say this is very basic because I could've easily made a seven-page outline for this and it still wouldn't be large enough to cover every scenario you may run into. You just have to dive in, follow a good method, and allow your professionalism to shine.

Initial Response
Recognize that a crime may have occurred and begin an investigation
⬇
Preservation of the Crime Scene
Lock down the area or cell(s)
⬇
Preservation of the Evidence
Do not resume normal operations until evidence is collected
⬇
Chain of Custody
Every person who has had access to the evidence is logged
⬇
Isolation of Perpetrator or Victims
Preserve evidence and stop victimization
⬇
Evidence Collection
Collect photographs, video, audio, biological, physical, and criminal history
⬇
Witness Statements
Get them if possible
⬇
Interview or Interrogation
Advise them of their rights before questioning them about a crime
⬇
Victim's Rights
Make sure you are in compliance with the state's victims' rights statutes.
⬇
Reports
They need to be completed fully and within a decent timeframe
⬇
Arrest Workbooks
Affidavits, booking forms, warrants, etc.
⬇
Filing Charges
Follow your agency's policies and procedures as well as state statutes
⬇
DA Meetings
For felony cases or other cases that may need another eye before filing

COURT PROCEEDINGS

In the vast majority of cases, if your work is professional, timely, accurate, well documented, and presents a strong case for conviction, the defense attorney will advise their client to take a deal. However, if you're subpoenaed to court, it's likely that the DA sees holes in your work as well as the case itself, or maybe the citizen just really wants to take the case to trial. If you have the ability to go to your county court to watch a few criminal proceedings it will be of great benefit to you.

AN HIGH VOLUME SYSTEM

If you haven't filed charges before or gone to the DA's office to speak about a case, then you really have no idea of the sheer volume of cases out there. In my county alone, there are at least seven different agencies that bring people to the jail. This means that each person in the jail already has at least one charge from one of those agencies. Often, additional charges are filed a short time after they arrive.

Should the incarcerated citizen also break the law while an inmate, your case gets added to those already in process. One example of this is a violation of a protection order. If a man is brought in for having a verbal altercation with his wife, he likely has charges of harassment with a domestic violence enhancer. There will also be a protection order put into place to protect the victim. If the man contacts his victim, he has now violated a protection order, and these charges will be added by the jail investigator. In the overall scope of this person's criminal case, the charge of a violation of a protection order may be seen as a very small component of their case, and it could be used as a bargaining chip to sweeten a plea deal.

The system relies on these plea deals because there aren't enough attorneys or judges to make going to trial desirable. So, expect a plea deal and a lesser sentence for those who have earned criminal charges.

CHALLENGES TO INVESTIGATIONS IN A JAIL

My jail houses a little over six hundred inmates when at full capacity. It's large enough that we could run two to four full-time investigators, but we don't have the funding for that. Most agency budgets are tight enough that they must focus their dollars for maximum effect, and this doesn't always include funding for additional investigators or training for the jail.

I can tell you from experience that working a criminal case at the jail comes with many challenges. First, you're still responsible for running your housing area. You may have up to one hundred inmates or more to observe, protect, and ensure that they have access to their constitutionally protected activities. Every minute spent focusing on your investigation while still operating your housing area means less attention on those in that area. It's also difficult to focus on preparing a criminal case when you still have an area to run, which means there are meals to serve, medical, counseling, and attorney visits, programs, maintenance, county services, general operation, and loads of inmate questions.

Should it become too challenging to do your investigation during your shift, then you must work on it during your time off. Since jailers are often already working overtime, your supervisors may frown on you for doing this. In addition to this, you're spending even more time away from your family.

LEARN TO THINK LIKE A DEFENSE ATTORNEY

It's useful to learn to think like a defense attorney when conducting an investigation because it helps to see how doubt can be cultivated or even manufactured. Career criminals rely on doubt to get out of being held accountable. These criminals also sow doubt in their victims' minds in order to dissuade them from testifying or to question their own recollection of events.

Defense attorneys are there to ensure that the due process is fully followed and that the DA proves their case beyond a reasonable doubt.

As a law enforcement officer, you have a duty to preserve and collect all the evidence in a case. Some of this evidence may cast doubt on the guilt of the accused. Thinking like a defense attorney will help keep you grounded and looking for both the exculpatory evidence as well as the incriminating evidence. In essence, it helps you maintain a more objective approach to an investigative question.

Beyond the collection of evidence and report writing, learning to see the case from a DA's point of view helps you understand and counter the techniques and tactics that destroy credibility and create reasonable doubt. After you work on this skill for a while, deceptive speech and writing will begin to stand out, making it clearer where you should investigate further. It will also make it clearer when you don't have enough evidence to prove your case beyond a reasonable doubt. The downside to this is that sometimes this makes you feel that further investigation is a waste of your time.

Below is a diagram on how difficult proving guilt can be, as it's only after a case is proved beyond a reasonable doubt that you can get a conviction.

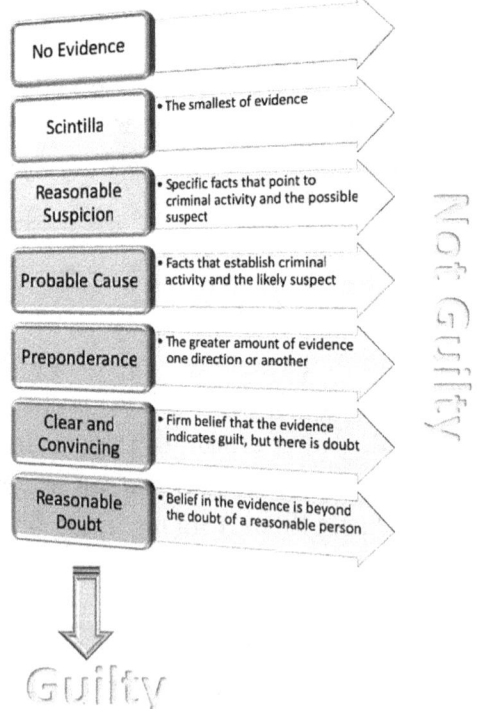

LEARN TO ARGUE YOUR CONCLUSIONS AND EXPECTATIONS

Sometimes, you may be required to have a meeting with the DA before filing charges. The evidence of the case will be gone over, questions will be asked about the evidence, and the DA may ask you what you'd like to see happen in the case. Remember, they see thousands of cases in a year and you may have to argue for prison time over probation. By argue I don't mean yelling, but by articulating that the evidence supports the charges filed and the severity of the situation requires prosecution and sentencing that reflects this.

The DA's office is very busy with their caseloads. Over time they become accustomed to reading about, investigating, and prosecuting the worst crimes imaginable. This happens so much that, to a DA, a "simple" assault case may seem hardly worth the time or costs associated with it. Plea deals are made all the time that benefit the defendant, the DA, and the taxpayers. However, sometimes your argument makes the difference between the defendant getting probation or four years in the department of corrections.

LEARN TO "FIRE AND FORGET"

So now you've completed your investigation, preserved the evidence, and sent your case to the courts. The rest of this process is largely out of your hands. Should your case be plead down or dismissed, it's hard not to take it personally. If you forget how busy the DA's office is, or how plea deals are a very necessary part of the process, then you might think that your efforts don't make a difference. These thoughts might make it that much harder to work your cases with the highest precision.

A good way to try and offset this possibility is to "fire and forget"—in other words, do your best, "fire" it off to the courts to sort out, and "forget" the results (unless you're using that information to learn to be a better criminal investigator). The results aren't really your concern unless it was you or your investigative process that were the direct cause of a case being dropped. Remember, it's "the people" who decide innocence or guilt. Move on to the next case.

CHAPTER 19 PREP

Incarcerated citizens with mental health issues seem to be on the rise or are being more recognized than ever before. If your agency sees enough inmates having mental health issues, you'll likely need to take a course in critical incident training or some other type of mental health communication training that will greatly assist you in your work. In the next chapter, we will look briefly at this issue.

Chapter 19: Mental Health and Jail

MENTAL HEALTH HOSPITALS AND THEIR operation, funding, capacity, and capabilities vary from state to state in the U.S. The access to mental health treatment in general is fragmented, and this causes some interesting challenges for communities and their jails. More and more jails are becoming the first-line mental health triage hospitals for their communities. Citizens who refuse to take their medication, and suffer from dysfunction as a result, tend to end up in jails. However, jails aren't designed as treatment centers.

In Colorado, there is one main state mental health facility and many behavioral health centers (spread out across the state) linked with non-profits, hospitals, and community programs. However, the resources for those who can't pay (such as incarcerated citizens) are very limited. When it comes to those who need close supervision to function, there are too few beds and resources, leaving a large treatment gap.

County jails only have a certain number of beds they can fill at the state hospital, severely limiting the number of inmates that can be treated at any one time. Even if inmates do secure a bed at the state hospital, they may be turned away because of physical illnesses—these institutions don't have enough funding to deal with medical needs on top of psychiatric ones. There are also lengthy legal processes required to force treatment at a state facility, even when severe dysfunction is obvious. All of these factors mean that most inmates with mental health problems stay in the jail until they're released.

Where I work, the majority of serious assaults on staff seem to happen in our mental health section. This mental health section has grown dramatically over the last five years, and the amount of mentally ill inmates with violent tendencies has grown with equal measure.

IDLE HANDS AND MINDS

Sitting and sleeping does a person little good while being in jail. We offer many programs to occupy their minds and attempt to prepare them for release to the community. It's important for people to focus on changing their life path and building up support so they can leave the jail system without being pulled back in by some violation of the law or their probation.

When a person has little to do, their mind runs wild. While sometimes this leads to great creativity, more often than not I've seen it lead to depression and bad behavior. As a result, educational and recreational programs are essential in providing a distraction for the mind and a task for the body as an inoculation to discourage depression and prevent bad behavior from taking root.

However, those with more severe mental health challenges isolate themselves a great deal of the time and act out just enough to be ineligible to attend these programs. As a result, they present a more significant challenge to the mental health professionals working inside the jail. This also severely limits the jailers' options when attempting to manage them safely.

Jail is an extremely challenging environment in the first place, and there are those that no amount of programs, direction, or home support will help or change. Through accident, birth, or the decisions they've made (particularly drug use), they have some sort of dysfunction that greatly increases bad behavior, depression, or aggravates mental illness. As a result, for many coping with mental illness, jail can have a decompensating effect, or a deterioration in their daily functioning and coping skills.

MENTAL HEALTH CARE IN JAILS: A COMMUNITY ISSUE

When a person is brought to the jail by street officers, whatever is going on in their lives and minds has often been going unchecked and allowed to worsen. Once stabilized, the person will go through the legal system to find out what will happen to them. The triage and stabilization that mental health professionals do in the jails is critical for the continuity of care of those who will be moving on to the department of corrections. However, there are also those who will be released only to return to the dysfunction that resulted in their arrest in the first place. There's a definite belief, by those I work with, that there needs to be a stronger push by communities to ensure some sort of continuation of care.

More and more there's an understanding by county jails that efforts toward a continuation of care will benefit the inmate, reduce recidivism, and keep the community safer. There are citizens whose lack of continuous mental health care directly contributes to their dysfunction in the community. This increases contact with law enforcement and the chances of being jailed. The same people can have the chances of this happening to them decrease with programs designed to maintain care.

Partnerships with local behavioral health resources are a must, and working relationships between the jail and these resources have to be maintained. After all, it's in the best interest of citizens that those who need treatment get treatment, and don't victimize or get victimized by others or have negative interactions that result in being taken to the jail.

An additional challenge is that many mentally ill citizens don't want to be helped. They have to want help because it's very difficult to get court-ordered treatment and medication. Because of the difficulty in getting court-ordered treatments, inmates are released from jail every bit as dangerous, or more so, than when they entered. But we can't hold people in jail because of things they "might" do.

MENTAL HEALTH TRAINING

When working with a dysfunctional person, using the same verbal and physical tactics or techniques that work on those without dysfunction will likely not end well. Each type of dysfunction will have its own best practices. Even then, some individuals are further challenged by the personality behind their dysfunction.

I can say, without any hesitation, that mental health professionals working inside a jail are very valuable members of the team, and they have great insights on generating voluntary compliance. They'll also likely reinforce the use of security policies for those with whom words don't work, who have higher levels of dysfunction, or who are unable to hear others over the voices in their mind.

It's a very good idea to get additional training on dealing with people who have some type of dysfunction. Here are some basic tips to get you started.

Practice Your Verbal Skills

If you use clear and short sentences, you're more likely to get the result you're looking for. Even still, every once in a while, verbal skills will be inadequate. If at all possible, attend a crisis intervention training (CIT) course, as they often cover speaking to those who are having a mental health crisis or continuing mental health issues.

Don't Play into Delusions

It's best to not play into an inmate's delusions because it only causes more issues in the long run. Your badge of authority will only reinforce these delusions if you purposefully treat them as real. Sometimes you can get people to start taking medication when you're straight with them. Other times, you have to wait for a narrow window of reasonability in order to get through to the person and get compliance.

Give Them Extra Time

Some people are dealing with mental health issues in addition to having a difficult personality. Give them extra time to comply to your requests and orders. As some point, though, you'll have to act, and it doesn't hurt to have a mental health professional there as another set of eyes. This person can let you know when you're more likely dealing with the difficult personality side rather than the mental health side.

Hold Them Accountable

Holding them accountable doesn't mean giving multiple lockdowns to a person who isn't in a culpable state of mind. It means that you document their decisions, actions, and rule violations because this may come into play in competency hearings, court-ordered treatments, or to outline dangerous behavior by the inmate so staff can be informed and prepare accordingly. Such documentation may also reinforce or justify the safety and security practices that restrict the inmate's movement and access to items that can be turned against you.

Maintain Officer Safety

Although the vast majority of those with mental health issues are non-violent, those who are violent don't process the consequences of their actions or decisions like a normal person. Be as relaxed in body posture and tone as possible, but position yourself to be ready for an assault that will likely have little to no warning. Be aware of your surroundings and use the building's architecture, your tactics training, and your communication skills to your advantage in order to keep yourself safe.

ANECDOTES FROM THE JAIL

Below are some stories outlining how challenging inmates with behavioral or mental health issues can be.

"Crazy Strong"

One night, without any indication or provocation, a violent mental health inmate attacked one of our deputies. Fortunately for us, this deputy was one of the most physically built, fit, and competent deputies in the facility. The inmate was able to remove his radio in the first two seconds of the attack. The attack lasted several minutes, until the deputy was able to finally make a radio call for help and assistance arrived. He was left with damage to his hand and a concussion from the encounter.

There was little doubt that the inmate was trying to kill him and no doubt that if he had attacked anyone else the outcome would likely have been tragic. Around two months later, the same inmate bit off his own thumb, chewed it beyond repair, and pulled out the ligament with his teeth without seeming to feel any pain. Despite the clear evidence that this person needed help, even if there was a bed available at the state hospital, because he had a physical injury that could become infected (and the hospital doesn't accept those with medical conditions), it is highly likely that he wouldn't have been admitted.

"Clean the Window"

One person was arrested and brought into booking with instability. As a result, he was placed into a cell with a glass wall so he could be observed continuously despite the business of the area. While in this cell, the person decided to defecate on the floor and then smear the feces onto the glass. Over time, the person became more lucid and was able to have a conversation. Since the glass was smeared, causing visibility to be diminished, the jailer asked him to clean off a section of glass, thinking he would use one of the articles of issued clothing on the floor but not giving that direction. The inmate proceeded to lick the fecal matter off of the glass, much to the disgust of those present.

"I'll Prove to You That I Am Crazy"

One person was placed into a cell and was making a spectacle over being crazy. Most individuals who do this type of thing aren't really crazy, but are putting on a show for all to see. Over time, the inmate pounded on the glass, sang for an extended length of time, told anyone who came by the cell that they were crazy, and pounded on the door and glass.

When this didn't appear to work, the inmate defecated on the floor and told the jailer, "If I wasn't crazy, why would I do that?" Rather than keep silent, as is customary when dealing with such individuals, the jailer thought they were replying cleverly by stating, "Well, if you were really [truly] crazy you would have eaten it" (referring to the feces on the floor). Without delay, the inmate picked up the feces and took a bite, much to the disgust and horror of the deputy, who then regretted speaking to the inmate.

"Watch This, Deputy"

One particularly disturbed inmate was brought from one housing area to segregation due to his behavior. After he was put into a new cell he waited on all fours, naked, with his rear facing the door. He watched the glass and waited for jailers to check on him. As they passed his cell, he would start to defecate. This happened until he was "empty," at which time he tore his mattress apart and used it to wipe himself before pushing the remnants out the bottom of his door.

CHAPTER 20 PREP

Although you have to be physically prepared for this work, you have to be even more mentally prepared. You should be aware of the stressors and challenges that you may face and come up with some good methods for stress management. If you want to have a career lasting more than two or three years, you should give the next chapter on psychological stress some serious thought and work toward a consistent and built-in method of stress management.

Chapter 20: Psychological Stress and Assaults

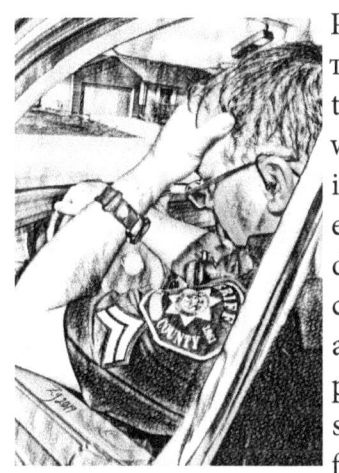

PSYCHOLOGICAL ASSAULTS ARE DESIGNED to tax the mind and emotions and influence the behavior and decisions of the person to whom they're directed. The stress this brings is like adding a flash flood to a nearly full reservoir of challenges and emotions, making it difficult to take in stride. Jailers like a good challenge, and this one is often as good as it gets—it's really difficult to maintain professionalism and a rational mind when someone is threatening the lives of your family members, for instance. However, an overblown reaction is what inmates are looking for.

Deputies and jailers did choose to take on the challenge of working in a jail—they're public servants working under difficult circumstances. However, just because they love a challenge and chose to work in a jail doesn't mean that they signed up expressly for the physical, psychological, and emotional abuse that they'll experience from their fellow citizens.

"YOU CHOSE TO WORK THERE!"

Working in a conflictual environment does not mean being a "voluntary" victim to repeated psychological attacks. If I had a dime for every person who's told me that being psychologically abused was part of the job and I signed up for it, I could've bought an airplane by now. However, to me, this type of statement is ignorant, and it blames the victim. In essence, they're saying you asked for the abuse by choosing your career.

Let's apply this logic to some other jobs. Military personnel join for the express purpose of being killed by the enemy. EMTs become EMTs in order to be traumatized by the injuries and deaths they see. Therapists become therapists so they'll be psychologically abused by their patients. Bankers become bankers in order to be injured or traumatized in a robbery.

Of course, these statements are absurd. So, too, is the belief that police and corrections officers go into the field "wanting" to suffer physical, emotional, psychological, or spiritual abuse. However, there's little public empathy and, in some cases, outright hostility for those who work inside a jail or correctional facility. Thanks to Hollywood and the poor decisions of a few individuals inside the correctional system, jailers are represented as being oppressive and prone to sadistic abuses of authority visited upon the "innocent" criminal.

The reality is that a jailer is entrusted with the authority to maintain order and safety inside the jail by the people of the state. This means keeping the micro-society inside the jail from devolving to a *Lord of the Flies* scenario, as well as preventing vigilantism and ensuring due process. Furthermore, jailers demonstrate to those inside that impulsive decisions often result in long-lasting individual and societal consequences.

VIOLENCE IS INFLUENTIAL

In studies of the politics of nations, much is made of the idea that the monopoly of force must be maintained by the state or nation. Although we don't like to think of our society in this way, this monopoly of force is what allows a legal system to operate by removing vigilante violence on the promise that the state will impose the rule of law. Otherwise, "might makes right," and those willing to kill win.

Some of the inmates I've seen were exposed to violence in their childhoods and learned the influential power of violence firsthand. Perhaps the dominant influence in their young lives didn't care about what was right, only that the child did as they were told or else suffered the violent consequences. As a result, violence became a viable option for their everyday life, including predatory violence on others.

Many such violent predators are successful enough that they're difficult to catch. In areas where the state doesn't have the monopoly of force, there are "no go" areas for law enforcement where the crime lords are in control. Since violence and fear control behavior so effectively, it baffles me that there are people out there who think you can legislate away violent behavior by removing "tools" used in crimes. Even more baffling to me is the belief that violent offenders will stop being violent if the police appear less able and willing to bring violence and force.

However, having the monopoly of force doesn't mean that violence should be the first or standard approach to policing or jailing. This is why the field continues to grow, with alternative philosophies and approaches to generating voluntary compliance with law enforcement. It isn't appropriate to try and scare everyone you meet into submission. However, a law enforcement officer also doesn't want to invite an attack from a predator simply because the predator mistakes "manners" for weakness or incompetence.

What does all of this have to do with psychological abuse in a jail? Since violence and the threat of violence is the preferred method of violent criminals, it's a tactic that is commonly used en masse by those career criminals inside the jail. Although criminals, in general, have no real allegiance with one another, they're unified against the jailer and sometimes with that elusively defined entity known as society.

As a result of this, instead of one verbal or psychological assault per day, a jailer is subjected to many, from a wide variety of individuals. Therefore, it isn't a surprise that jailers attempt to build emotional armor in an attempt to extend their careers. Sometimes this is done at significant cost to the person.

PSYCHOLOGICAL STRESS

Having been a jailer for an extended amount of time, I can safely say that the environment can be one of near constant psychological stress. Fortunately, most of us receive some sort of training on how to deal with stressors or diminish their effects. However, this training isn't always enough, and there's a delayed recognition of the need for training on new causes of stress. The thing about stressors is that what stresses you out may not have an effect on another person.

Psychological stressors are a norm for the job, and it's a big reason why not everyone can have this career. The mental and emotional aspects of this work are far more challenging than the physical demands, but since the mind and body are linked, the stress often manifests in physical ways. Plus, like physical stressors, the duration and intensity of psychological stressors can significantly impact a person's ability to process them in a healthy way. Stress management is the key to career longevity.

PSYCHOLOGICAL ASSAULTS

Predatory inmates know how taxing threats can be on one's psyche. They know that you're already dealing with stress, and because they're watching you, they can visibly see when you're already taxed to the max. They can perceive your vulnerability and, if it suits them, they'll increase it with a psychological assault.

Sometimes these assaults are routine business for such inmates and they don't realize they're doing it. Others make it a spectacle for all to see because it makes them feel more empowered or powerful. Because such assaults happen so frequently to law enforcement, there's an expectation that those who work in the field are supposed to be immune to it. The reality is that we work on developing an armor that is plainly visible when we don't react like a normal person does in these situations. The jury is still out on whether this is healthy or not.

In 2015, the Washington State Supreme Court ruled that verbal abuse from the public directed toward law enforcement is protected freedom of speech (State of Washington v. E.J.J.). In one respect, this makes total sense. I believe a person should be able to voice an opinion, but when does voicing an opinion evolve into a psychological assault?

There are generally three laws that may be applied to such behavior: verbal menacing, harassment, and disorderly conduct. The intention behind someone's speech is measured in these statutes, and if the person's intention was to cause fear for safety or provoke a physical response, one of those laws could apply.

For example, I don't think "fuck the police" is an expression of an opinion; I think it's designed to provoke a negative response inside the officer. This doesn't mean that the officer should turn around and arrest someone for saying such things. I just think that the officer shouldn't lose the rights and protections a normal citizen has just because they work in law enforcement.

STOCKHOLM SYNDROME

If you work in a jail where direct supervision is the dominant philosophy, there are numerous interactions with inmates and jailers where the "professional line" between the two may be blurred. As a result, the jailer may develop more than a working relationship with the inmate(s). Often, those that work in jails are as isolated as those they watch over and should they have difficulty in maintaining a healthy level of empathy. As a result, some people may begin to identify more with those inside than out.

As outlined in a previous chapter, for many professional criminals, the development and exploitation of relationships is a primary strategy. This is why many jails rotate staff through housing areas as frequently as practicable.

TRAUMATIC TRANSFERENCE

During World War I, psychologists treating soldiers from the front noticed that, over time, they were developing symptoms of shell shock without ever having been there. Although I'm unaware of any studies of this within jails, my suspicion is that it likely plays a significant role in the psychological stress carried by jailers.

I've noticed that nearly everyone comes to the profession with a standard or high level of empathy for those who have become incarcerated. They empathize and go out of their way to assist people. As I've outlined before, these new jailers will eventually get "burned" by a criminal who uses their empathy to manipulate them. However, this isn't as bad as one might think. The true transference happens with "regular" interactions where empathy may, over time, seem like a masochistic emotional response.

For example, in a given day you may hear (and feel) ten stories about how someone's kids are faced with dealing with challenges alone because their parent is incarcerated. You'll hear multiple stories about how someone's life is over. You'll hear how someone has lost everything, including their pets. You'll be there when someone is accused of molestation or incest and feel for the victims. You'll be there when someone attempts self-harm or is assaulted by another inmate.

It isn't the one story here or there that's the issue, it's the volume and consistency of these stories that are, in my opinion, a likely cause for this traumatic transference and the resulting callous or cynical responses by jailers. Since stress management is vital, jailers will seek a way to protect themselves from the emotional onslaught that comes with empathy. As a result, jailers will seek to avoid these conversations and make statements designed to shut down such conversations.

ANECDOTES FROM THE JAIL

Implied Threats

Some inmates will use an implied threat as their psychological weapon. This relies on giving the jailer just enough information to know that they're being threatened, but not enough that they can respond with criminal charges.

"I Know Where You Live"

One deputy was conducting her walk through the pod to ensure the safety of the individuals there. One of the inmates came up to her, told her that he knew where she lived, and then provided her with her own address. That individual was already under investigation for stalking a program staff member and he had her address, too.

Another inmate expressed concern that the threatening inmate would find the staff member after his sentence was completed and, if she rejected him, would harm her. The question is, why would you look up a deputy while you were in jail and then let them know that you have their address? There were no direct threats made, but clearly it was meant to cause alarm about the unknown probability of him showing up at her house while she was sleeping.

How many of these types of threats would you find appropriate coming from individuals showing up at your workplace? These types of threats are creepy and very concerning to the law enforcement professional.

"Outgoing Mail Threat"

A deputy scanned an outgoing letter from an inmate that contained aggressive verbiage aimed at jail deputies, specifically saying that "it takes all of my self-control not to throw one of these lil' punks over the tier." In addition, it contained a statement that returning to a segregated status wouldn't concern him. The deputy believed that this message was a result of confiscating property from the inmate's cell earlier in the day, and the letter was an attempt to indirectly threaten the deputy.

Direct Threats

Some inmates know and can see how direct threats affect those around them. When given an opportunity, they'll wield them like a weapon on a jailer's mind. Often, they're trying to make the deputy lose their cool and respond inappropriately. Their other intent is to leave a long-lasting wound to the psyche as the deputy may see this threat as a real possibility, thus altering their behavior and perhaps isolating themselves further.

In any case, it isn't easy to weather a direct psychological assault. Below are some stories that show this.

"I'm Going to Kill and Rape Your Kids"

It seems that every other week, some angry predator is yelling that they're going to find a deputy's family and harm them. One inmate, who had a propensity to verbally abuse the nursing staff, began attempting to intimidate a nurse while I was on duty. I told him to lock down and that I would notify him later of what discipline he would receive. This type of discipline runs from a verbal warning to five days of lockdown.

The inmate became enraged that I stepped in, interrupted his behavior, and gave him a consequence for his decisions. For the next eight hours, he proceeded to bang loudly inside his cell. When I mean loudly, I mean that the neighboring pods, through the concrete and steel, thought someone was banging in their areas. While doing this, he was shouting, "You want a war? I'll give you a war!" He also shouted, "I'm going to kill you," and, "I'm going to rape your wife and children with a buck knife!" repeatedly throughout that time.

However, this was not all. Knowing that we would have to go into his cell to prevent self-harm, he cut himself in order to put blood everywhere inside the cell so we couldn't help but be exposed to it when we went into the cell.

If it was just him, maybe it wouldn't be overly stressful, however, he was also urging the remainder of the pod to act out as well, and two others did join in with making banging noises and yelling threats at staff.

"Arranged Husband"

An inmate brought the housing deputy an inmate request as soon as the housing area came off of lockdown. After skimming through it, the deputy informed him that the request wouldn't be sent on because it was inappropriate. The inmate said, "I understand," and walked away.

The inmate's request was for a meeting with a female deputy to tell her that he was her "arranged husband." Much of the request was unreadable and included a line of symbols. The inmate ended the request by writing, "I am your love pet. You own me. Wouldn't your gift to yourself and the rest of the family. Your pet Tigger." Naturally, the incident was documented and the deputy in question and a supervisor were notified.

CHAPTER 21 PREP

Despite the clear challenges outlined throughout this book, this can be a good career. If you like being challenged like I do, working in a jail will likely satisfy that need. But like many careers, you have to prepare yourself physically, emotionally, and mentally. And before you can prepare for something, you have to get an idea of what it is that you'll be doing. Education is a big part of this process, and this extends to your support base, such as family and friends.

The next chapter isn't a comprehensive guide to ensuring that you'll be totally prepared for this job, but it's a good place to start.

Chapter 21: Challenges and Preparation

Almost anyone can sit in a chair, hand out toilet paper, and walk around once every fifteen minutes. If that was all that being a jailer required, there would be no need for a training program. The reality is that only a few will get through the selection process. A few more will leave within the first year of service. By five years, many more will have left the jail or the law enforcement career in general. Even fewer make it to ten years. It's rare for a person to last twenty or more years working a jail housing area—most who have made it that long have spent several years in a duty that doesn't require working a housing area.

So, what is the challenge of working as a jail deputy? In general, it's to do the job well, manage your stress, and not lose yourself in the process. It's sometimes easier to break this larger challenge into four subcategories: competency, identity, worldview, and stress management.

COMPETENCY CHALLENGE

If you've made it through the previous chapters, you know that the learning curve for a career as a jail deputy can be steep. There are many new skills you'll need to learn in order to become competent at this job, and it takes even longer to master them. Many times, people will focus on completing this phase of the challenge to the extent that they neglect dealing with the other challenges. While it's okay to focus the bulk of your efforts on competency for a short time, not dealing with the other challenges can come back to haunt you.

IDENTITY CHALLENGE

The change in identity you'll experience in this job can be another great challenge. Most of us have one idea about what it means to do a certain job until we actually do that job. We also have the expectation that a certain job will bring with it the societal acceptance and respect that helps us feel legitimate and of benefit. However, sometimes we take this too far and make our occupation our identity.

As a jailer, you will experience a change in identity when you become a sworn deputy and then again when you retire back to civilian life. If you make poor decisions or mismanage stress, it's possible that you could even go from sworn deputy to inmate. Furthermore, if your identity revolves completely around law enforcement, then where is the room for husband, wife, parent, friend, skydiver, hiker, mountain climber, pilot, cook, carpenter, and all the other things that make you unique?

WORLDVIEW CHALLENGE

Although you could roll this into identity, I'm listing it as a separate challenge because it's harder to see it happening. It's stressful to see the world so differently than you did before you worked in the field, and managing that stress is a big part of the challenge. You might find yourself resisting changes in worldview at first, then becoming flabbergasted by them, and if they aren't dealt with in a healthy way, they can lead you into a skeptical worldview or to a view that is misanthropic (a general dislike, distrust, or hatred of humankind). A change in worldview is inevitable; the true challenge lies in guiding that change into something that doesn't result in depression and misanthropy.

STRESS MANAGEMENT CHALLENGE

In my opinion, the biggest challenge of working as a jailer is stress management in the face of constant, semi-rotating, and shape-shifting stressors. And since every person is different, what works for me may not work for you.

Stress management takes a multidisciplinary response as the mind, spirit, and body tend to be linked. Good exercise, eating, and sleep habits impact mood and motivation, which impact training and preparedness, which can then impact your response to a critical situation.

The following is a list of possible stressors that you may run into while working this job. Earlier chapters have already discussed many potential strategies for mitigating these stressors, but so far we haven't seen them all put together. This list may seem overwhelming at first, but it doesn't have to be. Some of these stressors are part of any job. In a few cases, deputies who've come from other fields have said that working as a jailer was less stressful than their previous job!

Words

Words can help or hinder you. Your words can escalate someone, so you should attempt to avoid escalating language and work on using de-escalation techniques while maintaining authority.

Beyond this understanding of the power of words, there's the use of a lie. By lying, I don't mean misremembering; I mean a purposeful deception to avoid taking responsibility. Lying just once will end your career because you'll no longer have any credibility.

Actions

Everything you do is up for scrutiny and criticism. Your decisions and actions can result in praise or criminal charges, depending on situation.

Item Accountability

Accidentally leaving keys out or papers face up on a desk (showing security sensitive information) or losing your handcuff key will cause you stress!

All Eyes on You

You're being watched by many predators who will learn about you and your habits. You may also be watched by your supervisors via camera. As a result, you have to get used to the constant idea of "being watched."

Proximity

You will be within physical striking distance of many people very frequently. Some of them will use body language indicating that they're getting ready to fight you, so you must constantly be on alert. Every shift I work, I have at least two encounters where someone's body language causes me to wonder if I'll have to fight to get home.

Saying No

Saying no to a normal person isn't usually that hard, but saying no to a violent predator takes a conscious effort because there may be a cost in doing so. You never know how they'll respond to it, but you have to do it because it's your job and you must maintain your authority. If you can't say no, you really can't work as a jailer.

Conflict

Conflict is everywhere inside a jail. To many of these citizens, it's part of their everyday language, and pushback is often seen as necessary to them. You'll likely have conflicts regarding law, policies, and the limitations of your influence.

Duration

Our shifts are more than twelve hours a day. This is a long time, and it's often for three, four, or more days a week. On top of this, consider how much time you'll spend behind the walls in a year. If you work a forty-hour week (the bare minimum), in a year you'll spend roughly eighty-seven twenty-four-hour days behind the steel doors. With overtime, a jailer can easily spend four months or more of their year locked up with the inmates.

Physical Discomfort

You will likely have to wear a uniform, stab-resistant vest, belt, radio, and other equipment. Moving around leaves you in a state of perpetual heat and sweat. To top it off, you can't just leave to go to the bathroom. In some cases you'll be waiting quite some time for someone to relieve you so you can answer the call of nature. You'll likely become very familiar with these types of physical discomforts.

Psychological Discomfort

As outlined in the previous chapter, I can safely say that the jail environment can be one of near constant psychological stress. Fortunately, most of us receive some sort of training on how to deal with stressors or learn how to diminish their effects. Keep in mind, though, that what stresses you out may not influence another person.

Inmate Numbers and Quality

Sometimes the sheer volume of inmates causes stress. One jailer to seventy or more inmates is rough. However, sometimes the "quality" of the inmate is so poor that watching fourteen of them is worse than watching one hundred twenty "standard" inmates. Also, overcrowding in a jail causes stress all on its own.

Staff Shortages

Many times, there aren't enough jailers to fill the slots. In our jail, for instance, it once took nearly nine months to fill a vacancy. By then there were even more vacancies to fill. Because of the stresses of the job and the high turnover, there's always talk of recruitment, retention, and retirement.

Deadlines

Rotating between days, nights, and being on call through holidays, birthdays, school events, and the like can be disorienting and inconvenient. You may also have to work extra hours or days when staffing is short (which is often the norm).

Many Demands and Requests

You're the go-to person for everyone who is housed in or visiting the housing area. In addition to inmate questions and demands, there are those from other staff members, attorneys, medical and counseling teams, program leaders, volunteers, and the families of the inmates. This doesn't take into account the demands and requests you have from your own family and the other people in your life.

Deadlines

You must complete training, criminal investigations, projects, inmate movement, and routine paperwork in a timely manner. Some are critical and come with supervisory or public pressure.

Training

Over time, jailers become more aware, and possibly more stressed, by what they know. They'll also become stressed by what they may not know and how that can hurt them and their families. Also, training comes with its own set of stressors, including evaluations by peers and the need to meet expectations.

Exposure Risk

As a jailer, you risk being exposed to hepatitis A, B, and C, tuberculosis, MRSA, the flu, colds, parasites, HIV—not to mention drugs and needles. We have homeless people brought in who are sick. Drug dealers and abusers come in with dangerous drugs or materials that can cause death from exposure. Incarcerated people with HIV sometimes chew on their cheek so they can spit their blood on you. This is a real mental stressor.

Death of a Coworker

We always feel for those we lose in the line of duty, even if they're from other agencies. However, when the loss is closer to home it hits especially hard. When those close to you die in accidents or by their own hand it can shake you to the core.

Injuries and Physical Assaults

Training and work injuries can end your career, or even your life. They can also lead to post-traumatic stress that will need to be dealt with. It's said that a person who works in the corrections field can expect to suffer two serious assaults in their career. Some say the rate of traumatic events for those who work at jails is about three per person in a six-month period.

Verbal Assaults

Some people intend to cause you psychological and emotional harm. This negative energy and vitriol cause stress that is felt in the core. Often, you will feel anger or defensiveness.

Sometimes there are general shouts and taunts from closed cells, and you have no idea who said them. These aren't shouts of encouragement, but rather echoes of those who want to harm your self-esteem and confidence. They use the same techniques on their victims outside of the jail to great effect; otherwise they wouldn't use these tactics.

Workers' Compensation

Most of the time, on-the-job injuries can be treated and you can get back to work. However, if a doctor states that your injury isn't work-related, you'll have the stress of fighting for workers' comp while trying to preserve your job. Also, if you're receiving treatment, you may have the stress of wanting to be cleared to work so you aren't seen as useless to the team. Some jailers will risk their careers by coming back too early and perhaps causing a more permanent disability in the process.

Isolation

Jailers spend a lot of time at work. They're known by many members of the community but won't remember all the people they run across. As a result, many seek to not be so visible in public. You'll get a great deal of dirty looks by those who recognize you. If you're out with your family, you may feel as if you're endangering them. Due to this isolation, jailers generally don't get the opportunity to receive the occasional thank you from the public that street officers do. This isolation has a stressful impact.

Legitimacy

Some jailers may not be given legitimate law enforcement status. As a result, they do hard work while feeling that those who work the streets look down on them or that they're valued less than a street officer. Many more see working in the jail as a stepping stone to the street. In my agency, our sheriff and captain work hard to show the legitimacy of those who work in the jail, to great effect.

Supervisor Support

When supervisors are supportive, you feel empowered and cared for. When they aren't supportive, your stress may increase considerably as you may be uncertain of your supervisor's motives. If supervisors are too hands-off and never see their staff, stress will increase as the feeling of isolation grows. The opposite of this is micro-management, where a person may feel like they're getting it from both inmates and supervisors.

Change and Information Overload

Policies, procedures, laws, the agency's focus, the leadership team, and staff members are constantly changing. Information overload is the norm, and a small, forgotten piece of information can have life-or-death consequences.

Professional Wrongdoing

The microscope will be upon you if you're accused of wrongdoing, and rightly so. The agency's best interest is in maintaining integrity and the public trust. You should expect, at least once in your career, to have a wild accusation thrown your way because you angered an inmate. Fortunately, most of the time, inmate accusations are later recanted by the inmate or aren't supported by the evidence. However, the stress they cause is very, very, real.

Lawsuits

Even if you've done the best job you can, there's a possibility that you may be sued for actions that were justified. Sometimes, agencies will settle these because the cost of fighting them is far more than settling out of court. The settlement, in most cases, is purely a business decision and not mean that you or the agency has done anything wrong.

Paperwork

Jails are almost always leaving a huge paper trail to pass on vital information, assist in the prosecution of criminal cases, and inoculate against litigation. The information must be accurate and professional. There's nothing like having to take the witness stand after having written a poor report and sounding like a complete buffoon.

Other Staff

You will always have that coworker who drives you crazy, or that you have trouble working with because of their personality, work ethic, or other issue. Sometimes you grow used to staff members and then they make a really poor decision and have to be escorted out of the building. The rumor mill goes into overdrive as people try and figure out what that person did wrong or if there was misconduct or illegal activity. It's natural to feel that these individuals are betraying the profession with their misconduct.

Other Professionals

Occasionally, some psychologist, therapist, defense attorney, or other professional can seem every bit as entitled as a badge-heavy law enforcement officer. It's amazing how some people think that your safety, and that of the other citizens in the area, pales in comparison to their momentary wishes. More troubling is that sometimes their complaints to a higher level can result in real and negative consequences. As a result, dealing with some of these "professionals," although they're the exception, not the norm, may cause additional stress and make for more conflicted priorities while working an area.

Specific Inmates

Some inmates will inherently cause you more stress than others. These inmates find it pleasurable to make your day as long as possible. Personality conflicts with inmates are an additional stressor in an already stressful environment.

Professional Challenges

Having difficulty in transferring to another assignment, moving to the street, getting additional training, or getting promoted may also cause additional stress on a jailer.

Maintenance Issues

When things don't work or function as intended, stress can increase. Staff and inmate restrooms have to function or stress increases. Showers have to work or inmates become agitated. Clogged plumbing will increase stress as well as up the chances of being exposed to biohazards. Cameras, lights, doors, and other basic safety equipment have to function. We need to be able to rely on our equipment.

Agency Culture

I've always felt that the agency I work for is constantly moving forward and looking for the next effective change on the jail-operations horizon. Our sheriff wants to get ahead of these trends rather than be reactionary. I feel this is a sign of a good agency culture.

However, agency culture can also be stressful. I've trained staff coming in from other agencies who have talked about a culture of isolation if you were seen treating inmates as anything other than lowdown criminals. My agency, while stressing a strong separation of staff and inmate personal lives, encourages communication as opposed to isolationist behaviors. After all, we can't help inmates get the resources they need if we don't talk to them.

Prejudice and Bias

We all bring biases with us, and that includes inmates. If you're a jailer of an ethnicity other than "white," some inmates will attempt to manipulate you or call you a traitor. If an agency is largely of one ethnicity and has a particular political affiliation, there may be biases that become evident in the workplace through jokes and stereotypes of who the "bad guys" are.

Either way, a clearly voiced ethnic or economic bias that is tolerated among the leadership will make the whole environment more stressful and even hostile. In my agency, leadership makes it clear that there's no place for bias because it only serves to discredit our profession and limit our ability to protect and serve. If a person doesn't like it, they don't have to serve.

Gender Bias

Gender bias is another area that our society and community should continually work on. It's no different inside our governmental institutions. Every now and then I will hear someone's bias emerge about female deputies. I challenge them to see that those differences also provide the team with advantages as well. We have worked hard to help others recognize the strengths that female staff often bring, such as communication, teamwork, and leadership. Still, depending on the agency, there may be times where a gender bias can cause additional stress or create a more hostile environment.

Political Slants

If the agency has far more people of one political belief and they're vocal about it, there can be stress in voicing differing thoughts and opinions. Some people turn their political views into a weapon and marginalize or chastise those with differing viewpoints. I've seen the political environment in the country voiced among staff members in the jail, and it makes the atmosphere hostile. Fortunately, it tends to drop off quickly after an election year.

Public Personal Life

Everything you do and don't do reflects on your agency, so you have to think over many things you would've just said or done automatically in the past. Your private opinions may suddenly become national news because you're a representative of your agency and law enforcement in general. This is something that most professions don't have to deal with.

Public Perception

Most of the community has no idea what it's like to work in a jail. Many have views on this that are informed by the media, Netflix shows, rumors, and so-called reality TV. Some people's education about law enforcement comes from when they've been questioned by a patrol officer. Some are educated by incarcerated or formerly incarcerated family members. And because incarcerated people *never* lie, their accounts of incarceration often portray themselves as victims of the justice system.

Familial Perceptions

Most of us try hard to not bring work home. If your spouse hasn't worked in a jail before, chances are, even if you speak about it, they won't understand. I've avoided bringing work home as much as possible because when I've spoken about it, I can see the transfer of stress to my spouse. I would rather have her and my children be as happy as possible. They've watched the physical effects of stress on me but have shown strong support and appreciation. Without their love and support, the job would be so much harder.

The Rest of Life

The same stressors that an average person has go on top of everything else. This stress includes housing, health, extended family issues, illnesses, immediate family issues, deaths, vehicle problems, bad neighbors, home repair, and financial stressors, to name a few.

You're unlikely to have more than a few of these stressors impacting you at any given time. Still, it's important to develop stress management strategies in advance of some of these, and that includes building your knowledge base and professionalism. The more you know, and the more professional you are technically and ethically, the more you'll likely be able to redirect stress appropriately. It's important to maintain and build your support mechanisms for those times when life events beyond your control add more to your plate than you're used to.

PREPARING FOR THE CHALLENGE

The first element to starting work as a jailer is to understand that the job will change you, but the question is, how and to what degree? There are many thoughts on preventative measures and education for what happens to your physical and mental health as a result of needing to sustain a higher level of vigilance for hours on end. In the end, the reactions and solutions are as varied as the individual.

However, I've found that there are some helpful and general responses and solutions. Here are a few:

Do Inoculate Yourself Regularly

You can insert your own joke about drinking alcohol here, but I don't recommend attempting to drink your troubles away. Instead, you'll have to develop healthy habits that are carefully cultivated and then maintained. Being mindful and using these healthy habits and techniques will be part of your inoculation and preparation for those times that are really challenging.

Do Talk

Many people in law enforcement are introverted. As a result, they isolate themselves in order to recharge. However, isolation also serves to further separate us from our support systems. Instead, when you're no longer upset about an event, talk to your friends, family, or significant other. You can let them know about your day without compromising confidentiality. Leave out the names of individuals and talk about the situation. Just be aware of how often you do this because you can transfer your stress to others.

Do Educate

Just because we work in law enforcement doesn't mean we're blind to issues faced by the field. It will be difficult to educate those in your life who aren't working in the field because it's a contentious topic, feelings can run high, and people seldom find time to really dive into understanding something. As a result, media and anecdotal evidence is offered, and unfortunately accepted, as the reality.

Most of us working in law enforcement take our responsibilities seriously and avoid abuse. A fear that some people have is being under the control of an abusive law enforcement officer. The law enforcement officer is supposed to enforce the laws passed by governmental representatives in as unbiased a way as possible, not antagonize citizens through enforcement.

The trick is to conduct this education in a way that isn't seen as being totally biased toward law enforcement. It's amazing how many people shut down on discussing these serious matters because your explanations may be seen as biased toward law enforcement. It also amazes me how some citizens think that there's a centralized police academy that trains all police the same exact way.

I've always found it useful to compare police departments with fire departments. Fire departments on opposite sides of the country study fire science, tools of the trade, and tactics, yet they're separate entities and they have their own culture. That is why people don't protest New York City fire department mishaps in downtown Denver. It's the same for law enforcement, but people don't seem to realize this.

Also, educate yourself and your loved ones on the emotional and physical toll that working in this field does to a person. Do yourself a favor and read a book on emotional survival for law enforcement—it will help you and your family understand what is happening to you. I have a recommendation for such a book in the Resources section.

Do Appreciate

When you're very busy and stressed, it's easy to forget about those things in your life that are good or going well. There are times where our challenges result in a powerful negative emotion that can overshadow these great things in life, causing a temporary loss in appreciation. Remembering to appreciate what's important helps inoculate you from becoming entitled and allowing the stress to overshadow the good in your life.

Do Check Yourself

I tell those I train to pay attention to their own behavior in the presence of those they're most comfortable with. One tip I have in this regard is to reflect on your behavior at home. If you find yourself treating the serial child rapist better than your family, you're not dealing with the stress appropriately.

In a jail, we must maintain our professionalism—we often don't look up an inmate's charges because it lessens the possibility of treating people differently based upon their charges. At home, pent-up frustrations can reveal themselves if not dealt with appropriately. Leave work at the jail. When you get off a shift, get into your car and use the time from there to home to decompress and change gears.

Another thing to beware of is getting too used to the authority entrusted to you. This usually presents itself outside of the jail when you get upset and think of using your status as a law enforcement officer to give you influence or control. When this happens, ask yourself if you've become too used to the authority granted to you. Remember, you're a citizen who's been granted authority because of the public's trust that you won't abuse it. Try to be a regular citizen until something happens that requires your intervention because of a law violation or a danger to public safety.

Do Work Out

It may not seem like it, but getting some exercise at the end of shift really will help you sleep better and get rid of any psychological stress that's manifesting in some sort of physical way. Working out is the last thing you want to do after a tiring day, but it really can help. What do you have to lose? Give it a chance!

Do Maintain Your Hobbies

One of the first things that go out the window when a person is stressed is their hobbies. It's very difficult for a person working in law enforcement to maintain hobbies because when they aren't at work, they're focused on de-stressing. If your old hobbies aren't working, try new ones.

I've found that so many people who work in this field are highly creative. I've known jailers who could out-sing performers who get paid millions. In addition to jailers, they're artists, woodworkers, pen makers, leather workers, armorers, solar charger designers, product designers, world-class bakers, musicians, flint knappers, rocket builders, pilots, photographers, filmmakers, mountain climbers, and the list goes on. I'm always amazed at what other talents my coworkers bring to the table.

Do Maintain Friendships Outside of Law Enforcement

Conversations with coworker friends almost always devolve into shop talk. Most of the time it can be kept to a minimum, but it seems unavoidable. After all, that's the world you spend most of your time in when you're not at home, and your coworkers know exactly what you're talking about.

It's important to be available for peer support, but it's also essential to have other friends who keep you tethered to the life and person you were before working as a jailer. Your view on just about everything may change, but it's important to maintain these friendships—even if there are disagreements. Most of the time these disagreements are caused by a lack of education or understanding, but changes in your worldview and your higher stress levels may also play a part.

Use your experience to help educate your friends, but remember not to alienate them. They help keep you grounded.

Do Avoid Entitlement

This one is easier said than done. Good leaders want "buy-in" for their agencies. Buy-in usually means that sweat equity is built within the organization. The nature of this hard work usually means that those responsible for it feel that they have part ownership. Part ownership can sound like or manifest itself as entitlement when there's a difference of opinion with leadership.

The advice I give most people is to do extra things or duties because you enjoy them, and your efforts will in turn benefit the agency. This sounds strange at first, but it does help inoculate yourself against entitlement while also being much healthier and more sustainable. There are times when the agency does need a person to go above and beyond, especially during emergencies, but usually all hands are on deck for such events.

Do Learn Who You Are

Inmates will learn who you are quickly. You need to do the same so you can avoid their manipulations and getting your "buttons" pressed. It's also important to know when you need additional help, and whether or not you're the type to avoid asking for it. Be prepared to level with yourself so you know when it's time to retire before you begin to make decisions or mistakes that result in a demand for your resignation.

Do Remember What's Important

Many people get so focused and busy with work that they put off things that are important to them. Some people go so far as to use work as a means to drown out the other challenges in their lives. I recommend asking yourself a simple question every so often: "What was important to me before I got so busy?"

Keep asking yourself this question, and then find a way to make the important things a higher priority. Often it's our relationships we neglect, and it's these relationships we need to maintain our grounding as to who we are.

Do Seek Guidance and Support

It's always important to recognize when you need additional guidance and support. As I've said before, it's seen as a strength to know when you need a hand. Many employers have an employee assistance program that pays for a limited number of counseling sessions for their employees and their immediate families. In law enforcement (which includes corrections) there's growing recognition that there needs to be a concentrated effort or program to reduce work stress. However, not every agency has the resources to support a separate program to do this.

In our agency, we have a peer support team (PST). This team is made up of coworkers who have received additional training in regard to guidance counseling and confidentiality. Since PST members are working the same job as you, they're more likely to understand the challenges you're going through and give you an outlet and some direction.

Do Seek Additional Knowledge

Believe it or not, there are a few resources out there that can help you. Whether it's just getting a feel for what it may be like for a citizen to be incarcerated or the personal experiences of jail and corrections staff, those books are out there. A few of these are listed at the back of this book. If you feel like you want to learn more about body language, interviews, interrogations, manipulative tactics, and criminal minds, those resources are also out there. This book is a primer, and it can't stand in for training, experience, and further study.

Don't Be Unnecessarily Hard on Yourself

Many a self-driven person knows what I'm talking about. We're our own worst critics, which sometimes drives self-improvement and being better. However, you don't have to be perfect and you definitely don't need to be masochistic in order to get better. Be kind to yourself and cut yourself some slack. Remember, life gives you plenty of chances to be miserable, so there's no sense in practicing!

CONCLUSION: THE CRUCIBLE OF SERVICE

Working in a jail is a challenging endeavor. If you take on the challenge, a new you will be forged in the crucible of service. Some of the elements in the crucible are beyond your control, but how you respond to them is always your choice. This career is life-altering, and your choices within it can make you a better person, a more well-rounded person, and likely a more skeptical person. You don't have to lose touch with who you are. You don't have to take the stress and keep it in. Rather, redirect this energy and emotion and channel it into stress management strategies and professional development.

If you've chosen this career path, a few more words of wisdom may still help. At the back of this book I've listed some other resources that can help you extend your career and get better at your job. Since you've come this far, I hope my words have helped you in some way, whether it's getting to know the field, gaining practical advice, or understanding what your deputized loved one is going through.

Additional Resources

ONLINE RESOURCES

"The Locust Effect: Why the End of Poverty Requires the End of Violence" By Gary Haugen.
Accessed March 6, 2019. https://www.ted.com/speakers/gary_haugen

BOOKS

The Social Contract, by Jean-Jacques Rosseau (translated by Maurice Cranston)
A work by Rosseau on preparing a person for citizenship by arguing that a contract exists between the citizen and the state.

Inside the Criminal Mind, by Stanton E. Samenow
This work in on a profile of the criminal mind that challenged perceptions about the origin of crime.

The Hate Factory, by Georgelle Hirliman
This book is an account of a riot at a corrections facility written by a reporter who witnessed it.

Verbal Judo: The Gentle Art of Persuasion, by George Thompson
This work discusses and demonstrates verbal techniques that are effective in de-escalation and rapport building.

Nonverbal Communication in Human Interaction (8th Edition), by Mark Knapp
A resource on nonverbal communication and how this impacts a variety of fields. It comes with theory and research from a variety of scholars.

Spy the Lie, By Philip Houston, Michael Floyd, Susan Carnicero and Don Tennant
A book takes readers through anecdotes and shows how to recognize deceptive behaviors both verbal and non-verbal.

The Gift of Fear, by Gavin de Becker
This work provides information on how to see signs of danger, particularly of violent acts in advance. It also gives advice on how to prepare and protect yourself.

Emotional Survival for Law Enforcement, by Gil Martin
This work explains changes that a person who works in law enforcement may experience and how it affects others in their lives. It also gives ideas on how to mitigate the stressors of law enforcement work.

The Art of the Con, by Gary Cornelius
Geared for those who work in a corrections environment, it offers ways to understand behaviors and cultures and prevent inmate manipulation.

Corrections Officers' Guide to Understanding Inmates, by Larone Koonce
This work is a guide on working with people inside correctional facilities. It provides information on how to maintain influence with inmates on the inside.

Games Criminals Play, by Bud Allen and Diana Bosta
This work is geared towards helping a person recognize common techniques and tactics used by inmates to first select, and then manipulate certain officers.

Hell on Fire, by Sara Lunsford
> This is a personal account of a female officer and both the personal and professional challenges she faced.

Doing Time Eight Hours a Day: Memoirs of a Correctional Officer, by James R. Palmer.
> A memoir of a seasoned corrections officer who spent a great deal of time working solitary confinement.

I Love a Cop, Revised Edition: What Police Families Need to Know, by Ellen Kirschman
> This work describes the challenges for those who have loved ones working in law enforcement. It also provides suggestions on how to address the challenges they will face.

Bibliography

"America's Founding Documents." National Archives and Records Administration. Accessed March 6, 2019. https://www.archives.gov/founding-docs.

"Colorado Revised Statutes." Colorado General Assembly. Accessed March 6, 2019. https://leg.colorado.gov/colorado-revised-statutes.

"Corrections Yearbook 2000, 2002" Criminal Justice Institute. Accessed October 2018. https://www.ncjrs.gov/app/publications/abstract.aspx?id=18715.

"Sourcebook of Criminal Justice Statistics 2003" Bureau of Justice Statistics. Accessed October 2018. https://www.ncjrs.gov/pdffiles1/Digitization/208756NCJRS.pdf.

"Suicide Risk Among Correctional Officers" Archives of Suicide Research. Accessed October 2018.https://www.researchgate.net/publication/240238125_Suicide_risk_among_correctional_officers_A_logistic_regression_analysis.

www.ingramcontent.com/pod-product-compliance
Lightning Source LLC
Chambersburg PA
CBHW071223080526
44587CB00013BA/1481